DEMOCRACY IN THE POST-TRUTH ERA

DEMOCRACY IN THE POST-TRUTH ERA

Restoring Faith in Expertise

Janusz Grygieńć

Translated by Dominika Gajewska

EDINBURGH
University Press

Edinburgh University Press is one of the leading university presses in the UK. We publish academic books and journals in our selected subject areas across the humanities and social sciences, combining cutting-edge scholarship with high editorial and production values to produce academic works of lasting importance. For more information visit our website: edinburghuniversitypress.com

Edinburgh University Press Ltd
The Tun – Holyrood Road
12(2f) Jackson's Entry
Edinburgh EH8 8PJ

Typeset in 11/13 Adobe Sabon by
IDSUK (DataConnection) Ltd, and
printed and bound in Great Britain

A CIP record for this book is available from the British Library

ISBN 978-1-4744-9730-5 (hardback)
ISBN 978-1-4744-9732-9 (webready PDF)
ISBN 978-1-4744-9733-6 (epub)

CONTENTS

═══════════

TABLES

ACKNOWLEDGEMENTS

This book is the outcome of many years of research. Therefore, it is impossible to mention all the people who have had an impact on its creation. I will therefore focus on the most important individuals.

First of all, I am very grateful to the authorities of the Institute of Philosophy and the Faculty of Philosophy and Social Sciences of the Nicolaus Copernicus University in Toruń for giving me six months sabbatical leave to complete work on this book. I am incredibly grateful to Zbyszek Nerczuk whose support and patience were invaluable.

Over the years I presented parts of this book at many conferences, including in Krakow, Poznan, Paris, Nancy, Cardiff, and during the face-to-face ECPR in 2019 and the online ECPR in 2020. I want to thank all the contributors to the discussions on my papers (and there were many). Their comments repeatedly forced me to rethink critical parts of my narrative. I especially thank Rikki Dean, who shared insightful comments on the outline of this book with me.

I am incredibly grateful to the anonymous reviewers from Edinburgh University Press. They have done a fantastic job. They accurately tracked down and pointed out the weak links in my narrative. They encouraged me to take a precise stand, especially in Chapters 3 and 5. This book would have been much worse without their comments.

I also want to thank everyone at Edinburgh University Press for the smooth running of the publishing process, their professionalism and the friendly atmosphere of cooperation. In particular, I would like to thank Ersev Ersoy for her constant help.

Finally, special thanks are due to my wife, Ewa. She was the first to read the manuscript and to point out its weaknesses and strengths. Writing this book did not come easily to me. I have never been so immersed in academic work. Without Ewa's help, I would not have been able to complete the task. In fact, I could not have done much else.

The contribution of all the above people to all that is inspiring and interesting in this book was decisive. I take sole responsibility for the average, weak and mediocre aspects of my work.

INTRODUCTION: POST-TRUTH AND THE DAWN OF ILLIBERAL DEMOCRACY

EXPERTISE IN CRISIS

Scientists and journalists have increasingly been calling our attention to an alarming drop in our faith in the authority of expertise.[1] Although doubt in the good intentions and competence of experts has been on the rise since the 1970s, it seems to have reached unprecedented proportions lately. A whole host of factors are to blame for this, including spectacular expert gaffes, as seen in the failure to predict political and economic crises, to understand their nature and repercussions, and to come to agreement on most of the problems discussed in the public realm. On the other hand, the increasing privatisation of scientific research has bolstered the view that experts who are financially dependent on private sponsorship are simply biased. The social dynamics of this crisis have been brought into stark relief by the COVID-19 pandemic. The worldwide health crisis has shown just how much both citizens and politicians are dependent on expertise. Expert opinions on how the pandemic would develop and how to combat it were suddenly in huge demand. It is true that on many occasions politicians made instrumental use of expert authority to justify the measures they were taking in order to avoid political responsibility for the consequences of their actions.[2] However, it is now the norm for politicians to comply with the recommendations of scientific advisory bodies. The pandemic has also mercilessly laid bare the flaws of scientific communication. The lability and multiplicity of expert opinions; the evolution of hypotheses and forecasts; contradictory positions with regard to the existence, thresholds and possibility of achieving herd immunity; changing recommendations regarding the effectiveness of protective measures, including masks and face shields – all of these combined to create a chaotic communication environment

1

that citizens found hard to navigate.[3] New reports on the side- effects of the AstraZeneca vaccine generated alternating waves of readiness and unwillingness to get vaccinated. The pandemic also revealed how populist politicians were ready to flout expertise and the sorry consequences that this eventually produced.

The COVID-19 crisis exposed an entire macrocosm of inflammatory points at the intersection of expertise, political power and public opinion. It highlighted the fact that expert institutions and pharmaceutical companies may pressure political authorities by dictating vaccine prices and delivery dates. It witnessed the debacle of state-funded research institutions in competition with private companies that were able to patent successive vaccines. It unmasked the role of expert-staffed regulatory agencies such as the European Medicines Agency (EMA) which authoritatively decided if vaccines were safe or whether the risks associated with the occurrence of vaccine adverse reactions were admissible.

The pandemic also exposed public fears, concerns and disbelief regarding the scope and consequences of the crisis. In just one year we saw ample evidence of the huge role experts play in our lives and of the public's alarmingly low trust in their competence and good intentions. On the one hand, studies such as 3M 2020 Pandemic Pulse have shown that the pandemic increased people's trust in science.[4] Some scholars claim that trust in science was in much better shape than generally assumed prior to the pandemic. Aside from a few exceptions, such as climate change or vaccines, trust in science had been steadily growing.[5] However, some sources point to the opposite phenomenon.[6] A survey commissioned by the European Council on Foreign Relations (EFCR) in nine European Union countries with two-thirds of the EU's population shows that despite the pandemic 65 per cent of respondents do not trust the experts, blaming them for deliberate concealment of important information. Of my own compatriots, 20 per cent trust experts, while only 15 per cent of French people trust them.[7] This decline in confidence seems to be deepening. It is uncertain if the COVID-19 pandemic will alter this picture in any way. At least not for the better.

POST-TRUTH AND ILLIBERAL DEMOCRACY

The crisis of confidence in expertise coincides and resonates with the phenomenon of post-truth. When writing about this phenomenon in 2004, Ralph Keyes used the term 'post-truth' to refer to an increasing acceptance of and acquiescence to lies in the public sphere. According to Keyes, we lie more often and with less compunction.[8] We also increasingly get away with it. The years 2015–16 and the victories of illiberal democrats in Europe and the United States only confirmed these claims. The political success of the Polish United Right, the Hungarian Fidesz, the Italian Five Star Movement, the French Front National, the Swedish Democrats, the German AfD and PEGIDA, Donald Trump, Recep Erdoğan and Jair Bolsonaro were largely driven by the same trends. One of these is the eloquent questioning of the content and relevance of the scientific consensus, citing controversial slogans contrary to science and hailing the 'the triumph of the visceral over the rational, the deceptively simple over the honestly complex'.[9] Illiberal democrats counter facts with desires, hopes and fears. This is why Trump could unabashedly claim that his swearing in had attracted the largest crowds in history and that climate change was simply a hoax disseminated by the Chinese government; Bolsonaro could mock statements about the anthropogenic origins of climate change; while Modi's government in India could officially announce the end of the COVID-19 pandemic just before its third wave hit; and Brexit supporters could decry the United Kingdom's purported weekly loss of £350 million (according to Boris Johnson) due to its EU membership. Illiberal democrats suggest that fiction can be equivalent to truth, expertise is relative, and that the existence and importance of the scientific consensus is debatable. This allows them to practice 'science denial', to equate science with business and private (usually foreign) corporations that band together against ordinary people. Experts who do not agree with the illiberal democrats are considered to be either corrupt or succumbing to the scientific fashions of 'useful idiots' who kowtow to medical multinationals.[10] When politics is reduced to pandering to popular opinion, the scientific narrative becomes problematic. Science counters freedom of expression with methodological rigour, and hasty conclusions with the careful weighing of evidence. If the illiberal democrats capitalise on prejudice, fears and desires, then scientific narrative becomes their natural enemy. This is why an alliance between the illiberal democrats and science is impossible, and conflict between them is inevitable. We could multiply the examples. The French Front National warned against leaving the 'destiny of the people in the hands of unelected experts'. Beppe Grillo denounced 'supposed experts' in 'economics, finance, or labour'.[11] Michael Gove famously stated that 'the people of this country have had enough of experts'. I come from a country where the last decade has seen a spectacular rise of illiberal democrats and where apolitical and expert bodies have been treated dismissively, if not with outright criticism. In his 2015 presidential campaign, Andrzej Duda announced the programme of the Law and Justice government, highlighting its anti-elitist and anti-expert character. He described economic experts as biased and defeatist, and said that dismissing their advice was a hallmark of courage and patriotism. In a demographically shrinking society, Duda promised to lower the retirement age. In mining regions, he openly stated that it is hard to tell if human beings are responsible for climate change. Courting young voters, he shared his anti-vaccination proclivities. Battling elites, including scientific ones, has become one of the main points on the new government agenda.

Scientists rarely emerge victorious from such skirmishes. They do not enjoy privileged platforms and access to citizens, and their narrative is doomed from the outset. It is boring and requires cognitive effort to be understood, or at least a high level of trust in the scientific community. It is 'mysterious, magical, or dangerous', as Marilee Long and Jocelyn Steinke put it.[12] It has a hard time capturing the attention of citizens if the particular issue under discussion does not concern them directly and to a large degree. Paradoxically, the advance of science and technology only makes the situation worse.[13]

ILLIBERAL DEMOCRACY VS. UNDEMOCRATIC LIBERALISM

Liberal democrats (both theorists and practitioners) are just as ineffectual at responding to populists. They react to the phenomena of post-truth, manipulation and propaganda by seeking refuge in the declining authority of science and expertise. Liberals mock the incompetence of their opponents and condescendingly chastise the enemies of the scientific consensus. They call for greater confidence in experts and scientific institutions instead of pandering to the opinions of the democratic majority. They see hopes of overcoming post-truth in delegating the most specialised decisions to expert institutions. This is why Yasha Mounk claims that liberal democracy today has not one but two enemies.[14] The first of these is illiberal democracy, which calls for heeding the populist-defined voice and communal interest. The other is widespread 'undemocratic liberalism', an elitist form of liberalism that would gladly see all technical decisions delegated to institutions not subject to democratic oversight. This strain of liberalism tends to rely on the opinions of technocrats rather than ordinary citizens.[15]

Historically, the alliance between liberalism and democracy is neither long-standing, nor particularly permanent. It is therefore hardly surprising that a growing number of scholars point to the inevitable tensions between them. After Fareed Zakaria,[16] who blamed the rise of illiberal democracy on the increasing democratisation of successive aspects of the political reality, the theoretical and practical contradictions between liberalism and democracy have been pointed out by Jan Zielonka, Mark Lilla and Adrian Pabst, among others.[17] Some of these authors have identified undemocratic tendencies in liberal thought and practice.[18] Mounk notes that the effectiveness of a political system depends on expertise, but significantly limiting citizens' influence on the system must lead to a loss of political legitimacy.[19] The postulates of reclaiming power, agency and sovereignty put forward by illiberal democrats therefore fall on fertile ground and are not baseless. This diagnosis is shared by Zielonka, in whose view 'across Europe, politics [is] increasingly presented as an art of institutional engineering and not as an art of political bargaining between the elites and the electorate'.[20]

Undemocratic liberalism is hostile to liberal democracy not only because it rejects the idea of civic empowerment, but also because its narrative plays into the hands of populism. It allows populists to proclaim themselves defenders of the interests of the average citizen. They promise to reclaim agency and sovereignty for the citizens. Their criticism targets independent central banks,[21] especially the European Central Bank,[22] as well as a range of other institutions not subject to democratic oversight but having a fundamental influence on the social reality.[23] Most of these are supranational organisations,[24] for example, EU institutions such as the European Food Safety Authority (EFSA), the European Medicines Agency (EMA) and the European Chemicals Agency (ECHA).[25] The illiberal critique of apolitical courts and tribunals follows the same pattern. For decades, American conservatives have accused the Supreme Court of instigating liberal social revolutions that would have been practically impossible to bring about via the normal legislative route.[26] In Poland, courts and judges who pass sentences that do not conform with the authorities' expectations are considered to be biased, representing the voice of the elite or morally degenerate. Critics of such institutions invariably state that the unhindered freedom of the elected parliamentary majority to shape public life is the essence of democracy. Majority rule should be subject to no constraints.

WHEN DID IT ALL GO WRONG?

It does not seem possible to pinpoint the exact causes of the current crisis of faith in the authority of science and expertise. There are many hypotheses, some of them more popular than others. One of the most popular focuses on the role of social media and the information noise they generate. Phenomena like information bubbles, group polarisation and the quick proliferation of hard-to-verify information and conspiracy theories have become widespread as the use of Facebook, Twitter and Instagram has increased. This is skilfully exploited by merchants of doubt, who successfully disseminate information that undermines faith in the existence and content of the scientific consensus. The psychological profiling of social media users makes sowing doubt even easier and eradicating it next to impossible.

The second culprit is said to be the increasing complexity and unpredictability of political, social and economic processes. The quantity of information one must consider when making a decision has skyrocketed, as has the degree of interdependence between political and economic actors. Not only has the character of intra- and inter-state relations changed, but so has man's relationship with nature. Climate change is accelerating, bringing global chains of dependence into relief. Weather anomalies, pandemics and mass climate migration – phenomena never seen before – have followed suit. Expert prognostics with regard to these unprecedented phenomena are inevitably imprecise. Science has no simple and quick answers here, only estimates and general recommendations. This makes it seem as though it is unable to grasp the nature of these changes and propose effective solutions. This consequently leads to the conviction that science is helpless against the present challenges, so one might just as well trust common sense.

Thirdly, post-truth and the collapse of scientific authority are blamed on post-modernism and relativism – currents developed within the framework of social constructivism which have significantly informed the social sciences.[27] After all, the good reputation of science has never depended on the degree to which it was understood by laypeople. It has always been based on trust in the genius of scholars personifying the efficacy of science – as seen in its 'cartoon' version, where science connotes perpetual progress and the consistent and methodical solving of humanity's problems.[28] The spread of the idea that scientific processes are essentially social in nature and that science does not differ from other social practices has thrown science off its pedestal, massively contributing to the crisis of faith in its authority. The spark that kindled the flame was the publication of Kuhn's *The Structure of Scientific Revolutions*.[29] The death blow was dealt by the writings of social constructivists and sociologists of scientific knowledge such as Sheila Jasanoff (the founders of the so-called Wave Two in social studies of science),[30] who claimed that science is political in nature and that extra-scientific assumptions and social prejudice play a key role in it.[31] These scholars examined research practices as a form of power-seeking political activity. Latour expressed this idea in his pithy statement that science is the pursuit of 'politics by other means'.[32] Science is not peer-reviewed journals, but the 'cognitive authoritarianism' of scientists.[33]

Other authors have looked for the origins of today's crisis in the erosion of the post-industrial 'knowledge-based society'[34] and the transition from academic to post-academic science,[35] leading to the renouncement of the Mertonian norms.[36] In their view, science has become first and foremost a vehicle for pursuing financial interests, rather than searching for solutions that best serve citizens. It has also ceased to be an arena of free and open discussion and has become a tool in the hands of private sponsors and shareholders.

I would like to explore another possibility in this book. I would like to reflect on whether the reasons for our faltering faith in the authority of science are rooted in the very nature of the relationship between experts and laypeople. If we assume that relations between laypeople and experts always involve the former trusting the latter, it may turn out that post-truth is not strictly a contemporary phenomenon but an unavoidable part of life in a democratic society.[37] According to the theory of epistemic dependence, which I will frequently refer to in this book, it does not matter how educated a society is and how willing and capable of deliberating because it will never be able to rationally solve technical dilemmas or problems with a strong technical component. These will always be beyond the grasp not only of citizens and politicians, but of most of the scientific community. A significant number of the issues debated in the public realm are of this kind, including climate change, COVID-19, pension and social insurance reform, the socio-economic consequences of migration policies, and so on. Laypeople will always be helpless when it comes to diagnosing these kind of problems, predicting the course they are likely to take and coming up with solutions. They will never be able to identify the best strategy for fighting the coronavirus, judge the effectiveness of social distancing, wearing masks and determine whether it prevents or merely postpones the inevitable – the development of herd immunity. Nor will they be able to say whether such immunity exists at all, starting at what threshold, what the long-term side effects of the COVID vaccines are, to what extent human beings are responsible for climate change, if they can slow it down, and how. To answer any of these questions one needs specialist scientific knowledge. And this is what laypeople lack. Confronted with mutually contradictory expert opinions, ordinary people are not only incapable of identifying the more reliable expertise – they cannot even determine which expert they should trust.

Illiberal democrats realise full well that such dependence exists. However, instead of expecting greater competence and knowledge from citizens, they skilfully exploit their ignorance. They cleverly question the competence and motivation of inconvenient experts. Liberal democrats do the opposite. They fervently believe in citizens' cognitive potential and have faith that their reason, capability and readiness to choose the best course of action will manifest themselves under the right conditions. This is why they rail against post-truth and the practice of pandering to the basest human instincts instead of inspiring citizens to greater cognitive effort. The theory and practice of liberal democracy cannot come to terms with civic incompetence. Most of the time it outright denies it. It shies away from discussions with climate-change sceptics, anti-vaccinationists or lockdown sceptics in the case of COVID-19. Liberals stigmatise and attack anti-expert sentiments. The enemies of expertise are condemned for their imprudence and irrationality, and they are not considered worthy discussion partners. Liberal theory is permeated by the Enlightenment demand for the autonomy of reason, individualism and empiricism. It is dominated by the scientistic paradigm – the conviction that scientific knowledge is fundamentally unproblematic, the only problem being how to convince citizens to embrace it.

WHAT CAN STS CONTRIBUTE TO POLITICAL THEORY?

Considering the above, I believe that the theory of democracy cannot do without a reference to social studies of science (SSS), science and technology studies (STS) and the philosophy of science.[38] It is actually quite surprising that it has managed to avoid these references thus far. The subjects of debates in the sociology of science and in political theory have overlapped since the 1970s. In both areas, the clash of two visions of the expert–lay relationship has been at the centre. The first vision posits competent citizens capable of independently deciding their fate and experts abusing their authority in order to maintain control over the public sphere.[39] The second envisions irrational masses of voters held at bay by a rational science that systematically solves humanity's burning social problems.

Supporters of the first vision – let us call it participatory – call for the greater involvement of laypeople in making decisions, including technical ones. They are not entirely in agreement as to the scope of civic empowerment. The moderates propose more frequent use of referenda and public consultations, setting up new spaces for civic participation in public debate and making scientific research (including information about its sponsors and procedures) more widely available. The radicals call for the direct involvement of ordinary citizens in the most important decisions or even in scientific research, making them co-responsible for politics and science.[40] As a matter of fact, they believe that the boundary between science and politics is not fixed. Some think that it is the experts who arbitrarily and authoritatively define that boundary, and by so doing exclude from public debate issues that should be examined and decided upon by the whole community. Supporters of the second vision – let us call it epistocratic – defend science and scientists against being politicised and rendered less effective. They are aware of the problems that plague science, but they believe it is possible to overcome them without 'throwing the baby out with the bathwater'. In their view, laypeople too easily fall prey to manipulation and cognitive heuristics, and have too little knowledge and experience to assess the credibility of scientific evidence. Their empowerment would inevitably bring about a waste of resources as well as precipitate crises and instability. Laypeople, therefore, should not decide on all matters. Strictly technical matters should be handled by apolitical expert bodies.

The points of convergence between the considerations debated by political theorists and science theorists are so striking that Philip Mirowski searches for their common origins in the philosophies of John Dewey and Walter Lippmann.[41] Dewey's thought is an archetypal example of placing trust in laypeople and opposing all forms of elitism.[42] Lippmann's thought, on the other hand, is permeated by a lack of faith in the cognitive capacities of ordinary people and by the hope that the expert elite will heal itself. In doctrinaire style, Dewey likens science to democracy, proposing to make citizens as empowered as possible. Lippmann, on the other hand, is sceptical about lay rule, but offers no clear recipes for lessening lay ignorance.

Aside from these similarities the perspectives of political and scientific theorists differ significantly. The former usually have a very simplified vision of science. They share an uncritical vision of infallible scientists and of cumulative scientific progress. A wholly different perspective informs studies of science, where science is viewed as having no privileged cognitive status. Science does not provide fail-proof, uncontroversial and universally correct answers. It is not par excellence a domain of rational, apolitical and meritorious cogitation. It is non-cumulative and rife with contradictions, while relations between scientists are often marked by ideological domination and competition for resources and status.[43]

As for scholars of science, their in-depth analysis of expertise is coupled with a rather simplified and generalised idea of political procedures. This may be why a consistent theory of democracy has never emerged in studies of science.[44] Here, democratic processes have tended to be identified with a kind of vague, undefined transparency and the direct empowerment of laypeople.[45] Advocates of a science open to the citizen enthusiastically equate democracy with the 'insiders' wisdom', with the self-determination of ordinary people, seen as a counterweight to hermetic circles of self-important scholars. Supporters of an autonomous science meanwhile tend to associate democracy with arbitrariness and the domination of private and short-term political interests over the common good. Both of these zero-sum visions produce equally over-simplified, radicalised political postulates which either call for full civic self-determination or the full autonomy of science vis-à-vis politics.

The benefits that could be obtained by merging these two perspectives are therefore considerable. It is all the more surprising that for a long time scholars in both fields – political theory and philosophy and studies of science – have studied very similar phenomena without drawing on one another's work. It was only at the beginning of the twenty-first century that the works of philosophers and sociologists of science like Philip Kitcher,[46] Steve Fuller, Stephen Turner, Harry Collins and Robert Evans, Michel Callon and Martin Kusch[47] began to pave the way for interdisciplinary studies combining an interest in science and politics. Some authors, like Fuller, have recognised ubiquitous reliance on experts as 'the biggest single problem facing the future of democracy'.[48] Turner has called formulating the rules of expert–lay democratic co-existence as the greatest political challenge of today, comparable with the establishment of the democratic system and the extension of voting rights to most adult citizens.[49] According to Collins, Evans and Weinel, the survival of democracy depends on whether citizens will be able to identify the real experts and trust them. Otherwise science will not be able to 'check and balance' politics.[50]

Political theorists have been much more reluctant to embark on interdisciplinary enterprises. It is only in the last decade and a half that a small number of them have turned their attention to STS and, thanks to this effort, they have begun to problematise the political role of expertise. Authors like Mark B. Brown,[51] Alfred Moore,[52] Darrin Durant, Catherine Holst and Anders Molander have pointed to the implications that discussions hitherto conducted within the framework of science studies could have for the practice and theory of democracy. They understand that expertise is a complex phenomenon that takes many forms but also has natural limitations. They are aware of the problematic nature of the expert–lay relationship, especially in the context of the post-truth society. Their analyses open up a new field for reflecting on democracy.

In this book, I want to follow in their footsteps. Like them, I want to examine the political implications of expertise as defined within the science studies tradition. I believe that theory of democracy cannot do without a fine-grained analysis of the phenomenon of expertise. Not only without taking into account the systemic impact of science on politics, already analysed by Jürgen Habermas or Michel Foucault, but also without epistemological reflection on the scope, object and limitations of expert knowledge. I especially want to focus on an aspect of the lay–expert relationship that is very rarely considered by theorists of democracy and which in my opinion is of key importance for the functioning of democratic societies, namely, the authority of science, and social trust as the foundation of that authority. There is a kind of paradox in the relationship between science and democracy. On the one hand, effective management makes it necessary to rely on the specialist knowledge of a small group of experts. On the other hand, the social legitimacy of political decisions requires that they be accepted by citizens who do not understand the scientific underpinnings of those decisions. Decisions based on specialist knowledge are socially legitimate only to the degree that expertise enjoys authority. But in a time of declining authority, with trust in experts plummeting, the legitimacy of policies based on specialist knowledge also drops. It is then that post-truth begins to resonate with the narrative proffered by populists.

I would like to see whether this is inevitable. That is why the aim of this book is to run a kind of intellectual experiment. What happens with the theory of democracy if we reject the fundamental liberal assumption that laypeople, ordinary citizens or their representatives, are capable of making choices that are better than random? What if we embrace the view that the layperson will never be capable of appreciating the relevance of the arguments put forward by experts? What if they will never be able even to identify the expert who is right? What if they will never be able to competently choose between supporters and opponents of theories concerning the anthropogenic origins of climate change, the effectiveness of vaccines or ways of resolving economic and social crises? What if the 'post-truth' era is not an undesirable anomaly but a natural state of affairs that sets in when blind societal trust in experts disappears? Is liberal theory of democracy able to come to terms with this vision? I will argue that in its present form it is unable to meet this challenge. I will also attempt to demonstrate that rejecting the assumption that laypeople are competent to make decisions necessitates a reshaping of liberal democratic theory. I will show that it is culture and an atmosphere of trust in expertise rather than rational deliberation that plays a key role in ending the era of post-truth and radical, axiomatic scepticism with regard to expert knowledge.

I am not arguing that liberal democratic theory must be rejected or radically revised. I am not speaking here as its sworn critic, but rather as an advocate of some level of change. I am arguing that liberal theory needs to revise some of its assumptions. Consequently, it will be able to assess more realistically the competencies of citizens at the grassroots level and to respond more effectively to the problem of post-truth and populism. The final proposals for change may not prove to be revolutionary, but changing the logic of liberal thinking about expertise can have far-reaching consequences.

Before I tell readers what they will find in each chapter, let me tell them what they definitely will not. First, there is no information on specific, practical methods of empowering laypeople or ways of using participatory budgets or various types of democratic innovations. There is no detailed discussion of any mechanisms for applying citizen science and no detailed analysis of different kinds of minipublics, citizens' juries, panels or deliberative polls. These will be discussed only to the extent necessary to describe the concept of inclusive epistocracy in Chapter 5. The available literature on these topics is so rich that it requires no elaboration. Or at least that is not my aim.

Nor will the reader of this book come across a complex analysis and comparison of arguments in favour of civic empowerment. The participatory turn in political theory, philosophy and in social studies of science that happened fifty years ago has produced a sufficient number of normative and epistemic arguments for the more frequent use of direct democracy. I will not be analysing the arguments in favour of participatory risk assessment popular in social studies of science. Nor is this book a collection of arguments criticising epistocracy or technocracy. Few contemporary thinkers openly defend expert government. Most scholars are critical of it. The relevant literature abounds in dozens of arguments against all forms of guardianship. So these will not be the subject of my investigations either.

What then is this book about? My reflections in the main will be devoted to lay epistemic dependence on experts. The relevant theory proclaims that understanding between laypeople and experts will never be possible. It does not matter how much time laypeople spend getting to know the theoretical underpinnings of expert opinions, in the end they will never be able to confirm their validity. My claim is that contemporary liberal thinkers too hastily assume that this kind of understanding is possible. For this very reason, they are incapable of coming up with a sensible solution to the increasingly commonplace problem of citizen manipulation and post-truth. Liberals too easily proclaim that citizens are capable of making fully conscious, rational political decisions in a fully autonomous manner. This is why in times like ours, when citizens are easily swayed by the narratives disseminated by merchants of doubt, liberals blame everything and everyone but themselves: new technologies, bad education, the tabloidisation of the press and of politics, or populist politicians' lack of respect for the basic values of democracy. I believe they sidestep one important issue, a kind of 'blind spot' in their own theory. Namely, they fail to consider the possibility that the problems with the contemporary liberal narrative stem from the very nature of scientific research and expert–lay relations. In this book, I would like to take a closer look at where contemporary research on the phenomenon of expertise appears to diverge from liberal theory. In my opinion, if liberals do not pay attention to the problem of expertise and fail to take epistemic dependence seriously, they will never be able to formulate a cogent strategy in response to the populist danger. To do this, however, they have to renounce their nonchalant treatment of experts and expertise.

This is why I shall begin by showing just how casually, if at all, liberals approach the issue of expertise and the role of experts in political decision-making. Analysing the works of Amy Gutmann, Dennis Thompson, Thomas Christiano and Hélène Landemore, among others, I will identify three approaches to the lay–expert relationship dominant in liberal thought and their undergirding methodological assumptions. The first sees citizens as capable decision-makers and considers their competence sufficient for most political decisions. The second assumes that although citizens are often ignorant, if put through the right educational process they can become competent decision-makers with relative ease. The third claims that citizens do not need to be involved in decision-making at all because experts and politicians can pursue desirable social goals on their behalf. My claim is that although each of these approaches is based on a different set of methodological assumptions, liberal theorists routinely mix them up. This puts them at risk of theoretical inconsistencies.

One of the main reasons for this state of affairs is the lack of a precise definition of expertise. This problem will be explored in more detail in Chapter 2, in which I analyse three mainstream definitions of expertise and the theoretical problems each of them brings up. The first definition equates the expert with an academic or theorist. The second takes the practical aspect of applying theory to practice into account (in addition to theoretical knowledge). In this context I discuss the controversies that erupted in connection with the definition of expertise proposed by Alvin Goldman. Finally, the third definition emphasises the expert's practical skills. I attribute it to Harry Collins and Robert Evans. In my view, it is saddled with the least theoretical difficulty and at the same time has the most heuristic potential. Its main advantage is that it also allows us to identify experts among those whom we customarily perceive as laypeople.

Chapter 3 is devoted to the concept of epistemic dependence. I discuss the two most popular interpretations of this kind of dependence. The first, more radical one proclaims that experts and laypeople cannot communicate or understand one another, and that even expert-to-expert communication is impossible. Increasing specialisation within science means that there are no systemic mechanisms in place for verifying research findings. All of science runs on trust. This vision undeniably deals a blow not only to liberal theories of democracy (which presuppose that citizens are capable of understanding the premises upon which each political decision is predicated), but also to the concept of epistocratic government. This is why the vision of science as an archipelago of discrete 'cognitive islands' is generally rejected in the literature. A more moderate version is usually embraced. According to the latter, epistemic dependence is a problem only in areas in which there are no indirect expert evaluation criteria. It is not a norm but a pathology of science. Most of the time, criteria for assessing expert competence that make it possible to circumvent the problem of epistemic dependence are available.

I then analyse five such criteria proposed by Alvin Goldman. Four of them are epistemic (they ultimately make it necessary for the layperson to assess the expert's competence) and one is non-epistemic. My claim is that the first four criteria will always be controversial and will never lead to the overcoming of epistemic dependence. In using them, the layperson can never be sure that they have made the right choice. Only the non-epistemic strategy, consisting of searching for proof of the expert's bias, allows the layperson to avoid the pitfalls of epistemic dependence. For it requires no specialist knowledge to ascertain if the experts are potentially biased and, having determined that they are, to question the credibility of their expertise.

In Chapter 4 I take another look at liberal democratic theory, this time taking into account possible definitions of expertise and the problem of epistemic dependence. From this standpoint, I re-examine the three approaches to the expert–lay relationship discussed in Chapter 1. In my opinion none of them survives the confrontation. The main problem, as we will see, is the impossibility of translating scientific theory into everyday language. I will discuss this problem using the example of the controversies around interactional expertise. According to Harry Collins, it is possible to acquire expertise by way of 'linguistic socialisation' alone. I will demonstrate just how problematic and contested this view is. I will argue that it cannot simply be assumed that laypeople are capable of communicating with experts without themselves taking part in research practices. This point is a huge problem for the concept of deliberative opinion polls which are predicated on the idea that such communication is possible. I will analyse the statements of some critics of this concept and I will uphold the view that epistemic dependence is one of the biggest challenges that must be dealt with here. Finally, I will show that the 'division of labour' model of the public sphere also loses its relevance if we accept that citizens essentially have to rely on trust (or lack thereof) in their interactions with experts.

In the final chapter, I draw practical conclusions from my earlier observations. I lay out the concept of inclusive epistocracy which empowers citizens only in areas where they can reasonably be expected to have relevant (contributory) expertise. I discuss the theoretical inspirations and practical limitations of this idea. I claim that overcoming epistemic dependence in political practice is possible only in a small number of cases. In the majority of situations we are doomed to trust or mistrust experts. This is why it is crucial to develop extra- or non-epistemic methods of verifying the motivations of our advisers. I believe that whistle-blowers can play a key role in this process. I also argue that it is necessary to remove narrative disproportions between experts and merchants of doubt, and that it is crucial to teach citizens to critically analyse sources of information. Only through these methods will it be possible to limit the negative phenomena linked to the era of post-truth. Limit – since it is wishful thinking to count on fully eradicating manipulation, pseudoscience, populism and fabricated controversies.

NOTES

1. Roger Koppl, *Expert Failure* (Cambridge: Cambridge University Press, 2018); Tom Nichols, *The Death of Expertise: The Campaign against Established Knowledge and Why it Matters* (Oxford: Oxford University Press, 2017); Gil Eyal, *The Crisis of Expertise* (Cambridge: Polity, 2019); Harry Collins, *Are We All Scientific Experts Now?* (Cambridge: Polity, 2014).
2. Cf. Andrea Lavazza and Mirko Farina, 'The Role of Experts in the Covid-19 Pandemic and the Limits of Their Epistemic Authority in Democracy', *Frontiers in Public Health*, 14 July 2020, available at: https://www.frontiersin.org/articles/10.3389/fpubh.2020.00356/full.
3. Cf. Julian Reiss, 'Why Do Experts Disagree?' *Critical Review* 2 (2021), DOI:10.1080/08913811.2020.1872948
4. See at: https://www.3m.com/3M/en_US/state-of-science-index-survey. Pew Research studies also indicate that a high level of confidence in science seems to be the norm, available at: https://www.pewresearch.org/science/2020/09/29/science-and-scientists-held-in-high-esteem-across-global-publics/, https://www.pewresearch.org/fact-tank/2020/02/12/key-findings-about-americans-confidence-in-science-and-their-views-on-scientists-role-in-society/. Cf. https://www.ukri.org/wp-content/uploads/2020/09/UKRI-271020-COVID-19-Trust-Tracker.pdf.
5. Steven Shapin, 'Is There a Crisis of Truth?', 2019, available at: https://lareviewofbooks.org/article/is-there-a-crisis-of-truth.

6. See at: https://issues.org/real-numbers-mixed-messages-about-public-trust-in-science; https://www.researchgate.net/publication/297569382_Trust_in_Science_and_the_Science_of_Trust.

7. Ivan Krastev and Mark Leonard, 'Europe's Pandemic Politics: How the Virus has Changed the Public's Worldview', available at: https://www.ecfr.eu/publications/summary/europes_pandemic_politics_how_the_virus_has_changed_the_publics_worldview.

8. Ralph Keyes, *The Post-Truth Era: Dishonesty and Deception in Contemporary Life* (New York: St. Martin's Press, 2004).

9. Matthew d'Ancona, *Post-Truth: The New War on Truth and How to Fight Back* (Ebury Press 2017), 24.

10. Cf. David Runciman, *How Democracy Ends* (London: Profile Books, 2018), ch. 1.

11. Both statements cited after: Koppl, *Expert Failure*, 6.

12. Marilee Long and Jocelyn Steinke, 'The Thrill of Everyday Science: Images of Science and Scientists on Children's Educational Science Shows in the United States', *Public Understanding of Science* 5 (1996): 101–19.

13. Cf. José van Dijck and Donya Alinejad, 'Social Media and Trust in Scientific Expertise: Debating the Covid-19 Pandemic in The Netherlands', *Social Media and Society* 2020: 1–11, DOI: 10.1177/2056305120981057.

14. Yascha Mounk, *The People vs. Democracy: Why Our Freedom is in Danger and How to Save It* (Cambridge, MA: Harvard University Press, 2018).

15. Mounk, *The People vs. Democracy*, ch. 2.

16. Fareed Zakaria, 'The Rise of Illiberal Democracy', *Foreign Affairs* 76(6) (1997): 22–43.

17. Jan Zielonka, *Counter-Revolution: Liberal Europe in Retreat* (Oxford: Oxford University Press, 2018); Mark Lilla, *The Once and Future Liberal: After Identity Politics* (New York: Harper, 2017); Adrian Pabst, *The Demons of Liberal Democracy* (Cambridge: Polity, 2019).

18. Pabst, *The Demons of Liberal Democracy*, ch. 2; Frank Vibert, *The Rise of the Unelected: Democracy and the New Separation of Powers* (Cambridge: Cambridge University Press, 2007).

19. Mounk, *The People vs. Democracy*, 95.

20. Zielonka, *Counter-Revolution*, 5.

21. Cf. Charles Goodhart and Rosa Lastra, 'Populism and Central Bank Independence', *Open Economies Review* 29 (2018): 49–68.

22. See Jacqueline Best, 'Technocratic Exceptionalism', *International Political Sociology* 12(4) (2018): 328–45; Jacqueline Best, 'Bring Politics Back to Monetary Policy', *Foreign Affairs* 6 December 2017, available at: https://www.foreignaffairs.com/articles/world/2017-12-06/bring-politics-back-monetary-policy, last accessed 30 March 2020; Ian Bruff, 'The Rise of Authoritarian Neoliberalism', *Rethinking Marxism* 26(1) (2014): 113–29.

23. See Adam William Chalmers, 'Getting a Seat at the Table: Capital, Capture and Expert Groups in the European Union', *West European Politics* 37(5) (2014): 976–92; Kevin M. Esterling, *The Political Economy of Expertise: Information and Efficiency in American National Politics* (Ann Arbor:

University of Michigan Press, 2004); Claudio Radaelli, 'The Public Policy of the European Union: Whither Politics of Expertise?' *Journal of European Public Policy* 6(5) (1999): 757–74.

24. Ulridh Beck, 'World Risk Society as Cosmopolitan Society? Ecological Questions in a Framework of Manufactured Uncertainties', *Theory, Culture & Society* 13(4) (1996): 18; cf. Boris Holzer and Mads P. Sorensen, 'Rethinking Subpolitics: Beyond the "Iron Cage" of Modern Politics', *Theory, Culture & Society* 20(2) (2003): 80–1.

25. Elena Madalina Busuioc, *European Agencies: Law and Practices of Accountability* (Oxford: Oxford University Press, 2013); Elena Madalina Busuioc, 'Blurred Areas of Responsibility: European Agencies' Scientific "Opinions" Under Scrutiny', in Monika Ambrus et al. (eds), *The Role of 'Experts' in International and European Decision-Making Processes* (Cambridge: Cambridge University Press, 2014), 388–94; cf. Julia Metz, *The European Commission, Expert Groups, and the Policy Process* (Basinstoke: Palgrave Macmillan, 2015); Magdalena Góra, Cathrine Holst and Marta Warat (eds), *Expertisation and Democracy in Europe* (New York: Routledge, 2018).

26. See Jack Greenberg, *Crusaders in the Courts: Legal Battles of the Civil Rights Movement* (New York: Twelve Tables Press, 1995); Michael J. Klarman, *From Jim Crow to Civil Rights: The Supreme Court and the Struggle for Racial Equality* (Oxford: Oxford University Press, 2004).

27. Harry Collins, Robert Evans and Martin Weinel, 'STS as Science or Politics?' *Social Studies of Science* 47(4) (2017): 580–6; Harry Collins, Robert Evans and Martin Weinel, *Experts and the Will of the People* (London: Palgrave, 2020). Cf. the opposite view, promoted by Sergio Sismondo, 'Post-Truth?' *Social Studies of Science* 47(1) (2017): 3–6.

28. Collins, Evans and Weinel, *Experts and the Will*, 47–59.

29. Collins, Evans and Weinel, *Experts and the Will*, 48; Philip Mirowski, 'Democracy, Expertise and the Post-Truth Era', 2020, draft.

30. Harry Collins and Robert Evans define their position on, inter alia, expert knowledge in reference to other currents within social studies of science. They divide the development of these studies into three stages (waves). The first wave covered the period from the end of the Second World War until the end of the 1960s. This period was characterised by a linear and unproblematic view of scientific progress and the strict division between experts and laypeople. The second period lasted from the early 1970s to the early twenty-first century. Its representatives were sociologists of scientific knowledge and social constructivists, who questioned the attribution of a privileged cognitive status to science. They considered it to be a social construct similar to other social institutions. This belief led to the abolition of the strict division between laypeople and experts. Wave Three, to which Collins and Evans attribute their authorship, retains the belief in the 'real' and not merely relational nature of expert knowledge, but also recognises the existence of people who do not belong to the scientific community, though they have expertise. Cf. Harry Collins and Robert Evans, 'Third

Wave of Science Studies: Studies of Expertise and Experience', Social Studies of Science 32(2) (2002): 239–40.

31. Frank Fischer, *Technocracy and the Politics of Expertise* (London: Sage, 1990); Frank Fischer, *Citizens, Experts, and the Environment* (Durham, NC: Duke University Press, 2000); Frank Fischer, *Democracy and Expertise; Re-Orienting Policy Inquiry* (Oxford: Oxford University Press, 2009); Angela Liberatore and Silvio Funtowicz, '"Democratising" Expertise, "Expertising" Democracy: What Does It Mean, and Why Bother?' *Science and Public Policy* 30(3) (2003): 146–50; Helga Nowotny, 'Democratizing Expertise and Socially Robust Knowledge', *Science and Public Policy* 30(3) (2003): 151–6; Helga Nowotny, Peter Scott and Michael Gibbons, *Re-Thinking Science: Knowledge and the Public in an Age of Uncertainty* (Cambridge: Polity, 2001); Thomas F. Gieryn, 'Boundary-Work and the Demarcation of Science from Non-Science: Strains and Interests in Professional Ideologies of Scientists', *American Sociological Review* 48 (1983): 781–95; Sheila Jasanoff, '(No?) Accounting for Expertise', *Science and Public Policy* 30(3) (2003): 157–62.

32. Bruno Latour, 'Give Me a Laboratory and I Will Raise the World', in Karin Knorr-Cetina and M. Mulkay (eds), *Science Observed: Perspectives on the Social Studies of Science* (London: Sage, 1983), 142–69; Sheila Jasanoff (ed.), 'Ordering Knowledge, Ordering Society', in *States of Knowledge: The Co-Production of Science and Social Order* (London: Routledge, 2004), 13–45; Sheila Jasanoff, 'Breaking the Waves in Science Studies: Comment on H.M. Collins and Robert Evans "The Third Wave of Science Studies"', *Social Studies of Science* 33(3) (2003): 395–6; Mark B. Brown, 'Politicizing Science: Conceptions of Politics in Science and Technology Studies', *Social Studies of Science* (2014): 7–9; Karl Rogers, *Participatory Democracy, Science and Technology: An Exploration in the Philosophy of Science* (Basingstoke: Palgrave Macmillan, 2008), 5.

33. Steve Fuller, *Social Epistemology* (Bloomington: Indiana University Press, 1991), ch. 12.

34. Eyal, *The Crisis of Expertise*, 19.

35. John Ziman, *Real Science: What It Is, and What It Means* (Cambridge: Cambridge University Press, 2000).

36. Cf. Piotr Sztompka, *Zaufanie. Fundament społeczeństwa* (Kraków: Wydawnictwo Znak, 2007); Jamie Carlin Watson, *Expertise: A Philosophical Introduction* (London: Bloomsbury, 2021), 8–10.

37. Cf. Steve Fuller, *Post-Truth: Knowledge as a Power Game* (London: Anthem, 2018); Steve Fuller, *A Player's Guide to the Post-Truth Condition: The Name of the Game* (London: Anthem, 2020).

38. Cf. Rogers, *Participatory Democracy*, 143, 217.

39. Carole Pateman, *Participation and Democratic Theory* (Cambridge: Cambridge University Press, 1970); Peter Bachrach and Ariel Botwinick, *Power and Empowerment: A Radical Theory of Participatory Democracy* (Philadelphia, PA: Temple University Press, 1992); Peter Bachrach, 'Elite Consensus and Democracy', *Journal of Politics* 24(3) (1962): 439–52; Crawford Brough

Macpherson, *Life and Times of Liberal Democracy* (Oxford: Oxford University Press, 1977); Benjamin Barber, *Strong Democracy: Participatory Democracy for a New Age* (Berkeley: University of California Press, 1984). Cf. Mark Stears, *Demanding Democracy: American Radicals in Search of a New Politics* (Princeton, NJ: Princeton University Press, 2010).

40. See Rogers, *Participatory Democracy*, ch. 5; Daniel Kleinman (ed.), 'Democratizations of Science and Technology', in *Science, Technology and Democracy* (Albany: State University of New York Press, 2000), 139–65.

41. Mirowski, 'Democracy, Expertise', 35.

42. It should be noted that some authors attribute the exact opposite position to Dewey, that is, a technocratic vision of politics in which it is experts who develop solutions to major social problems on behalf of and at the initiative of citizens. This is partly justified. In a famous passage from *The Public and Its Problems*, Dewey openly states that 'the man who wears the shoe knows best that it pinches and where it pinches, even if the expert shoemaker is the best judge of how the trouble is to be remedied'. It can be concluded from this that Dewey would have been at least an advocate of an autonomous science and politics (cf. Jeffrey Friedman, *Power Without Knowledge: A Critique of Technocracy* (Oxford: Oxford University Press, 2020, ch. 2.4)). However, the prevailing opinion among scholars is that Dewey was anti-technocratic. For example, Richard J. Bernstein argues that 'Dewey certainly recognizes that there is a positive role for expert knowledge in a democratic society . . . But, ultimately, democratic citizens must judge and decide, not the experts' (R. J. Bernstein, 'Dewey's Vision of Radical Democracy', in Mooly Cochran (ed.), *The Cambridge Companion to Dewey* (Cambridge: Cambridge University Press, 2010, p. 293)). On this subject, Dewey's position contrasts so sharply to Walter Lippmann's approach that some scholars draw a straight line leading from Dewey to the radical political demands of the New Left. As Robert Westbrook has stated, 'perhaps nowhere did Dewey's ideals echo more resoundingly than in the "Port Huron Statement" (1962) of the Students for a Democratic Society' (Robert B. Westbrook, *John Dewey and American Democracy* (Ithaca, NY: Cornell University Press, 1991, p. 549)).

43. Authors representing SSS have not put out an unequivocal assessment of this state of affairs. Some believe that regardless of the imperfections of the research process we should see scientists as having privileged access to reality. The alternative is post-truth, chaos, manipulation, inconsistent and ineffective political action. This view is held by Harry Collins, according to whom even the most reliably unreliable discipline of econometrics should be treated with the respect due to the most exact scientific endeavour. 'Remember, the big danger is not the rejection of any specific claim coming out of the scientific and technological community, and certainly not the surreptitious and hypocritical rejection of any particular expert finding. The big danger is the explicit rejection of expertise per se as a moderator of governmental power and a source of checks and balances; such explicit rejection is an attempt to change the basic civic epistemology upon which collective decisions are

based' (Collins, Evans and Weinel, *Experts and the Will*, 82). 'A problem arises only if increasing the diversity of expertise is confused with the democratisation of expertise.' (Collins, Evans and Weinel, *Experts and the Will*, 83). Others, including Sheila Jasanoff, believe that we should also stop privileging the expert perspective over the allegedly lay perspective. Expert status, the rules of scientific demonstration, methods of data collection and analysis are defined culturally (cf. Mirowski, 'Democracy, Expertise', 20). This is why everyone, including laypeople, should decide which parts of the research process can and should be subjected to social critique and discussion. Science should be assessed and reflected upon by a much larger group of people than just experts.

44. Cf. Brown, 'Politicizing Science', 13–16.
45. Mirowski, 'Democracy, Expertise', 5.
46. Philip Kitcher, *Science, Truth, and Democracy* (Oxford: Oxford University Press, 2001); Philip Kitcher, *Science in a Democratic Society* (Amherst, NY: Prometheus, 2011).
47. Martin Kusch, 'Towards a Political Philosophy of Risk: Experts and Publics in Deliberative Democracy', in Tim Lewens (eds), *Risk: Philosophical Perspectives* (London: Routledge, 2007), 131–55.
48. Steve Fuller, 'The Constitutively Social Character of Expertise', in Evan Selinger and Robert P. Crease (eds), *The Philosophy of Expertise* (New York: Columbia University Press, 2006), 348.
49. See Stephen Turner, *Liberal Democracy 3.0: Civil Society in an Age of Experts* (London: Palgrave, 2003), ch. 5.
50. Collins, Evans and Weinel, *Experts and the Will*, 80.
51. Mark B. Brown, *Science in Democracy: Expertise, Institutions, and Representation* (Cambridge, MA: MIT Press, 2009).
52. Alfred Moore, *Critical Elitism: Deliberation, Democracy, and the Problem of Expertise* (New York: Cambridge University Press, 2017); Alfred Moore, 'Deliberative Democracy and Science', in Andre Bächtiger et al. (eds), *Oxford Handbook of Deliberative* (Oxford: Oxford University Press, 2018); Alfred Moore, 'Democratic Reason, Democratic Faith, and the Problem of Expertise', *Critical Review* 26(1/2) (2014): 101–14.

Chapter 1

EXPERTISE IN LIBERAL POLITICAL THEORY: PROBLEMS AND DISCREPANCIES

Contemporary liberal political philosophers are not especially interested in the topic of expertise. In *A Theory of Justice*, whose content has been informing philosophical debates for half a century, Rawls only addresses the subject once, and very peremptorily at that.[1] He simply does not consider it a philosophical problem in the strict sense – perhaps something which, at best, fits within the scope of non-ideal theory. It has to do with the application of ideal theory to reality, but it does not essentially impact Rawls' considerations regarding his primary philosophical interests: justice, equality and liberty. In other words, the problem of expertise is technical in nature. So let it be handled by political and social scientists. Philosophers should focus on more fundamental issues,[2] such as the aims of a political system rather than ways of arriving at one. Of course, one cannot tell to what extent Rawls bears responsibility for today's liberal thinkers' neglect of the problem of expertise. It is certain, however, that unlike leftist thought, contemporary liberal thought is noticeably reluctant to deal with the subject.[3] Starting with John Dewey's famous discussion with Walter Lippmann, through the manifestos of the New Left, to the Frankfurt School, from the beginning of the previous century the left has grappled with the role of experts in public debate, the decision-making competence of voters and the *raison d'être* of participatory democracy. In our time the value and significance of expertise has also been recognised by advocates of epistocracy. Thinkers like Jason Brennan have no doubt that experts are destined to govern because of their competence. The only problem, as they see it, is how to legitimise expert rule in the eyes of citizens.

I believe – and I will adhere to this view throughout this book – that in spite of sustained efforts to do so, liberal thought cannot go on ignoring the problem of expertise indefinitely. Like other theories of democracy, it cannot avoid examining what makes democratic government work. Without in-depth reflection on the nature, agent (who is an expert?), object (what is expertise about?) and limitations of expertise, a comprehensive and consistent examination of the problem of political power becomes impossible. Any instrumental defence of democracy invoking the salutary consequences of resorting to this form of government makes it imperative to define the competence and knowledge required to govern effectively. Regardless of whether one considers democracy to be about showing respect to the citizens,[4] creating good conditions for economic growth,[5] maintaining peace,[6] protecting the natural environment,[7] upholding human rights and avoiding the *'primary bads*: war, famine, economic collapse, political collapse, epidemic and genocide',[8] attaining these goals requires expertise and the support of those who have it. Some thinkers have also argued to the contrary, of course. Supporters of what is known as pure proceduralism claim that the value of democracy inheres in the very procedure proper to this form of government (as an expression of liberty and equal respect for all citizens), whatever the consequences. *Fiat justitia et pereat mundus.* Democracy must remain faithful to its normative ideals and procedures, and cannot sacrifice them in the service of any goal. Usually, pure proceduralists claim that upholding democratic values boils down to ensuring equality and political impartiality (sometimes interpreted as equality of opportunity).[9]

Pure proceduralism does not have many supporters among theorists, who are usually aware of the need to ensure compliance with other conditions of political legitimacy, such as the rationality of the solutions implemented in the wake of applying the democratic procedure.[10] David Estlund has convincingly shown that no political system can be legitimised on procedural grounds alone. A coin flip will always be the most procedurally impartial method of settling controversies.[11] If anyone claims to have a better solution, they must justify it on grounds other than impartiality alone. They must have a theory of how the form of government they propose is actually more effective. This is why pure proceduralism has more avowed proponents among political practitioners, in particular among populists.[12] For this attitude fits in perfectly with the anti-elitist rhetoric. Calling for uncritical submission to the will of the people, regardless of the consequences, lets populists successively dismantle systemic safety devices like independent judiciary and supervisory institutions, or to ignore the recommendations of international organisations.[13] However, as they gain power, populists tend to abandon procedural arguments in favour of substantive ones. When the will of the people ceases to align with their purposes, they part ways with it without qualms.

The substantial justification of democracy, invoking the effectiveness of this form of government, turns out to be integral to the political narrative on the practical level.[14] Even when explicitly ignored, it usually lurks beneath the theoretical and practical assumptions. A good method of uncovering such assumptions is to ask about the limits of democratic government. Can the democratic majority shape politics and social life as they see fit, with no constraints? How one answers this question usually reveals one's vision of the purpose of democratic government and at the same time the criterion by which to judge its efficacy. It also shines a spotlight on the type of expertise that is essential to the pursuit of this aim. Most of the time the expertise in question concerns moral issues – a specific definition of the common good, liberty or social justice. These limits imposed on democratic power are supposed to protect that which should never depend on the changing will of the majority: human rights, essential values like personal liberty, the political liberty and security of citizens. However, these assumptions are concerned not only with moral competence but also with the technical and specialist competence needed in order to govern.

Nor are these assumptions foreign to liberal thought. They usually undergird definitions of rationality and public reason. It is here that the liberal vision of the type of competence that is indispensable to participation in political life is ordinarily implicit. The ideas of Rawls are a perfect example. As already mentioned, Rawls made only perfunctory reference to the problem of expertise.[15] The subject almost never appears in *Theory of Justice*. In the hypothetical original position it is simply assumed that individuals behind the veil of ignorance are familiar with the basic facts of social, economic and political life. The question of how they came to have this knowledge, whether any parts of it are controversial, and whether everyone understands it to the same degree are outside Rawls' interest. Any asymmetries in access to information are ruled out *a priori*, and so also any expertise. Where there are no laypeople, there are no experts either. Since everyone is an expert in the original position, there are no experts, period. 'Here the experts are rational legislators able to take an objective perspective because they are impartial.'[16]

Rawls did not consider the problem of expertise particularly important in *Political Liberalism* either, although he did not disregard it entirely. He assigned scientific controversies to the category of 'burdens of judgement', that is, reasons why even reasonable people might disagree.[17] Pushed out of the spotlight of political reflection, the problem of expertise however resurfaces in another area: the definition of reasonableness and of the admissibility of statements in public debate.[18] According to Rawls, an opinion must meet three conditions in order to be taken into account in the public sphere, namely:

1. it must respect the rules of proof and argumentation generally accepted by the members of a given conversational community;[19]
2. it has to be consistent with scientific findings (if they are largely uncontested) and common knowledge, both of which impose material constraints on the debate – their denial is a ground for deeming the argument irrational;[20]
3. the arguments it uses must be in a public form – arguments that openly advance the interests of a particular individual or group are not admissible in the public sphere.[21]

From the standpoint of public discussion it is therefore crucial for all the arguments raised to be formulated in such a way as to be admissible within a given argumentation community. This does not mean that it is necessary to limit oneself to stating the bare facts. References to one's personal experience, storytelling or even the use of rhetorical devices is admissible provided the community in question accepts it.[22] Secondly, arguments cannot appeal to one's personal interest so that a conflict of interest between discussants does not become an obstacle to agreement. Lastly, and most importantly to us here, only arguments supported by commonly recognised facts (scientific ones and those generally accepted as true) are considered reasonable. Arguments contradicted by the scientific consensus cannot be used in public debate.[23] The reasonableness of a statement is therefore predicated upon its being consistent with the knowledge authorised by the scientific community.

Of course, such a laconic definition of what makes a statement reasonable raises several doubts.[24] How can we tell that an issue is not contentious/disputed? What if the scientific community is divided on an issue? What if the scientific findings defy common knowledge? There is no way of solving any of these quandaries by taking recourse in the ideas of Rawls alone. The only thing that remains undoubted is that rationality requires that scientific knowledge be taken into account in public discussions. This opens the door to expert participation in the public sphere. However, where experts stand in relation to other citizens remains unclear.

THREE VISIONS OF CITIZENS' DECISION-MAKING COMPETENCE

Such doubts continue to haunt post-Rawlsian liberal thought as well.[25] For example, Gutmann and Thompson are aware that democratic rule must invariably rely on expertise,[26] but they see no problems with using the latter. When claiming that 'Citizens are justified in relying on experts if they describe the basis for their conclusions in ways that citizens can understand',[27] they presume that the complex meanders of scientific thought can be explained to citizens without running into any major problems. In fact, they do not discuss situations in which there are scientific controversies at all and in which citizens or politicians need to choose among two (or more) similarly well-justified courses of action.

The above cursory treatment of the problem of expertise takes its toll on liberal thinkers when they try to specify the role of ordinary citizens in the decision-making process. Confronted with this problem, they usually opt for one of three theoretical approaches or some combination thereof.

The First Approach: Scientific Knowledge is Not a Political Problem

Some liberal theorists claim that citizens are sufficiently competent to take part in solving not just normative, but to a large extent also technical problems. Admittedly, no one claims that the average person will be able to discuss the prospects of cold fusion competently with a nuclear physicist. There are several issues that no one without specialist scientific training will understand. The way viruses spread and mutate, the level of carbon dioxide in the atmosphere, the rise in global temperatures are all examples of issues where the layperson cannot judge for themselves the correctness of scientific estimates. No one in their right mind would argue otherwise. Nor do any liberals claim it. Instead, they claim that expertise is not a fundamental problem from the perspective of democratic procedures. On the contrary, it provides invaluable support for citizens in taking the most important decisions. The presence of experts in public debate improves citizens' decision-making competence. For example, during the COVID-19 pandemic, public knowledge about the sources, consequences and ways of countering the spread of viruses increased. Citizens filter scientific knowledge through their own experiences and integrate it into their worldview.

John Dewey is rightly considered one of the precursors of this view. His experimentalist vision of democracy warned against excluding anyone from public debate. In Dewey's opinion, democracy is a self-perfecting mechanism that allows citizens to make bad political decisions and to learn from their mistakes. This is why the decision-making competence of ordinary citizens only increases continually in democracies.[28] It is also the reason why all voices should be heard in the public arena. Politics, like science, needs 'the unimpeded flow of information and the freedom to offer and to criticise hypotheses'.[29] A better understanding of reality is born out of the multiplicity of views. Both politics and science suffer when opportunities for criticism are restricted.[30] When ordinary citizens are deprived of the opportunity to question expert recommendations, the narrow scholarly perspective produces disastrous political consequences.[31]

Expert knowledge is not a fundamentally political problem, because most issues, even the most complex ones, can be explained to ordinary citizens in an accessible way. How to prevent a pandemic, the causes and consequences of economic crises and the passing of specific laws are all exoteric knowledge, comprehensible to all. Esoteric scientific knowledge is of little relevance to democratic procedures.

That is why some liberals argue for the wide use of direct democracy. Hélène Landemore is a scholar who is rightly identified with this postulate. According to Landemore, the superiority of democracy to other forms of government stems from its better effectiveness at solving political problems. This effectiveness is due to democracy's ability to exploit citizens' cognitive diversity and socially dispersed knowledge.[32] Her argumentation is simple. Familiarity with scientific theories does not suffice to solve political problems. Politics is decision-making in conditions of uncertainty, constantly facing new problems or well-known problems in a new guise. Under such circumstances, we can never be sure who has the knowledge that will enable us to make the right decision.[33] That is why restricting the group of decision-makers is like closing one eye when driving a car. It narrows one's perspective and shrinks the pool of potentially useful ideas, leading to a disaster.[34] The more people who take part in public debate and decision-making, the greater the chances of finding an optimal solution to problems.[35] As Landemore states:

> there are good reasons to think that for most political problems and under conditions conducive to proper deliberation and proper use of majority rule, a democratic decision procedure is likely to be a better decision procedure than any nondemocratic decision procedures, such as a council of experts or a benevolent dictator. I thus defend a strong version of the epistemic argument for democracy. In my view, all things being equal otherwise, the rule of the many is at least as good as, and occasionally better than, the rule of the few at identifying the common good and providing solutions to collective problems. This is so, I will suggest, because including more people in the decision-making process naturally tends to increase what has been shown to be a key ingredient of collective intelligence in the contexts of both problem solving and prediction – namely, cognitive diversity.[36]

There is no room in this vision for doubt about the role of experts in the public arena. Instead, there is a Condorcet's Jury Theorem-like conviction that:

... under the right conditions and all things being equal otherwise, what matters most to the collective intelligence of a problem-solving group is not so much individual ability as the number of people in the group.[37]

Effective decision-making requires cognitive diversity. As Lu Hong and Scott Page (whose works Landemore heavily draws on) claim, choosing decision-makers based on whatever criterion, whether non-epistemic (race, religion, gender, social status) or epistemic (intelligence, education, professional specialisation, experience) will make them converge in their viewpoints, heuristics, interpretations and predictive models.[38] In those circumstances, the number of original ideas that they bring to the table will still be limited. There is only one way to increase the group's diversity, and that is to increase its numerical size.[39]

However, the diversity of decision-making bodies cannot be increased by making them more socially representative. Representativeness always reduces cognitive diversity. It inevitably means that the voice of some minorities will be neglected. Moreover, we usually do not know what kind of cognitive diversity is important from the standpoint of a given problem.[40] What kind of representativeness is essential when deciding how to fight COVID? Should the same group of decision-makers deliberate on climate change and on the EU budget? According to Landemore each separate problem would require the formation of a new, representative decision-making body. And since that is unfeasible, we should create a single, inclusive space of public discussion in which all voices will be heard.

Landemore occupies one of the most radical positions on the issue of civic empowerment in the liberal tradition. The majority of liberal theorists actually share a more moderate faith in the decision-making capacity of citizens.[41] They believe that although citizens often lack the competence to make the best decision, they should nevertheless participate in all decisions affecting them. Amy Gutmann and Dennis Thompson suggest that in most cases having or not having specialist knowledge cannot be a ground for granting political privilege to any specific group. Gutmann and Thompson provide two arguments to support this view: normative and epistemic. First, they invoke the oft-cited argument about the moral dimension of political decisions and the non-existence of anything akin to moral expertise.[42] Since there are no moral experts, and since all political decisions essentially boil down to pursuing different sets of values, there are no epistemic grounds for epistocracy.[43] Gutmann and Thompson cite examples from healthcare:[44] with regard to issues like transplants or abortion, specialist knowledge alone does not suffice when making decisions that affect other people.[45] Epistocratic theories meanwhile presume that objective, non-controversial choices can be made in such situations – a view that masks real, existing conflicts of value. Meanwhile, putting any expert recommendation into practice will bring about a different set of social consequences. This is why citizens should always be involved in making decisions, including very technical ones. Democracy should emphasise and illuminate places where conflicts of value occur,[46] rather than leave these for the experts to solve. It should problematise that which appears to be essentially uncontroversial at first glance.[47]

This argument is echoed by many theorists of liberalism, including Robert Dahl,[48] in whose opinion every decision, including those that seem strictly technical, has a normative component. This can take a variety of forms: from a decision regarding trade-offs, through an assessment of the long-term consequences of a policy, the identification of stakeholders, to the assessment of individual stakes.[49] In each of these variants, however, it means sacrificing some visions of the world for the sake of the single vision suggested by the experts. According to Julian Reiss, this is particularly true of the social sciences, including economics. In economic analysis, values not only determine the content of proposals, but also the research methodology. 'Values are involved in measuring GDP, the theories of rational choice that are often employed in modelling economic relationships, the testing and acceptance of scientific hypotheses, among other things', he writes.[50]

Secondly, Gutmann and Thompson argue that citizens, even without expertise, can judge the relevance of expert recommendations for themselves. All that is needed is for these recommendations to be comprehensible. Experts should communicate their knowledge in a way that is accessible to everyone. This is not only possible but necessary. The comprehensibility of argumentation should be a precondition of its admission into the decision-making procedure.[51] The problem with the lay–expert relationship is therefore technical: 'The conclusions and the essentials of the reasons that support scientific authority may be made publicly accessible.'[52] Once this is achieved, there will be no obstacles to effective democratic governance.[53] Thomas Christiano similarly recommends that the scientific grounds of every decision be explained to laypeople in a sufficiently accessible manner. In his opinion, the key to success is for part of the academic community to be interdisciplinary.[54] This allows the emergence of overlapping understanding:

> First, it enables the complex and remote theorizing of the expert in a special science to communicate with persons who are not at all experts. The economist can explain much of what they understand to the policy analyst. The analyst can explain what they understand of this, coupled with a knowledge of the legal and political background, to the politician or staffer

or perhaps to relatively sophisticated journalists. The journalists and politicians can explain what they understand to ordinary citizens. These chains of overlapping intelligibility enable politicians and citizens to have some appreciation of the reasons for and against particular policies.[55]

Naturally, not all theoretical subtleties can be explained to laypeople in an equally clear and comprehensible way. It is much more difficult to 'translate' theoretical physics into everyday language than the theory and practice of international relations or economics.[56] Much of the meaning will be lost or misunderstood, but what does get across should allow people to understand the nature of the problem and the main expert claims so as to make conscious political decisions possible.

From the standpoint of this approach to the expert–lay relationship, the structure of deliberative bodies is much more important than the skills of the individual citizens involved.[57] It is not the talents and knowledge of these individuals that count, but the number of perspectives represented by them.[58] So the effectiveness of democracy does not depend upon the education of the citizens, but on the way the knowledge dormant inside them is utilised.[59]

The Second Approach: Every Problem can be Solved by Better Education

Advocates of the second approach, rate the decision-making potential of citizens with somewhat less optimism. They recognise the extent to which effective decision-making depends on taking scientific facts into account. They also accept that citizens do not possess such knowledge, nor do they acquire it (or at least not sufficiently) through participation in public debate. Advocates of this position seldom share the optimism characteristic of the Deweyan experimentalist approach.[60] Most of them are sceptical about the 'automatic' increase in citizens' decision-making potential. Following J. S. Mill, they are more inclined to view education as the means of bringing about these improvements. The better that citizens understand the technical underpinnings of political decisions, the more capable they will be of making informed decisions. It is for this reason that proponents of this view often blame lay ignorance on the esoteric framing of scientific claims. Ordinary people do not have the time to independently look for information and grapple with its intricacies. One should therefore provide them with knowledge that is as user-friendly as possible under conditions that will allow them to assimilate this knowledge. Scientists are usually incapable of communicating their expertise clearly.[61] Moreover, citizens often hear only snippets of the arguments of scientists in the media or from other citizens. Also, citizens usually spend an insufficient amount of time expanding their knowledge on a given subject.[62] It is therefore unsurprising that left to their own devices, without basic knowledge and interpretive tools, resources and time, citizens are easily manipulated by populists and merchants of doubt.

Citizens must be allowed to continuously acquire information and discuss it with experts under optimum conditions. Formal education will not do. Expert knowledge is evolving, the problems discussed are often much more complex than those discussed in schools, and mostly unprecedented. Citizens cannot be expected to deal with them without the continuous development of their competence. The best tools for this are democratic innovations, especially in the form of minipublics. They are based on the idea of 'translating' expertise into lay language. In their most often discussed variant – that of deliberative polling – a randomly selected, socially representative group is supposed to understand the core ideas in expert recommendations by discussing them with experts and amongst themselves. Such discussion is supposed to help laypeople understand the nature and consequences of the alternative solutions proposed by the experts: 'that deliberating citizens will weigh the merits of competing arguments for themselves. And to the extent they are doing so, they are deliberating.'[63]

As Jane Mansbridge states, 'participatory innovations allow citizens to develop their own expertise and provide channels through which the citizens' own expertise can influence policy'.[64] By having the opportunity to talk to experts and encounter exponents of different scientific paradigms, the participants in democratic innovations will be able to understand the nuances of the issues under discussion better than other citizens, which will allow them to present their conclusions to the latter. Representatives of non-governmental organisations are especially well-suited to this task: 'political parties and interest group associations are designed to be communities of like-minded persons in which the persons have a lot of overlapping expertise'.[65]

The Third Approach: Everyone Do Their Job and We'll be Just Fine

Lately theorists have increasingly been embracing another position. They do not claim that citizens are sufficiently competent to take part in decision-making, nor that they should be educated so they can become competent. Instead, their idea is to divide citizens into groups of varying decision-making potential, each such group presiding over a different stage of the decision-making process. Let us call this a 'division of labour' model of decision-making.[66] Its proponents usually recommend creating two separate domains: an expert one (for technical matters) and a civic one (for normative matters). When a strictly normative issue is at stake, the decision should belong to everyone. When examining the matter requires special competence, the opinion of experts should prevail. This division of tasks is supposed to achieve two aims. First, it gives high social legitimacy to the political system.[67] Democratic procedures are retained, while citizens maintain their influence on public life, which in turn generates social trust. Secondly, the epistemic division of labour renders the political system as a whole more effective. Freeing the experts from the pressures of public opinion and politics is supposed to guarantee the disclosure and inclusion of relevant scientific knowledge in the legislative process. The 'division of labour' model is thereby supposed to reconcile political legitimacy with political effectiveness – democracy with epistocracy. It responds to the will of the citizens, on the one hand, and takes into account difficult-to-understand expertise, on the other. To quote Jean-Jacques Rousseau, it is a strategy conducive to 'taking men as they are and laws as they might be'. It is pointless to strive for an ideal; instead, one should exploit the epistemic potential already present in different parts of the social structure. Take from all public participants – citizens, politicians and experts – the best that they have to offer. Thanks to this, the 'division of labour' model is not exposed to the charge of utopianism with which normative political theories often have to contend.

There are many versions of this model. The classical one described above presupposes the existence two autonomous domains in the decision-making process.[68] The first of these is civil society, which is supposed to identify socially prized values and ends deemed worthy of attainment, and to arrange these ends, including the trade-offs between them, into a hierarchy.[69] The second domain is the state apparatus supported by expertise. It is supposed to pursue the values and goals indicated by society. Each of these domains is characterised by domain-typical types of reflection and deliberation. The first is dominated by deliberation of social values and goals, undertaken by ordinary citizens through all available channels: in the public and private sphere, inclusively and exclusively, between citizens within the framework of the non-governmental sector, in interpersonal communication, and via traditional and social media. The outcomes of this deliberation can be gleaned using public opinion polls, consultations and referendums. On the other hand, the deliberation proper to the expert domain is purely instrumental and is conducted in closed, exclusive forums. Together, the two domains realise 'democratically institutionalised will-formation and informal opinion-formation'.[70]

A prototype for such an approach was Habermas' model of the public sphere. Habermas argues for the creation of distinct spaces for wide-ranging discussions within the framework of civil society and for specialist deliberation by politicians and experts. A major role in this process is played by voluntary associations which:

> specialize . . . in discovering issues relevant for all of society, contributing possible solutions to problems, interpreting values, producing good reasons, and invalidating others. They can become effective only indirectly, namely, by altering the parameters of institutionalized will-formation by broadly transforming attitudes and values.[71]

Thanks to this division of labour, experts, politicians and citizens can systemically solve social problems. Habermas' model was expanded by Bohman, who sees a competence-based division of labour as necessary in today's world of hypercomplexity.[72] Any attempts to centrally manage complexity by decision-making bodies limited to the political elite are bound to fail. Managing complexity requires a skilful separation of epistemic roles, while this means often having to rely on expertise, rather than questioning or denying it.[73] 'The epistemic division of labour as such is not inherently undemocratic and anti-egalitarian.'[74] The claim that the inevitable epistemic disparities between citizens justify epistemic government is erroneous because 'effectiveness is a matter not merely of superior knowledge but of greater access to the relevant forum'.[75]

In social studies of science Collins and Evans have expressed a preference for a similar kind of 'division of labour'. They propose that decision-making be divided into a technical and a political phase in which different rules of civic participation and different criteria of recognising a valid testimony would apply, and a different degree and type of legitimacy would be sought.[76] The technical phase would be apolitical, without any room for representation, manipulation or emotional appeals. Its participants would be chosen on account of their competence, belonging to the 'core-set' of a research area. Participation would be direct. Meanwhile, the political phase would be open to citizens, whether through their representatives or via polling and referenda. The only condition of participation would be to be a stakeholder.

As we can see, even in their classical version the various visions of the 'division of labour' model differ, albeit slightly. In the post-Habermasian approaches, the entire society is the agent in the political phase.[77] Collins and Evans, on the other hand, include only stakeholders in this group,[78] which significantly reduces the number of deliberators. Thomas Christiano includes 'interest group associations' in the expert, rather than the civic phase.[79] The citizens brought together within such associations would not so much reveal the values shared broadly in society, as bring correction to the erroneous views of experts and point to the practical limitations of their theoretical models,[80] while being 'the source of anomalies for social scientific theories',[81] 'on the basis of long experience with certain kinds of social structures'.[82]

Non-classical versions of the 'division of labour' model can go even further in proposing reforms to the political system. Landemore, convinced of the decision-making competence of ordinary citizens, would like to see the latter take part in all three phases of decision-making. In the first phase, society would identify the most important social problems. In the second (deliberative) phase, citizens (along with experts) organised into prediction markets would select the two best available solutions to the problems. In the final phase (aggregative/majoritarian), all citizens would democratically choose one of the two solutions.[83] Landemore therefore radicalises the 'division of labour' model not only when it comes to the scale of empowering ordinary citizens, but also to the form of their participation. Most proponents of this model support a more moderate vision. They are usually convinced that parliamentary elections and political representation suffice to identify socially pregnant goals. According to some authors, this should be supplemented with cyclical referendums and public opinion polls (Collins/Evans). Other scholars recommend using democratic innovations. Only a small number call for the inclusion of ordinary citizens in the expert domain as part of prediction markets.

Supporters of the 'division of labour' model also hold different views regarding the role of experts in decision-making. For example, Jason Brennan has proposed a model of 'universal suffrage with epistocratic veto'.[84] The main role here would be played by an epistocratic council made up of citizens selected through a complicated examination procedure. The council could veto any democratically passed law. Thanks to this, all laws would enjoy social legitimacy (as outcomes of applying a democratic procedure), but they would also be more effective (since the least effective laws would be eliminated by the epistocratic council). The overwhelming majority of supporters of the 'division of labour' model, however, do not endorse the idea of giving experts veto rights or direct influence over the course of the decision-making procedure. For example, the only thing that Collins and Evans want is for the opinion of the scientific community to be heard in public debates regarding any political decision. The final decision should be up to democratic bodies.[85] If politicians deliberately ignore the opinion of the scientific community, the citizens should be aware of this fact, and the political decision-makers should be the only ones held to account for the consequences of such decisions.

Currently, the most popular interpretation of the 'division of labour' model is the deliberative systems conception.[86] It is based on the belief that deliberative democracy is neither a philosophical utopia,[87] nor in fact a minor reform of the political system,[88] as some have judged in the past. For it requires neither rational behaviour nor the capacity for reasoned conversation, nor civic virtues from citizens. Nor does it require symmetrical relations between the participants of public debate, nor that everyone be as well informed as possible.[89] Advocates of deliberative systems do not believe it is possible to eliminate manipulation from politics, overcome polarisation and inculcate citizens with the proclivity to respect, consider and accept well-argued views if these happen to be at odds with their personal world view. However, they believe that if we ensure the existence of institutions that guarantee that the current state of scientific knowledge is taken into account in the decision-making process, then voters may remain scientifically ignorant. If regulations are in place that allow everyone to take an active part in politics, there is no need to force all citizens to engage in such activity. As long as there are spaces for the judicious exchange of arguments, there is no need to eliminate partisanship, polarisation and the blind loyalty of voters.[90] If there are institutions that allow citizens to form rational opinions, then citizens should also reserve the right to ignore them and stick with their often irrational and inconsistent preferences. After all, deliberativeness is a characteristic of a political system as a whole, and not of its component parts.[91] If every element of the deliberative ideal is realised by institutions and practices, then the entire system can be said to be deliberative in nature. 'Parts of a system may have relationships of complementarity or displacement. In a complementary relationship, two wrongs can make a right. Two venues, both with deliberative deficiencies, can each make up for the deficiencies of the other.'[92] The elitism of experts, their failure to understand the living conditions of citizens and the social value hierarchies may be balanced by a populist policy responsive to every change of public opinion, and vice versa. From this standpoint, two minuses make a plus.

This position obviously rests on the idea of the epistemic division of labour.[93] Not all citizens want to and are capable, and therefore have to conscientiously assess the soundness of every argument raised in public debate. All members of society can take part in politics, but their roles should differ, in line with their individual aptitudes. Ordinary citizens are competent with regard to the values they hold and the problems they face on a daily basis. Let them therefore pass this information on to politicians and, via the latter, to experts, whose task will be to work out how best to realise those values. Politics must be 'truth-sensitive', but at the same time it must involve citizens in decision-making. That is why an intellectual division of labour does not endanger democracy: 'citizens are essentially in the driver's seat in the society as long as they choose the basic aims the society is to pursue'.[94] If only they do so, they remain the efficient cause behind all political processes.

PROBLEMS AND DISCREPANCIES

In summary, the first approach sees no problem at all with the participation of experts in democratic processes. It assumes that most issues can be explained and understood without recourse to esoteric expert knowledge. Moreover, most politically problematic issues are so normatively entangled that only citizens are predisposed to resolve them. Expert recommendations should be presented to them, and they will judge the value of each on their own. There are therefore no significant obstacles to citizen participation in all political decisions. The more voices, the better. Citizens have common sense and life experience which will always enrich the decision-making process.

The second approach is less optimistic. It sees citizens' lack of expertise as a problem, but not a very serious one. It can be remedied by allowing citizens to hold discussions with experts within the framework of democratic innovations. In this manner, citizens will continually improve their knowledge of the issues discussed. These simple solutions should eliminate the threat of manipulation and irrational, ineffective decisions.

Finally, according to the third approach, expert knowledge is not a major threat to democratic processes, as it can be integrated into the political system in such a way that citizens retain their causal role. It is enough for them to evaluate the effects of the implementation of expert recommendations, and politics loses nothing in its democratic character, but gains in effectiveness.

All of these approaches ignore the problem of citizen incompetence to a greater or lesser extent. Each of them is based on different epistemic assumptions. The first presupposes that citizens are by and large competent enough to take part in decision-making on an independent footing. Their individual experience provides them with insights that they can use to shine a new light on political problems. This is why everyone deserves to be included in the decision-making process. The second approach presupposes that citizens are admittedly not competent enough, but they can gain competence if only complicated scientific theories are presented to them in an accessible way. The third approach assumes that the effectiveness of a political system as a whole requires no competence on the part of citizens whatsoever. It is the experts who must be competent, while citizens can go about their own business and focus on their own problems. It is important to note that the three methodological approaches cannot be reconciled or reduced to a common denominator. According to the first, educating citizens may prove harmful, since it will produce uniformity. It will limit the diversity of viewpoints and by the same token the pool of worthwhile ideas. According to the second, it is imperative to educate citizens if democracy is to be effective. Only educated citizens can grasp the choices they face. The first approach involves a vision of an active citizenry that questions expertise based on their own experience. The second approach rests on a vision of passive citizens, mere recipients of the expert narrative.[95] The first approach is reminiscent of the participatory and constructivist perspective typical of the Second Wave in social studies of science (Jasanoff, Wynne, Irwin). The second approach is akin to the 'deficit model' of the lay–expert relationship typical of the First Wave. The two seem irreconcilable. According to the third approach, citizens do not have to be educated or for that matter included *en masse* in decision-making. Whether they are competent or not is irrelevant to how democracy functions. Familiarity with their own circumstances makes citizens sufficiently capable of assessing politicians and therefore of remaining the 'in the driver's seat in the society'. This vision seems to make little of lay ignorance, or at least not to see it as a major obstacle to a functional democratic system.[96]

Despite these differences, democracy theorists have routinely used the above three approaches in all kinds of configurations. For example, Landemore draws on all three when claiming that:

> there are good reasons to think that for most political problems and under conditions conducive to proper deliberation and proper use of majority rule, a democratic decision procedure is likely to be a better decision procedure than any nondemocratic decision procedures, such as a council of experts or a benevolent dictator . . .[97]

Landemore even advocates including citizens in decisions that are seemingly technical in nature – for instance, regarding nuclear energy or GMOs.[98] On the other hand, she suggests that it is reasonable to involve citizens in hybrid (deliberative) forums in which they consult experts. Finally, she recognises that the complexity of reality and the complicated nature of the decisions citizens face mean that 'professional politicians and experts will always be needed'. However, in her view:

> The recognition that a category of individuals labelled as 'experts' can legitimately speak for the people is not necessarily incompatible with the

view that ultimately the people know best and remain the underlying source of normative authority, not just on fairness grounds, but also on epistemic grounds.[99]

Christiano combines the second and third approach. Above all, he believes in the possibility of raising laypeople's decision-making competence. He recommends the use of democratic innovations as a way of taking advantage of the knowledge individuals already have while helping them to develop new skills.[100] He has on many occasions written that the main obstacle preventing laypeople from grasping the intricacies of the most important decisions is technical in nature and boils down to lack of time. Citizens desiring to make competent decisions 'would have to neglect all the other tasks they perform in the society in order to have the requisite knowledge'.[101] A society of engaged citizens would have to be like the Athenian *polis*, consisting of a small group of free citizens devoting their time to political affairs, while the majority of the people perform more down-to-earth tasks.

Relying on experts is a much simpler and more equitable solution.[102] As long as they do not tamper with the goals chosen by society, using their services will be much like using a word processor.[103] We do not need to know how a computer works as long as we can trust it to save the words we type. It does not matter that citizens cannot oversee experts or say which expert is the most competent.[104] They do not have to. This is why their interaction with experts is limited:

> (1) citizens can play some important role in determining what the aims of scientific research are; (2) different parts of the society can be the sources of different theoretical approaches to expert knowledge; and (3) citizens can do some checking on the defensibility of expert knowledge.[105]

Citizens are therefore supposed to set the goals of scientific research and assess findings.

Gutmann and Thompson recommend using all three strategies. Their works express a conviction that citizens are inevitably participants in all decision-making bodies, and the faith that if they ever lack specialist knowledge, they can acquire it thanks to the 'translation' of expert theorems into everyday language. Finally, they also propose a variant of the 'division of labour' model in which the citizens define social priorities and desirable social value hierarchies, while the political representatives and expert committees work to realise them.[106]

As a result, these authors often have to grapple with serious theoretical conundrums. One obvious point of contention is reconciling faith in the decision-making competence of citizens with the call to take expert opinions into account. The potential contradictions here are apparent all everywhere. For instance, Gutmann and Thompson sometimes claim that citizens will always be forced to rely on expertise. Reality is too complicated for them to grasp the processes governing it by themselves. On the other hand, however, these same authors do not endorse blind trust in experts. If democracy is not to turn into technocracy, citizens must have independent grounds for trusting expertise. This is precisely why expert statements have to be translated into a language laypeople can understand. Only then will ordinary citizens be able to compare them with the recommendations and opinions of other experts and to settle any disputes. And whenever it proves impossible to understand the experts, laypeople should assess the scholars' track record.[107] Understanding expertise and being able to assess the competence of its authors are foundational when it comes to the democratic use of scientific knowledge. Without these skills, citizens lose all political agency.

This framing of the subject gives rise to a number of doubts. First, it suggests that it is beyond laypeople's capacity to formulate theories or draft expert opinions, but that assessing the validity of such opinions is fully within their power. Even though citizens lack the theoretical basics to understand reality, once they learn them (and they are apparently capable of doing that), they gain the ability to independently assess their application. This seems to be an overly optimistic assumption.

Secondly, the expectation that expert recommendations be made universally understandable is at odds with the posit that expert competence should be assessed by laypeople. If it is possible to translate expertise into common speech, why would citizens need to additionally assess experts' competence or track record? And if expertise cannot be translated into everyday language then on what basis would laypeople be able to gauge experts' earlier achievements? If they are unable to assess the value of their current recommendations, how can they possibly be able to assess their track record? *Democracy and Disagreement* leaves these questions unanswered.

Thirdly, Gutman and Thompson posit the need for expert institutions, but they justify this mainly by invoking practical considerations and not the need to reduce the epistemic gulf between citizens, politicians and experts. 'Legislators cannot take an active part in, and inform themselves and the public fully on every issue on which they vote.'[108] Not every stakeholder can be heard and directly involved in the decision-making process.[109] There simply is not enough time, money and sometimes even willingness to participate. This is why Gutmann and Thompson opt for a variant of the 'division of labour' model in which citizens define social priorities and value hierarchies, while their political representatives and expert committees work to achieve them. For example:

> the choice of priorities in health care of the significance of those raised in this case should be at the center of 'the broad scheme of things'. The reasons for these priorities should be brought to the public's attention, and legislators should be open to public responses to their reasons.[110]

But putting the matter in these terms still leaves quite a lot of doubt. How are we to justify ceding some decision-making competence to undemocratic expert committees when at the same time it is assumed that citizens are capable of understanding the basis of even the most specialised expert opinions? How do we non-arbitrarily differentiate decisions that lie within citizens' competence from those that do not? And how do we differentiate seemingly purely technical decisions from those involving a normative component? Whom would it be up to to make such decisions: an expert council, a group of stakeholders (and who is to identify them?) or all citizens with no exception? It is hard to find an answer to these questions in Gutmann and Thompson's works.

Juggling a variety of methodological approaches forces Gutmann and Thompson to resort to a myriad different arguments in favour of assigning a dominant role in the legislative process to citizens. The reader therefore encounters the postulate of placing limited trust in experts and the requirement for expertise to be made comprehensible as well as the belief that political decisions involve a moral component and, therefore, citizens cannot be excluded from making them. We find both the 'division of labour' model here and arguments in favour of deliberative forums. There is the recommendation that experts confront other (independent) experts,[111] but no fleshing out of the mechanisms citizens could use to competently choose among competing opinions. Gutmann and Thompson's narrative seems to be characterised by a constant tension between the alleged decision-making competence of laypeople, including on technical issues, and the belief that it is necessary to develop objective criteria by which to judge expert authority.

None of the authors cited above convincingly explain how trust in expert opinion is to be reconciled with the empowerment of citizens, who are supposed to have the right to bring a corrective to the work of scientists. Nor do any of them say what citizens should do when the scientific community is divided. Following in Rawls' footsteps, they seem to assume that the experts will be unanimous with regard to the most important political decisions. Nor do they tell us what to do if the experts fail to persuade society to embrace their reasons.[112] In the coming chapters I will put forward the claim that these discrepancies are due to an imprecise definition of expertise and an erroneous understanding of its limitations.

NOTES

1. John Rawls, *A Theory of Justice*, rev. edn (Oxford: Oxford University Press 1999), § 54.
2. In *The Law of Peoples* in reference to the nuclear deterrence of outlaw states, Rawls says that 'How best to do this belongs to expert knowledge, which philosophy doesn't possess' (John Rawls, *The Law of Peoples* (Cambridge, MA: Harvard University Press, 1999), 9).
3. Cf. Fischer, *Democracy and Expertise*, 1–2, 17.
4. Amartya Sen, 'Democracy as a Universal Value', *Journal of Democracy* 10(3) (1999): 3–17.
5. See Adam Przeworski, 'Democracy and Economic Development', in Edward D. Mansfield and Richard Sisson (eds), *The Evolution of Political Knowledge* (Columbus, OH: Ohio State University Press, 2004); cf. Adam Przeworski, 'Institutions Matter?' *Governemnt and Opposition* 39(2) (2004): 527–40.
6. See Alex Mintz and Nehemia Geva, 'Why Don't Democracies Fight Each Other? An Experimental Study', *Journal of Conflict Resolution* 37(3) (1993): 484–503.
7. Michèle B. Bättig and Thomas Bernauer, 'National Institutions and Global Public Goods: Are Democracies More Cooperative in Climate Change Policy?' *International Organization* 63(2) (2009): 281–308.
8. David M. Estlund, *Democratic Authority: A Philosophical Framework* (Princeton, NJ: Princeton University Press, 2008), 160.
9. Cf. Fabienne Peter, 'Pure Epistemic Proceduralism', *Episteme. A Journal of Social Epistemology* 5(1) (2008): 34–5.
10. Peter, 'Pure Epistemic Proceduralism', 36. Cf. Fabienne Peter, 'Democratic Legitimacy and Proceduralist Social Epistemology', *Politics, Philosophy & Economics* 6(3) (2007): 329–53.
11. David M. Estlund, 'Beyond Fairness and Deliberation: The Epistemic Dimension of Democratic Authority', in James Bohman and William Rehg (eds), *Deliberative Democracy: Essays on Reason and Politics* (Cambridge, MA: MIT Press, 1997), 178.
12. Cf. Michael Kaplan, 'Prohibiting the People: Populism, Procedure and the Rhetoric of Democratic Desire', *Constellations* (2018): 1–22, DOI: 10.1111/1467-8675.12370.
13. After his actions were said to be unconstitutional, the Polish president, Andrzej Duda, stated openly in an interview that his mandate was stronger than that of the constitution, since more people voted for him than in favour of the constitution in 1997, available at: https://www.wsieciprawdy.pl/prezydent-zdradza-swoj-plan-pnews-3207.html, last accessed 15 March 2021.

14. Cf. Amy Gutmann and Dennis Thompson, *Why Deliberative Democracy?* (Princeton, NJ: Princeton University Press, 2004), 25–6, 130–1.

15. The subject is taken up by Darrin Durant, who interprets the dispute between the Wave Three and Wave Two in social studies of science from the standpoint of the opposition between Rawls and Habermas. In his view 'Discussion between Collins and Evans versus Jasanoff and Wynne is actually a case shaped by different positions within liberal democratic theory' (Darrin Durant, 'Models of Democracy in Social Studies of Science', *Social Studies of Science* 41 (2011): 692. Cf Harry Collins and Robert Evans, *Why Democracies Need Science* (Cambridge: Polity, 2017), 118–19).

16. Rawls, *A Theory of Justice*, § 54.

17. 'The evidence-empirical and scientific-bearing on the case is conflicting and complex, and thus hard to assess and evaluate' (John Rawls, *Political Liberalism* (New York: Columbia University Press, 1996), 56).

18. Cf. Gutmann and Thompson, *Why Deliberative Democracy?* 10.

19. Rawls, *Political Liberalism*, 224.

20. See Rawls, *Political Liberalism*, 67, 139.

21. Rawls, *Political Liberalism*, li, 137.

22. Cf. Lynn Sanders, 'Against Deliberation', *Political Theory* 25(3) (1997), 347–76; Iris Marion Young, *Inclusion and Democracy* (Oxford: Oxford University Press, 2000), 53, 72–6; Iris Marion Young, 'Activist Challenges to Deliberative Democracy', in James S. Fishkin and Peter Laslett (eds), *Debating Deliberative Democracy* (Oxford: Oxford University Press, 2003), 102–20; Iris Marion Young, 'Justice, Inclusion, and Deliberative Democracy', in Stephen Macedo (ed.), *Deliberative Politics: Essays on 'Democracy and Politics, Collective Intelligence, and the Rule of the Many* (Princeton, NJ: Princeton University Press, 2013), 95.

23. See Alfred Moore, 'Democratic Theory and Expertise: Between Competence and Consent', in Cathrine Holst (ed.), *Expertise and Democracy* (Oslo: ARENA Centre for European Studies, 2014), 59–60.

24. Stanley Fish, 'Mutual Respect as a Device of Exclusion', in Stephen Macedo (ed.), *Deliberative Politics: Essays on 'Democracy and Disagreement'* (New York: Oxford University Press, 1999), 88–102. Cf. Michael Walzer, 'Deliberation, and What Else?' in Stephen Macedo (ed.), *Deliberative Politics: Essays on 'Democracy and Disagreement'* (New York: Oxford University Press, 1999), 67.

25. Cf. Mark B. Brown, 'Expertise and Deliberative Democracy', in Stephen Elstub and Peter McLaverty (eds), *Deliberative Democracy: Issues and Cases* (Edinburgh: Edinburgh University Press, 2014), 53.

26. The principle of reciprocity requires deliberants to refer to knowledge that aligns with the scientific consensus (Amy Gutmann and Dennis Thompson, *Democracy and Disagreement* (New York: Cambridge University Press, 1996), 15).

27. Gutmann and Thompson, *Why Deliberative Democracy?* 5.

28. Elisabeth Anderson, 'The Epistemology of Democracy', *Episteme: A Journal of Social Epistemology* 3(1/2) (2006): 13–14.

29. Cheryl Misak, 'A Culture of Justification: The Pragmatist's Epistemic Argument for Democracy', *Episteme* 5(1) (2008): 96.

30. See Robert B. Talisse, *Democracy after Liberalism: Pragmatism and Deliberative Politics* (New York: Routledge, 2005), 104.

31. Dewey, *The Public and Its Problems*, 208–9.

32. Cf. Michael Fuerstein, 'Epistemic Democracy and the Social Character of Knowledge', *Episteme. A Journal of Social Epistemology* 5(1) (2008): 83–4.

33. Cf. Melissa Lane, 'When the Experts are Uncertain: Scientific Knowledge and the Ethics of Democratic Judgment', *Episteme* 11(1) (2014): 109–11.

34. Cf. Hélène Landemore, 'Why the Many are Smarter than the Few and Why It Matters', *Journal of Public Deliberation* 8 (2012): 1–14.

35. Hélène Landemore, 'Yes, We Can (Make It Up on Volume): Answers to Critics', *Critical Review* 26(1/2) (2014): 209.

36. Landemore, *Democratic Reason*, 3.

37. Landemore, *Democratic Reason*, 104.

38. Scott E. Page, 'Making the Difference: Applying a Logic of Diversity', *Academy of Management Perspectives* 21(4) (2007): 7–8; Scott E. Page, *The Difference: How the Power of Diversity Creates Better Groups, Firms, Schools, and Societies* (Princeton, NJ: Princeton University Press, 2007), 7.

39. Hélène Landemore, 'Deliberative Democracy as Open, not (just) Representative Democracy', *Daedalus* 146(3) (2017): 51–63.

40. Landemore, *Democratic Reason*, 111.

41. Mark Warren, 'Deliberative Democracy', in April Carter and Geoffrey Stokes (eds), *Democratic Theory Today: Challenges for the 21st Century* (Cambridge and Malden, MA: Polity and Blackwell, 2002); Mark E. Warren, 'Deliberative Democracy and Authority', *American Political Science Review* 90(1) (1996): 46–60; Joshua Cohen and Charles Sabel, 'Directly-Deliberative Democracy', *European Law Journal* 3(4) (1977): 313–42; Joshua Cohen and Archon Fung, 'Radical Democracy', *Swiss Journal of Political Science* 10(4) (2004): 23–34; Archon Fung and Erik Olin Wright, 'Deepening Democracy: Innovations in Empowered Participatory Governance', *Politics and Society* 29 (2001): 5–41; Bernard Manin, 'On Legitimacy and Political Deliberation', *Political Theory* 15(3) (1987): 352–3.

42. Gutman and Thompson, *Democracy and Disagreement*, 215. Cf. Robert Dahl, *Democracy and Its Critics* (New Haven, CT: Harvard University Press, 1989), 66–7; Cathrine Holst and Anders Molander, 'Epistemic Democracy and the Role of Experts', *Contemporary Political Theory* (2019): doi.org/10.1057/s41296-018-00299-4, p. 10.

43. Cf. Karen Jones and François Schroeter, 'Moral Expertise', *Analyse & Kritik* 2 (2012): 219–23.

44. Amy Gutmann and Dennis Thompson, 'Deliberative Democracy Beyond Process', *Journal of Political Philosophy* 10(2) (2002): 153–74; Gutmann and Thompson, *Why Deliberative Democracy?* 104–5.

45. Gutmann and Thompson, *Why Deliberative Democracy?* 11, 14, 21, 74–6. 'Although experts may be the best judges of scientific evidence, they have

no special claim to finding the right answers about priorities when degrees of risk and trade-offs of costs and benefits are involved.'

46. See Amy Gutmann and Dennis Thompson, 'Moral Conflict and Political Consensus', *Ethics* 101(1) (1990): 64–88; Gutmann and Thompson *Why Deliberative Democracy?* 153.

47. Amy Gutmann and Dennis Thompson, 'Deliberating about Bioethics', *Hastings Center Report* 27 (1997): 39–41; Gutmann and Thompson, *Why Deliberative Democracy?* 102.

48. Dahl, *Democracy and Its Critics*, ch. 5.

49. The technology assessment current also provides many examples of seemingly purely technical decisions which turn out to have a normative component. Technology can make one into an object, as in the case of reproductive technologies, exclude minorities (Robert Moses), disadvantage different age or social groups (see Langdon Winner, 'Do Artifacts have Politics?' *Daedalus* 109(1) (1980): 123–5; Wiebe Bijker, 'Why and How Technology Matters?' in Robert E. Goodin and Charles Tilly (eds), *Oxford Handbook of Contextual Analysis* (Oxford: Oxford University Press 2006), 682). Technologies can alter societies in the long term and set the tone of entire time periods (technological determinism). This is why Richard Sclove claimed that like the Old Amish, we should discuss, analyse, forecast and study the social impact of technologies on a small scale before making them widely available (Richard Sclove, *Democracy and Technology* (New York: Guilford Press, 1995), 56–61).

50. Julian Reiss, 'Expertise, Agreement, and the Nature of Social Scientific Facts or: Against Epistocracy', *Social Epistemology* (2019): 6, DOI: 10.1080/02691728.2019.1577513. Cf. Klemens Kappel and Julie Zahle, 'The Epistemic Role of Science and Expertise in Liberal Democracy', in Miranda Fricker et al. (eds), *The Routledge Handbook of Social Epistemology* (New York: Routledge, 2019), 399–401.

51. Gutmann and Thompson, *Why Deliberative Democracy?* 5, 146.

52. Gutmann and Thompson, *Why Deliberative Democracy?* 145.

53. James Bohman, *Public Deliberation: Pluralism, Complexity, and Democracy* (Cambridge, MA: MIT Press, 1996), 64, 192.

54. Thomas Christiano, 'Rational Deliberation Among Experts and Citizens', in John Parkinson and Jane Mansbridge (eds), *Deliberative* (Cambridge: Cambridge University Press 2012), 38–9; Jane Mansbridge et al., 'A Systemic Approach to Deliberative Democracy', in John Parkinson and Jane Mansbridge (eds), *Deliberative Systems* (Cambridge: Cambridge University Press, 2012), 15–16.

55. Christiano, 'Rational Deliberation', 39.

56. Christiano, 'Rational Deliberation', 39. See a similar view expressed by Michael Polanyi (Michael Polanyi, 'The Republic of Science: Its Political and Economic Theory', *Minerva* 1 (1962): 59–60).

57. Landemore, *Democratic Reason*, 106.

58. Jason Brennan, *Against Democracy* (Princeton, NJ: Princeton University Press, 2016).

59. Cf. Archon Fung, 'Putting the Public Back into Governance: The Challenges of Citizen Participation and Its Future', *Public Administration Review* 75(4) (2015): 517–18.

60. See Rogers, *Participatory Democracy*, 28–32, 120, 203.

61. Cf. Hugo Mercier, 'When Experts Argue: Explaining the Best and the Worst of Reasoning', *Argumentation* 25 (2011): 313–27.

62. Cf. Thomas Christiano, *The Rule of the Many: Fundamental Issues in Democratic Theory* (Boulder, CO: Westview Press, 1996), 176–7.

63. James S. Fishkin, *When the People Speak: Deliberative Democracy and Public Consultation* (Oxford: Oxford University Press, 2009), 47.

64. Mansbridge et al., 'A Systemic Approach', 16.

65. Christiano, 'Rational Deliberation', 40.

66. Cf. Kappel and Zahle, 'The Epistemic Role of Science', 367–70, 401–2.

67. John Parkinson, *Deliberating in the Real World; Problems of Legitimacy in Deliberative Democracy* (Oxford: Oxford University Press, 2006), 42.

68. Autonomy does not rule out criticism and control, as long as the latter are reciprocal. 'Despite the technocratic view, experts have not become sovereign over politicians subjected to the demands of the facts and left with a purely fictitious power of decision. Nor, despite the implications of the decisionistic model, does the politician retain a preserve outside of the necessarily rationalized areas of practice in which practical problems are decided upon as ever by acts of the will' (Jürgen Habermas, *Toward a Rational Society: Student Protest, Science, and Politics*, trans. Jeremy J. Shapiro (Cambridge: Polity, 1987), 67).

69. Christiano, *The Rule of the Many*, 170–1.

70. Jürgen Habermas, *Between Facts and Norms: Contributions to a Discourse Theory of Law and Democracy*, trans. William Rehg (Cambridge, MA: MIT Press, 1996), 308.

71. Habermas, *Between Facts and Norms*, 485.

72. Bohman, *Public Deliberation*, 160–1.

73. Bohman, *Public Deliberation*, 162–3.

74. Bohman, *Public Deliberation*, 165.

75. Bohman, *Public Deliberation*, 164.

76. See Robert Evans, 'Science and Democracy in the Third Wave: Elective Modernism, Not Epistocracy', in Cathrine Holst (ed.), *Expertise and Democracy* (Oslo: ARENA, 2014), 89–90. The authors offer a more detailed discussion of the difference between these two phases in Collins and Evans, 'Third Wave of Science Studies', 235–96. Cf. Harry Collins, Martin Weinel and Robert Evans, 'The Politics and Policy of the Third Wave: New Technologies and Society', *Critical Policy Studies* 4(2) (2010): 185–201.

77. Cf. Landemore, *Democratic Reason*, 91.

78. Collins and Evans, 'Third Wave of Science Studies', 262

79. Christiano, 'Rational Deliberation', 35. What is key is that 'It is important that not all citizens be required for this process of generating research agendas and anomalies' (Christiano, 'Rational Deliberation', 50). A key condition of participation in one of the two phases should be competence. The

overwhelming majority of people lack the competence to do anything but reveal their preferences. A small minority, concentrated in interest group associations, has sufficient insider knowledge (of social conditions) to point out the partiality of social theories (natural science theories are rarely biased). In the case of the social sciences, the uncertainty of research, the difficulty of studying the subject and of forecasting events is so great that, unlike in the natural sciences, intuition plays a large role (Christiano, 'Rational Deliberation', 49). Here citizens should be represented by political representatives and non-governmental organisations. 'As long as there are a wide variety of associations, the activist parts of these associations can communicate the issues of ordinary citizens to the policy experts, who in turn can communicate them to the social science experts' (Christiano, 'Rational Deliberation', 50).

80. Christiano, 'Rational Deliberation', 34.

81. Christiano, 'Rational Deliberation', 36.

82. Christiano, 'Rational Deliberation', 48. They are supposed to provide 'local insight into special problems faced by the members of that group'. They are also supposed to remedy the most negative phenomena accompanying exclusive expert deliberations – expert over-confidence and the tendency to rely on abstract models.

83. Landemore, *Democratic Reason*, 145–6.

84. Brennan, *Against Democracy*, 215–20.

85. See Collins, Weinel and Evans, 'The Politics and Policy of the Third Wave', 188–9.

86. Cf. John Parkinson, 'Deliberative Systems', in Andre Bächtiger et al. (eds), *Oxford Handbook of Deliberative Democracy* (Oxford: Oxford University Press, 2018); Michael A. Neblo and Avery White, 'Politics in Translation: Communication between Sites of the Deliberative System', in Andre Bächtiger et al. (eds), *Oxford Handbook of Deliberative Democracy* (Oxford: Oxford University Press, 2018); John Dryzek, 'The Forum, the System, and the Polity: Three Varieties of Democratic Theory', *Political Theory* 45 (2017): 610–36; Selen A. Ercan, Carolyn M. Hendriks and John Boswell, 'Studying Public Deliberation after the Systemic Turn: The Crucial Role for Interpretive Research', *Policy and Politics* 45 (2017): 195–212; Jane Mansbridge, 'Everyday Talk in the Deliberative System', in Stephen Macedo (ed.), *Deliberative Politics: Essays on Democracy and Disagreement* (New York: Oxford University Press, 1999), 211–39; Stephen Elstub, Selen A. Ercan and Ricardo Fabrino Mendonça (eds), *Deliberative Systems in Theory and Practice* (New York: Routledge, 2021).

87. This designation is sometimes – wrongly – applied to Habermas' proposals in *The Theory of Communicative Action* (see Estlund, *Democratic Authority*, 184–6).

88. As attributed to the deliberative incarnations of sortition democracy, for example, deliberative polls. See James S. Fishkin, *Democracy and Deliberation: New Directions for Democratic Control* (New Haven, CT: Yale University Press, 1991); James S. Fishkin, *The Voice of the People: Public Opinion and Democracy* (New Haven, CT: Yale University Press, 1995).

89. Mansbridge et al., 'A Systemic Approach', 5.
90. Mansbridge et al., 'A Systemic Approach', 6–7.
91. Mansbridge et al., 'A Systemic Approach', 1–2.
92. Mansbridge et al., 'A Systemic Approach', 3.
93. Mansbridge et al., 'A Systemic Approach', 2–3; Fuerstein, 'Epistemic Democracy', 81, 85; Habermas, *Between Facts and* Norms, 277–8, 305–8; Kitcher, *Science, Truth, and Democracy*, 118; Dennis Thompson, 'Deliberative Democratic Theory and Empirical Political Science', *Annual Review of Political Science* 11(1) (2008): 113–16; Collins and Evans, 'Third Wave of Science Studies', 235–96; Landemore, *Democratic Reason*, 145–6; James Surowiecki, *The Wisdom of Crowds* (New York: Anchor), 42–7; Cass R. Sunstein, *Infotopia: How Many Minds Produce Knowledge* (Oxford: Oxford University Press, 2006), ch. 4; Cass R. Sunstein, 'Deliberating Groups versus Prediction Markets (or Hayek's Challenge to Habermas)', in Alvin Goldman and Dennis Whitcomb (eds), *Social Epistemology: Essential Readings* (Oxford: Oxford University Press, 2011), 192–213.
94. Christiano, 'Rational Deliberation', 33, 34.
95. Cf. Brown, 'Expertise and Deliberative Democracy', 58.
96. David Owen and Graham Smith, 'Survey Article: Deliberation and the Systemic Turn', *Journal of Political Philosophy* 23(2) (2015): 213–34.
97. Landemore, *Democratic Reason*, 3.
98. Landemore, *Democratic Reason*, 14.
99. Landemore, *Democratic Reason*, 16.
100. Christiano, 'Rational Deliberation', 28–9.
101. Christiano, *The Rule of the Many*, 176, 123–4. Thomas Christiano, *The Constitution of Equality: Democratic Authority and its Limits* (Oxford: Oxford University Press, 2008), 146.
102. According to Christiano, letting citizens decide directly on the means used to pursue commonly valued goals would violate citizens' political equality. Since some people would have a better understanding of political processes, it would put them in a privileged position (Christiano, *The Rule of the Many*, 127, 177. Cf. Christiano, *The Constitution of Equality*, 3; Habermas, *Between Facts and Norms*, 325).
103. Christiano, *The Rule of the Many*, 175–6.
104. Christiano, *The Rule of the Many*, 126.
105. Christiano, 'Rational Deliberation', 47.
106. Gutmann and Thompson, *Democracy and Disagreement*, 227.
107. Gutmann and Thompson, *Why Deliberative Democracy?* 5, 146.
108. Gutmann and Thompson, *Democracy and Disagreement*, 227.
109. Gutmann and Thompson, *Democracy and Disagreement*, 30.
110. Gutmann and Thompson, *Democracy and Disagreement*, 227.
111. Gutmann and Thompson, *Why Deliberative Democracy?* 147.
112. Cf. Brown, 'Expertise and Deliberative Democracy', 58.

Chapter 2

EXPERTISE: PROMISES, PERILS AND LIMITATIONS

Nothing propels discussions on expertise like spectacular expert mistakes.[1] From disasters involving space shuttles (*Columbia*, *Challenger*) and nuclear power plants (Chernobyl, Three Mile Island, Fukushima, Sellafield, Saint-Laurent and dozens of others) to hundreds of noxious medications allowed to remain on the market for decades, science has frequently given citizens reasons to doubt and fear it. Mistakes have created fertile ground for contesting the scientific consensus and for the growth of suspicion with regard to the motives and competence of scientists. Some scholars blame them for the falling trust in science and hence for the crazy year 2016 which in many countries destroyed the belief that there is no alternative to liberal democracy: Donald Trump's successful presidential campaign, the Brexit referendum, and the successes of right-wing populism in Europe and other parts of the world. 'I think the people of this country have had enough of experts' – Michael Gove's words have been paraphrased by politicians from Poland to Brazil to France.

Paradoxically, the decline of public trust in science has coincided with a growing scholarly interest in expertise. Since the 1970s, works devoted to expertise have been written on social epistemology, cognitive science, social psychology and above all on the sociology of scientific knowledge. In political philosophy this interest has taken the form of a debate on the superiority of epistocracy to democracy. It has focused on the moral and political legitimacy of government by 'knowers', epistemic and ethical justifications, the political incompetence of laypeople, issues of equality and justice, and the effectiveness of expert government. Interestingly, the said discussions never touched on the definition of expertise. For some reason, none of the authors were tempted to explain what kind of technical knowledge it is that we should expect from alleged experts. Disputes between democrats and epistocrats centred on abstract 'knowers', quasi-Platonic philosopher kings, fictional characters endowed with supreme technical knowledge (whatever that is) and a moral motivation to use it for the good of the community. There was no room in these reflections for a nuanced approach to expertise. The division into experts and laypeople, democracy and epistocracy, was seen as obvious and unproblematic. The idea that laypeople may possess expertise in some domains and that experts may be like laypeople in many ways, clashed with these intuitions, as did the idea that there are degrees of expertise, and that the effectiveness of expert recommendations in different areas likewise falls on a scale. In other words, efforts were often made to defend democracy against an imaginary enemy. For Estlund, these were the 'knowers', those equipped with the highest possible knowledge, however defined. Jason Brennan, a defender of epistocracy, actually forgot to say whose government he was in fact defending. Experts, it was assumed, as the opposite of 'incompetent or unreasonable people'[2] are 'reasonable and reliable'.[3] For Caplan, experts are by definition people with academic degrees.[4] For many other scholars, the definition of an expert seems so obvious that they fail to even examine it.[5]

This lack of a precision is one of the original reasons for the misconceptions around expert knowledge. This is why we will now shift gears and consider the type of problems that attempts to define expert knowledge inevitably run into. These difficulties are for the most part twofold in nature. First, there are the controversies concerning what should be included in such a definition. Then, there is the counterfactual nature of most definitions, which happen to be richly contradicted by sociological analyses of what it means to be an expert. For example, Stephen Turner enumerates as many as five types of expert active in the public arena. 'Experts who are members of groups whose expertise is generally acknowledged'[6] may represent an esoteric domain or one commonly recognised as legitimate (for example, physicists, economists). The 'sectarian expert'[7] anointed by specialists in a particular field rather than by the public (for example, theologians). The expert anointed by laypeople – a celebrity whose authority is directly proportional to the number of his/her followers. He or she may represent the scientific community (A. Fauci) or a non-scientific one (for example, dietitians and nutrition experts, sports commentators). The 'lobbying expert' is anointed by interest groups and carries out their instructions. His or her aim is to influence public opinion in line with the expectations of his or her sponsors. The 'mole' also follows directives from sponsors but keeps a low profile, working within bureaucratic public institutions.[8] It would be hard to come up with a single definition covering all of these different aspects of experthood. Looking at them together, we are tempted to give in to the relativistic notion that an expert is simply someone whom others consider to be one.[9] They may be academics or not, have formal qualifications or entirely lack education and experience, be recognised by the masses or only by a handful of people.

WHAT MAKES ONE AN EXPERT?

Most of the definitional strategies offered in the literature do, however, share a number of recurrent features. These usually involve two beliefs. According to the first, expertise is specialised and belongs to the epistemic elite. It is therefore esoteric – the kind of knowledge that a layperson cannot acquire without lengthy training. As such, its opposite is common sense, while the expert can be considered the opposite of a layperson.[10] Due to the elitist and esoteric nature of his or her knowledge, the expert enjoys special recognition. The second widely held belief is that one needs expertise to answer difficult questions and solve emergent problems. Both of these beliefs give rise to a number of questions. Is specialist knowledge, supposedly contrary to common sense, the same thing as scientific knowledge? Is it concerned only with *theoria* (contemplative knowledge), or perhaps also with *techne* (practical skill)? Can expert knowledge be gained in any area of human endeavour? Is it a matter of degree and what is the threshold that a layperson must cross to become an expert? If we accept that an expert is highly competent and that, as Jamie Carlin Watson put it, it is 'someone who is in an especially good epistemic or technical position in a domain',[11] then what do the terms 'good' and 'especially' mean in this description? Who decides who is part of or excluded from the epistemic elite? And finally, does any person who has a following merit the name of expert? Are these features necessary or sufficient conditions of expert status?

What makes these questions even more difficult is the fact that research on expertise has been multi-pronged. On the one hand, expertise has been analysed as a psychological phenomenon having to do with the mental attitudes of those deemed to be experts and those who grant them such status. On the other hand, the sociological approach has focused on the relational dimension of expertise and its functions in society.[12] The sociology of scientific knowledge studies the activity structures and internal dynamics of epistemic communities.[13] Philosophical and epistemological analyses of expertise have focused on the epistemic qualities of experts, especially their ability to enounce true statements. There are also discussions about expert systems and the possibility of creating artificial intelligence that would be equipped with human knowledge but without taking part in human practices.[14]

And yet even within the framework of any these studies there is hardly a consensus as to what defines experts and expertise. This is well illustrated by the debate around the definition of expertise proposed by Alvin Goldman.[15] It is so entrenched and long-standing that even Goldman recently admitted, rather pessimistically, that 'it is plausible that "expert" is such a fluid term that different criteria for it are used in different contexts'.[16] In an even more disparaging tone, James Shanteau[17] once wrote that there are as many definitions of expertise as there are scholars of the subject.[18] Indeed, there is a truly impressive plethora of definitional strategies out there. Some people would like to define an expert by reference to symptoms of knowledge.[19] Others, alluding to Wittgenstein's idea of family resemblance, insist that the phenomenon of expertise should be considered only through the lens of actual examples.[20] Those siding with Goldman emphasise truth of claims as the leading attribute of expert knowledge. Their opponents' suggestion is to replace the truthfulness criterion with that of understanding one's domain or making consistent claims.[21]

There is little room here for agreement. The only common denominator in these portrayals is essentially the belief that lay ignorance is the rightful point of reference when it comes to defining an expert. Without laypeople, experts would not exist[22] and vice versa. Harry Collins describes the hypothetical Soviet city of Nobelskigrad, all of whose residents are experts:

> In 'Nobelskigrad' all the families are composed of scientists – mothers and fathers both – and scientists do all the menial work in their time off, such as collecting garbage, putting out fires and cleaning the drains. This community of scientists talks only science, day and night. Children born into the community hear only talk of science from the moment they are born . . . We can imagine that in this society, science would be a ubiquitous expertise and only the most intellectually challenged would fail to become a fluent mathematician, physicist, biologist, or whatever.[23]

In this hypothetical city no one is a layperson with regard to science. Nor, consequently, can anyone be called an expert. It would be just as absurd as to call an Englishman in England an expert in the English language. He could become one only upon leaving the country. Yet even this basic recognition causes problems. For it requires that we also define a layperson, and there is no reason to believe that while the definition of an expert is relational (with the expert being defined in relation to the layperson), that of a layperson is essential. We can find out as much by consulting a dictionary. Indeed, the Cambridge Dictionary defines a layperson as 'someone who is not an expert in or does not have a detailed knowledge of a particular subject',[24] and so by reference to expertise. Defining the expert as the opposite of a layman tells us nothing that we do not already know.

A TYPOLOGY OF EXPERTS AND EXPERTISE

In the light of the two beliefs informing most definitions of an expert, we can distinguish the three most popular strategies of defining expert knowledge in the literature:

1. expert knowledge is theoretical knowledge;
2. expert knowledge is theoretical knowledge with practical applications;
3. expert knowledge is practical knowledge.

1: This understanding of expert knowledge equates it with theoretical knowledge and the expert with the academic. To be an expert, one does not have to be able to apply one's knowledge in the world. One can be an expert in theoretical physics, theoretical mathematics, different varieties of logic, and a range of other disciplines that involve thought experiments as their main method. This category also likely includes some of the political discussions going on in the so-called ideal theory.[25] Although it is true that findings obtained in the course of such research can be applied by practitioners in other sub-disciplines, their application is not the proper object of the studies conducted by these theorists. The fact that such fields do exist leads some scholars to draw a strict distinction between the context in which expert knowledge is produced and the context in which it is applied, and similarly between the theorist (expert) and the practitioner (craftsman).[26] This is what Goldman, among others, does in his book *Knowledge in a Social World*, where he defines an expert as someone who 'knows more propositions in S, or has a higher degree of knowledge of propositions in S, than almost anybody else'.[27]

This definition has obvious advantages. It makes it easy to identify an expert by his or her external attributes or 'symptoms': that is, lab coat, university diploma or academic degree (the more advanced, the better), etc. It is what makes this understanding so popular. As we saw in the previous chapter, this view is commonly held by a large number of liberal political theorists.[28] But the majority of authors are quite critical of this strategy. They maintain, for instance, that having broad theoretical knowledge may actually make it difficult to be an expert. The longer a scholar's academic career, the more difficulty he or she may have in understanding new theoretical and practical discoveries and solving new problems. This applies to any scientific discipline undergoing a 'paradigm shift'. Areas prone to more frequent revolutionary changes of perspective, such as computer programming, are naturally more likely to face this situation. Few programmers 'survive' more than two major software overhauls. In this case, previous experience becomes problematic baggage and actually hinders one's understanding of successive changes. This is why some scholars believe that it is safer to consider the expert's most recent achievements as these count most. The grander these achievements when a new problem emerges, the better. Past competence and success, diplomas, publications and prizes are nowhere near as important as current skills and knowledge. Proponents of this view include Watson, who believes that the one-domain-at-a-time standard is crucial when it comes to expertise.[29] Most authors, however, simply remark that aside from theoretical knowledge the expert must possess implementation skills.

2: According to the second definitional strategy, expertise equals theoretical knowledge plus the skills required to put it into practice. Proponents of this approach believe that being an expert is first and foremost about the ability to solve problems. In 2001, Goldman added the 'implementation aspect' to his earlier definition. He now argued that the expert not only has extensive knowledge regarding basic questions and the discussion around these (so knowledge of the key facts pertaining to the discipline in question and of the potential interpretations of those facts), but is also capable of applying that knowledge to solve new problems in the relevant field[30]: 'an expert . . . in domain D is someone who possesses an extensive fund of knowledge (true belief) and a set of skills or methods for apt and successful deployment of this knowledge to new questions in the domain'.[31] Goldman later expanded this definition to include the number of true and false beliefs shared by the expert:

> S is an expert about domain D if and only if (A) S has more true beliefs (or high credences) in propositions concerning D than most people do, and fewer false beliefs; and (B) the absolute number of true beliefs S has about propositions in D is very substantial.[32]

This definition has been widely criticised. Essentially all of its components have been deemed controversial: the reference to truth, the criterion of having more true beliefs and fewer erroneous beliefs, as well as the requirement of being able to apply theory to practice.

The true belief criterion has actually proved to be the most controversial. Goldman is not alone in using it, however. A similar premise appears in Elizabeth Fricker,[33] Jimmy Alfonso Licon[34] and David Coady,[35] among others.[36] In their view, the objective dimension is of key importance in defining an expert. The expert must have more true beliefs than the majority of people. But the differences do not end there. Licon and Coady refute Goldman's criterion of having 'fewer false beliefs'. Coady actually doubts whether the expert has to be able to respond to new problems in his field.[37] Instead of truth, Fricker prefers to speak of a higher probability of a belief being true. Meanwhile, instead of referencing true beliefs Licon speaks of broader knowledge.[38] All three, however, agree that an expert is not just someone who is taken as such, but a person who deserves the title on account of their knowledge.

Several charges can be levelled against this position. The most basic one concerns the paradox of relativism. Any attempt to define an expert by recourse to the criterion of true beliefs, understanding or high probability of truth gives rise to a vicious circle. If the only way of recognising an expert is to look to whoever knows the truth, we must already have some prior notion of what assertions are true. But to determine this, we need to consult the expert, and so on indefinitely. This is not a particularly sophisticated argument but it does deal a fatal blow to the narrative. It is sufficiently problematic to drive scores of scholars to seek an escape into some form of externalism. Instead of truth as the criterion of expertise they propose an understanding of a given field,[39] better justification for their claims and more consistency to what they preach.[40] Some thinkers resort to procedural considerations. For example, they suggest relying on special procedures which allegedly lead to the identification of true claims or at least the best justified ones.[41] But they too cannot avoid circularity in their reasoning. Nor is the problem solved by recourse to even the most externalist criterion, that is, the practical success of a given expert claim, since success can be achieved even by those who make theoretical mistakes.

Another serious challenge to this narrative is the transitional nature of science. The scientific consensus is constantly changing and so is the truth quotient of scientists' beliefs. Those considered non-controversial authorities today will eventually lose this status. This is the inevitable fate of the scholar, although there are certainly fields in which such radical paradigm shifts and redefinitions of theoretical perspectives occur more slowly and less frequently than in others. Watson dubs this the 'shoulders of giants' problem. If the content of views considered to be true is constantly changing, then is it possible to maintain (or lose) one's expert status without altering one's views? Is Copernicus an expert in astronomy from our perspective, seeing as most of his claims have been falsified?[42] Is it enough to determine that someone had a greater number of true beliefs than their contemporaries to consider them an expert? What about the likes of Ignaz Semmelweis, who introduced the first antiseptics believing that childbed fever was caused by 'cadaveric poison'?[43] What of researchers whose practical solutions proved to be effective despite completely faulty theoretical assumptions?[44] Can one have a true belief but fail to argue it correctly? Many of the beliefs held by experts have much in common with the popular notions typical of the 'cartoon' vision of science. This phenomenon is studied by the sociology of scientific ignorance. There is no doubt that neither this simplified vision of reality, nor only a partial understanding prevent scientists from being successful in their narrow field. And yet if the majority of a scientist's beliefs are inexact, if not outright wrong, can a scientist be recognised as an expert in any domain? What about Joseph Weber, who believed that it was possible to detect gravitational waves, a belief that did not accord with the mainstream view? When enouncing his theories, was he the best expert in his field or no expert at all? And could that have been appraised at the time? Most of the above-mentioned criteria – whether we take the truth of one's beliefs or their efficacy – do not in practice allow us to decide who is an expert worth listening to. Even if we accept that truth equals scientific consensus, there is no way of telling if the said consensus is final and correct. Supporters of Goldman's veritism (defining an expert by reference to the truth of his or her beliefs) are conscious of these problems and extremely careful to avoid the relativism inherent in the view that one is only an expert at a specific point in time and from the standpoint of the agreed-on knowledge of the scientific community.

Also controversial is the view that an expert should have more true and fewer false beliefs than his peers. This statement seems to lack coherence on many levels. First, it is impossible to count the beliefs in question, since it is not at all clear how they should be differentiated. Nor is it obvious whether holding true beliefs is sufficient to make one an expert, and in particular to enable one to apply the said beliefs to solve new problems. It is as if knowledge of all the chess games ever played was equal to the ability to play chess, or rote knowledge of all the textbooks and scientific papers in a given field was enough to qualify one as an expert. Watson gives the striking example of someone who, for some reason, is unable to forget any of the information they have ever encountered.[45] Can such a person be deemed an expert in an area with which they have become thoroughly acquainted? Is it easier for people suffering from hyperthemesia to become experts, or harder? It does not appear to be the case that being familiar with the highest number of true facts makes one an expert. For that is not equal to actually understanding those facts or having an idea of their relative importance, or indeed to the capacity to deploy them in creative ways.[46]

The requirement of having fewer false beliefs (than others) turns out to be even more problematic. Aside from all the problems stemming from having to determine which beliefs are true, we face an additional challenge here. The number of false beliefs can easily be reduced by reducing one's overall number of beliefs. The less one knows, the less one can be wrong. Socrates stated himself to know nothing and therefore had fewer erroneous beliefs than all the other Athenians whom he was tormenting with his endless questioning. Similarly, most of us, who know nothing about the physics of gravitational waves have a great expert score if the number of false beliefs pertaining to the said field is the only criterion we use to make the assessment. Is that sufficient to rank us alongside experts in the field? After all, ignoramuses by definition hold no false beliefs and hence, according to Goldman's definition, meet one of the criteria conferring expert status. To avoid this absurd conclusion it is necessary to determine some optimal ratio of false beliefs to true ones. The problem is that whatever ratio we come up with will always be arbitrary.

And, finally, who are the people to whom we are supposed to 'compare' experts in terms of the number of true and false beliefs they hold? Do all epistemic communities count on equal terms? What if some of them draw conclusions, argue and substantiate claims in ways that differ radically from those in mainstream science? Should we treat phrenologists on a par with biologists, parapsychologists on a par with physicists, flat-earth theorists on a par with astronomers, anti-vaxxers on a par with immunologists and vaccinologists, or alternative medicine practitioners on a par with practising physicians? Are we to compare true and false beliefs only within the purview of particular communities, or more broadly between them? Can we consider parapsychologists experts in parapsychology? In terms of consistency of views or undergoing the peer-review process, authors who publish in journals such as the *Journal of Parapsychology* or the *Journal of the American Society for Psychical Research* are often no worse than scientists. Or perhaps we should question the truth of parapsychologists' claims by pointing out that the scientific mainstream considers them unscientific? The answers to such questions are not obvious at all.[47]

3: Many scholars, especially sociologists, seek to avoid these pitfalls by positing the ability to apply theory to reality as the only indicator of expertise.[48] This is precisely the road taken by Nico Stehr and Reiner Grundmann, who describe experts as 'persons of whom it is assumed that . . . they have accumulated experience in contexts relevant for taking action, and thus enjoy both trust and social respect'.[49] So expert status is not limited to academics but can also be enjoyed by members of other professions, such as farmers or travellers. Assigning such status is not dependent on having vast stores of theoretical knowledge, but only on the ability to 'perform knowledge-based activities that mediate between the context of knowledge creation and application'.[50] The task of professionals is to make scientific discoveries, while the task of

experts is to mediate between the context in which knowledge is produced and the context in which it is applied – between science, on the
one hand, and its patrons who are looking for ways to make the science
work to their advantage, on the other.[51]

The sociological currents that have most contributed to popularising
the notion of the expert as an effective practitioner include the sociology of science and the sociology of scientific knowledge. It is here that
the view (popular since the 1970s) that expert knowledge does not have
to go hand in hand with formal credentials and familiarity with scientific theories was first promoted. Expert status might well be enjoyed by
those we are accustomed to thinking of as laymen. This view is particularly typical of what is known as Wave Two in social studies of science.[52]
Its exponents believe that most people acquire expertise in areas of their
everyday experience.[53] This type of competence might be described as
life expertise or practical wisdom pertaining to one's job or place of
residence. It may be something as down-to-earth as being able to speak
one's mother tongue or a dialect thereof, or to follow social norms, for
example, accepted rules of social distancing, eye contact, touching, etc.
It may be a more local knowledge of where it is safe to go in one's neigh-
bourhood and which locations are better avoided, which streets tend to
have the most traffic and when, and what the best detours are. It may
be knowledge about one's neighbours, their habits and major problems.
This knowledge is often tapped by participatory budget planners, community policing or vigilante groups. It is the members of a community
who are the best informed about local risks or which parts of the local
infrastructure are most in need of investment or repair.

The optimal performance of any task requires familiarity with procedures that are usually inaccessible to theorists. These are often contextual
behaviours practised by small groups of people in response to infrequent
events – behaviours that do not readily lend themselves to scientific
analysis. A classic example of this type of competence was described in
the STS literature by Brian Wynne, who examined the dispute between
sheep farmers in Cumbria and experts from the British Ministry of Agriculture, Fisheries and Food (MAFF) concerning the decontamination
of sheep grazed in areas affected by radiation after an accident at the
Chernobyl nuclear plant in 1986.[54] Wynne discusses the problems that
the experts had in determining how long it would be before restrictions
on the sheep could be lifted. It turned out that the expert models were
almost ineffectual for the task at hand. The model sheep was nothing
like the real one. The models did not take into account the predilections
of the animals, for example, their feeding habits and location preferences. Only the farmers knew what type of grass the sheep liked best,

how much they would ingest, and where the sheep most liked grazing. These were key factors from the standpoint of digestive processes and, consequently, the decontamination effort. The farmers had knowledge they had gained through experience, not in the laboratory – the tacit knowledge characteristic of any practice. They could not be more unlike the MAFF experts: in their speech, gaps in theoretical knowledge, lack of diplomas and socialisation within research communities. But their expertise with regard to their job and their ability to solve emergent problems were undeniable. By the same token, Wynne argues, one could not deny them expert status.

STS theorists claim that it is tacit knowledge – fundamental when it comes to understanding real life and the practical application of theories and theoretical models – that should be decisive in the process of identifying experts. They underline its significance not only for daily practice but also for laboratory practice (B. Latour, S. Woolgar, K. Knorr-Cetina), especially within the context of replicating experimental results. Using the example of the invention of the TEA laser[55] and the detection of gravitational waves, Collins showed how the inability to replicate the conditions of an experiment as defined by its authors was due to the inability to pass on tacit knowledge through anything other than practice. Effective replication depends on the availability of tacit knowledge,[56] which can be acquired only through repeated participation in a given practice. It cannot be communicated verbally because not all of its aspects are equally conscious. Contrary to what 'cartoon' visions of science tell us, doing scientific research is not something we can learn from books.

THE THIRD WAVE IN SOCIAL STUDIES OF SCIENCE

The most elaborate take on expert knowledge, based on the claim of its universality, is presented by Collins and Evans, the authors and main proponents of what is known as Wave Three in social studies of science. Three of the many types of expert knowledge they distinguish are particularly important from the perspective of our considerations here. First, 'ubiquitous expertise', that is, the tacit knowledge enjoyed by members of a particular community simply by virtue of participating in that community's daily life. Using a native language and being familiar with cultural and social norms are examples of this type of knowledge. In Nobelskigrad (see above), scientific knowledge would be part of 'ubiquitous expertise'. Unlike 'specialist tacit knowledge', ubiquitous knowledge is non-elite. Acquiring elite knowledge requires conscious thought, training and practice. Collins and Evans distinguish two types of such expertise: contributory and interactional expertise.

Contributory expertise means having tacit knowledge linked to a specific specialist practice. It is acquired through socialisation within a discipline-specific scientific community and by performing the same actions as the experts in that field, through 'a full-scale physical immersion in a form of life'.[57] It has to do with the ability to run experiments and to propose new solutions to problems emerging in a given domain.

Different in nature is 'interactional expertise,' which amounts to familiarity with the research conducted in a given field (acquired by way of reading academic publications and having discussions with contributory experts), without taking part in the work carried out by the community of experts and therefore without acquiring the 'tacit knowledge' indispensable for skilfully applying theory to practice. This means having 'enough expertise to interact interestingly with participants',[58] 'the ability to converse expertly about a practical skill or expertise, but without being able to practice it'.[59] This type of knowledge does not allow one to solve problems emerging within a given field. But it suffices to make the interactional expert indistinguishable from the contributory expert not just in the eyes of the layperson but also of the expert. By taking part in a test of knowledge on gravitational waves (the so-called Imitation Game), Collins proved that although he lacked experimental experience in that field, he was nonetheless still able to answer questions on gravitational wave physics with the same degree of correctness as contributory experts in the said area.[60] A sociologist was able to pass for a gravitational wave physicist thanks to a grasp of the social *realia* peculiar to the discipline in question, its key narratives and theories, as well as 'second-hand' knowledge of research practices acquired solely on the basis of conversations with practitioners.

One can gain interactional expertise without ever stepping into a lab. But the same is not true of contributory expertise. From the standpoint of our considerations, the relationship between these two types of expertise is of key importance. Clearly, one does not have to have contributory expertise in order to be an interactional expert. But it is not at all clear whether interactional expertise is indispensable to a contributory expert. Not so, say Collins and Evans. One can be a contributory expert while having no notion of the relevant theories and experimental models. This is excellently illustrated by the above-mentioned example of the Cumbrian sheep farmers. The MAFF experts had both interactional and contributory expertise – they were familiar with both theory and experimental practice, and had some limited grasp of sheep grazing and soil decontamination. The farmers had no interactional expertise – they did not know the theories – but they did have contributory expertise when it came to sheep grazing. Their initial inability to come to terms with the MAFF experts stemmed from an asymmetry in the degree of inter-actional expertise. This, however, does not alter the fact that the dispute around sheep in Cumbria described by Wynne was a dispute between two groups of experts.[61]

A diploma or a lab coat do not automatically make one an expert. One becomes an expert thanks to skills acquired in the course of lengthy training. One can gain expertise in the most down-to-earth activities. One can be a contributory expert in sheep grazing, gardening, car repair, online shopping, writing, editing and reviewing academic papers, or even being sick. Each of these practices enables one to gain 'tacit knowledge' that may and should in fact add richness to theoreti-cal knowledge and serve as a check on overly abstract assumptions and theoretical or laboratory models. Especially when one is attempting to put such models into practice.[62]

The approach of Collins and Evans, while not without flaws, perfectly combines the previous positions. First, it says that one does not have to know how to apply theory to practice to be an expert; one may even expe-rience successive failures and still retain expert status (as in the 'reliably unreliable' field of econometric modelling whose expert status Collins and Evans unflinchingly defend).[63] One can also be an expert and have no knowledge of theory and theoretical or experimental models, only having a grasp of the practical side of their application. Finally, one can be an expert endowed with both theoretical and practical competence.

Secondly, academics and lab practitioners are not the only experts capable of responding to new questions and emergent problems. The group of those who can includes non-laboratory practitioners, often mistaken for laypeople. Most people develop some form of contributory expertise regarding their workplace or line of work through habits or familiarity with their immediate social environment. Their competence should be recognised, appraised and used to produce or apply theory to practice. In a sense, any person who participates in cultural practices of one kind or another can be deemed an expert. We are doomed to be experts, although not on every front. The effectiveness of science and expertise depends on the skilful exploitation of this knowledge.

Thirdly, one can be an expert without knowing it. In the case of expert groups 'nearly all of what their members know and believe they know and believe tacitly; unless they are unusually reflective, they will not even know what they know and believe'.[64] Expert knowledge is acquired not only intentionally by making a conscious effort to become more compe-tent, but also casually through atheoretical practice.

Collins and Evans' position is fundamentally important for a number of reasons. First, it is not entangled in the definitional problems afflicting the approaches to expertise presented above. Being an expert does not require simultaneous knowledge of theory and the ability to apply it. It does, however, require long-term cognitive effort leading to either theoretical expertise without the capacity for application, or socialisation within a scholar/expert community, or familiarity with the realia of a given practice. While positing elitism as the main ingredient of expertise, the said approach avoids controversial references to the verity (truth) of expert views. The practitioner does not have to rival the theorist or other practitioners in terms of the number of true beliefs he or she holds in order to expose the weaknesses of their views. It is enough for him or her to be familiar with a narrow segment of reality that has escaped their attention or been left out of their experiments.

It is for these reasons that I will use Collins and Evans' standpoint as my interpretive reference and springboard for further reflection. It allows us to see expert knowledge in places where we typically do not. Its heuristic potential is in my view vastly under-appreciated, especially in political theory and philosophy.

EXPERTISE AND ITS LIMITATIONS

There is one more issue that we must keep in mind. Even the best definition of expertise, accounting for the myriad ways in which it can be acquired and for its complexity, cannot safeguard us against misconceptions as to its role and epistemic status if we are not continually aware of the limitations of expert knowledge. These are twofold. The first type of limitation frequently described in the literature are 'thinking traps'. These are first and foremost cognitive heuristics. Paul Slovic was so convinced of the unreliability of expert cognitive attitudes that he advised experts:

> to recognize and admit [their] own cognitive limitations, to attempt to educate without propagandizing, to acknowledge the legitimacy of public concerns, and somehow to develop ways in which these concerns can find expression in societal decisions without, in the process, creating more heat than light.[65]

In the same vein Tversky and Kahneman argued that:

> The reliance on heuristics and the prevalence of biases are not restricted to laymen. Experienced researchers are also prone to the same biases – when they think intuitively. For example, the tendency to predict the outcome that best represents the data, with insufficient regard for prior probability, has been observed in the intuitive judgements of individuals who have had extensive training in statistics.[66]

Since these issues are explored in quite substantial detail in the literature, I would like to focus on another – systemic – aspect of the problem of the limitedness of expertise. What these systemic limitations mean is that in terms of effectiveness expert knowledge will never satisfy not just public expectations but even the 'formative aspirations' of science itself.[67] The existence of systemic limitations is overlooked by the public, which usually sees science as homogeneous as far as its methodology, object and effectiveness are concerned. This lack of nuance means that a failure or shortcoming in any scientific endeavour tends to undermine the public's trust in science altogether. For example, the failure to avert the 2008 financial crisis or the BSE epidemic eroded public trust in economists, vaccinologists and epidemiologists.

These misconceptions about expertise stem from the belief that science and expert knowledge are fundamentally homogeneous. We usually conceptualise them abstractly as the outcome of empirical research conducted in a perfectly controlled environment, an exact, precise and carefully planned and executed enterprise. In this picture, scientists never fail to put into practice all the Mertonian norms, regardless of what they are investigating. This simplified and streamlined image is in reality far from the truth. The conviction that science is homogeneous (popularised by Vienna Circle-style positivism) has been successfully challenged in post-Kuhnian thought.[68]

The heterogeneity of science means that different areas of scientific inquiry differ in subject matter, method and predictive power. James Shanteau makes the case that it is necessary to distinguish between areas of science and expertise in which predictions are generally correct and those where they are usually wrong. For example, polygraph testing, stock price predictions or long-term weather forecasting can hardly be described as accurate.[69] In other areas, such as astronomy or medicine, experts' work largely consists in interpreting information, so predictive power largely depends on the availability, accuracy, representativeness and reliability of data. The less complete and more general the data, the smaller the part of a phenomenon they describe, the fewer the chances of drawing up an accurate description or prediction of future events. There are also areas in which the individual competence and experience of the expert plays a key role (for example, livestock judges, grain inspectors, photo interpreters or soil judges[70]). Putting all these kinds of scientific practice into one basket with the label 'EXPERTISE' on it would be a mistake. Neither science nor experts are a homogeneous group. Failure to understand this fact negatively impacts people's attitudes towards science. The failings of econometricians or political scientists do not have to and should not make one sceptical about the effectiveness of vaccination or the anthropogenic nature of climate change. In many areas experts can do little more than 'recognize patterns and find consistencies in a dynamic problem space',[71] help organise ideas, identify alternative scenarios and point out the less obvious consequences of our actions. We must distinguish these areas from those in which we can expect expert opinions and recommendations to be much more precise.

Treating science as a monolith is not the only common mistake. The popular 'cartoon' vision of science also leads to the ubiquitous espousal of what Shanteau refers to as the 'experts-should-converge' hypothesis, which involves five components. First, is the assumption that there is a golden rule of behaviour in every situation. It is assumed that there is an optimal solution or solutions to every problem. Secondly, only experts can discover the golden standard thanks to the specialist, esoteric knowledge they have and are capable of applying. Neither discussion and lay voting, nor actions undertaken by political representatives (who themselves usually come from the lay strata of society), but only reliable, dispassionate, fact-based expertise is capable of taking on the task. Thirdly, since all experts draw on the same theories and empirical data, there is no way they can come to different conclusions. In other words, in an ideal world in which they had the opportunity to investigate a given issue in sufficient detail, they would always eventually converge. As a consequence, fourthly, any disputes among experts are a sign of someone's 'ignorance or incompetence'. A dispute, after all, simply means that one side is wrong. As a matter of fact, disputes between experts are a nonentity, since what they essentially demonstrate is that one side is not speaking from a position of expertise. It may even be that none of the parties are right and the quarrel is merely between proponents of erroneous views. Meanwhile, it is impossible for more than one side of a dispute to be right. And in the end, fifthly, 'since non-experts do not know which of the so-called "experts" are correct, the only safe course of action is distrust all of them. That is, disagreement between experts implies that we should be suspicious of their claimed special abilities.'[72] Put together, these five assumptions make us view expertise as a zero-sum game, and as a consequence erode social trust in expertise and science. From the standpoint of the present considerations, the first two of the above assumptions are of paramount significance (the three that follow are merely their logical conclusion): the presupposition that there is only one optimal solution to every question and the premise that experts are able to find it.

These assumptions are doubtful, to say the least, if not outright wrong. First, there is no one correct solution to most socio-political or even technical problems, but a whole variety of alternatives. These depend on how the problem has been defined and on what it might mean to solve it successfully. Situations in which the above is not true are quite rare. Even when there is essentially only one solution, it usually involves a number of competing variants. In the case of COVID-19, the only effective solution in the initial phase of the pandemic was to isolate all potentially infected individuals during the virus incubation period. Later, regular testing became a solution. Both of these solutions, however, proved to be impracticable due to their social, economic and political costs. There was also a whole slew of more realistic albeit 'second-best' solutions – from the mandatory isolation of vast geographic areas (China), through various degrees of lockdown (most countries), to letting the virus proliferate in the hope that the population would acquire herd immunity (Sweden, the UK).[73] The choice between these variants was not straightforward at all.

The second assumption, crediting experts with the ability to find effective solutions, is also wrong. There are at least a few reasons why experts will continually fail. The first and most important one is the casuistic nature of expert knowledge. Expertise is based on a systematic body of information about past events. This allows experts to look for patterns and similarities between current and past occurrences. The role of experts is therefore to look for similarities, which renders their opinions somewhat inaccurate. They must base their analyses on ideal types which are not readily applicable to the reality at hand. The ideal, abstract models developed on the basis of previous cases are not directly applicable. There is not even a single method for selecting cases based on their similarity to other phenomena. This is why those representing different epistemic communities or cultures can employ different cases as the interpretive model for entire classes of phenomena. For example, different models of economic and political transformation can be proposed in the same socio-political circumstances. As Reiss writes:

> Suppose, for instance, that . . . relatively large nations at a relatively low stage of development are ill-advised to enter into free-trade agreements with more developed countries. Suppose also that some nations have benefitted from entering trade agreements. These facts hardly determine what the answer is to the question whether contemporary Turkey should enter such an agreement. Is contemporary Turkey more like 19th century England or more like 19th century Portugal?[74]

Similarly, scientists forecasting the spread of the COVID-19 pandemic suggested that it was similar to a number of past epidemics. The fact that data on those was very scant made the task extremely difficult. As Jason Brennan, Chris Surprenant and Eric Winsberg write:

the ICL [Imperial College London] model assumes that when people
socially distance, their probability of getting infected at home increases
by 25%. But why 25%? Why not 35%? In fact, there is no data or
research to support any particular choice in the model, since we have
few well-established rates for any past virus, let alone rates for the novel
SARS-CoV-2 virus. ... There was enormous uncertainty concerning
nearly every parameter built into the model's coding. Most modelling
choices were relatively unconstrained by data or background knowledge;
when there was data, it was of poor quality.[75]

Selecting the best available case for comparison is not always easy and
may spark controversy. The failure to take into account a key feature
may render the whole analogy and the theoretical model based on it
irrelevant.[76] For example, given the increasing complexity and interdependence of systems and unprecedented climate change along with con-
comitant migration, political and economic crises, finding an analogy
for these events in the past is a prodigious feat. This is even more difficult with regard to especially rare events the likes of which have never
occurred before (the COVID-19 pandemic) or those in which highly
contextual, culture-specific factors are of paramount importance (for
example, democracy-building).[77] In these circumstances the practical
application of theory means venturing beyond the limits of expertise[78]
and the authority of science into the realm of trans-scientific casuistry.[79]

The other – quite banal – reason why expert recommendations are
not 100 per cent effective is the complication, complexity and interdependence of phenomena. Understanding the nature of discrete processes
increasingly requires a grasp of the social, political, economic and ecological system as a whole. Meanwhile, the increasing specialisation and
fragmentation of science prevents scholars and experts from seeing the
connections between seemingly different and relatively autonomous
environments or social, economic or technological systems.[80] As David
Colander and Roland Kupers note:

Too often, experts make arguments and design policy as if they know
exactly what they definitely know what they are doing, when they actually they don't. It's not that they aren't experts; it's that the problems they
are facing are so complex that no one fully understands them.[81]

An analysis of the rise of right-wing parties in Europe cannot fail to
take notice of factors like the migration crisis precipitated by the war
in Syria and therefore also the multi-annual drought that preceded the
conflict, as well as Russia's international policy. The more general the
nature of the problem, the more variables have to be examined. When
it comes to technological innovations, it may take decades to ascertain

their social, economic, political and ecological consequences, just as it took years to connect fossil fuel power plants with acid rain or to identify the fallout of DDT. In the case of more and more complex systems, the predictive powers of science gradually peter out. In weather forecasting the predictability limit is around 5–7 days. After this time it is virtually impossible to gauge the probability of most weather events. We expect models to work just as well in real life as they do in the controlled conditions of a science lab, but that is almost never the case.

A common error is to mistake trans-scientific problems for scientific ones. With regard to the former, science can indeed ask questions, but very rarely can it actually provide decisive answers. Alvin Weinberg gave a number of examples of these type of problems.[82] The first group includes problems for which it is not cost-effective to come up with predictive tools. It is impossible to check if the World Trade Center towers will collapse if they are hit by passenger airliners, or a bursting charge explodes in a mini-van parked in its underground parking lot, or to see if the Fukushima power plant will withstand a tsunami. An effective test would require building 'test' WTC towers and sacrificing two Boeings, or building a nuclear power plant only to flood it with an artificially provoked tsunami. Extremely rare events present a similar case. Here, we do not have sufficient data to identify regularities and so develop a theory of such phenomena, whatever they may be. An example is when several highly improbable factors occur simultaneously. Let us return to the attack on the WTC: the impact of the crash dislodged the fireproof insulation from the construction elements so the spilled aviation fuel was able to ignite multiple fires, ultimately causing the towers to collapse. There is no way of calculating the probability of such occurrences. Social phenomena are also trans-scientific problems. Reliably predicting the behaviour of masses of people would require predicting the behaviour of all the individuals and the dynamics of interaction between them.[83] That is too many variables. That is why one could not have predicted Arab Spring or the dynamics of the Polish women's protests following the introduction of stricter abortion law in 2020 during the COVID-19 pandemic.

It would seem that problems that have not been encountered before could also be assigned to the trans-scientific category. In this case we are dealing with something that Watson refers to as the 'new expertise problem'.[84] In the absence of earlier experiments and cases, and so of the possibility of gaining expertise, we are all laypeople with regard to the issue at hand.[85] All we can do is look for experts who specialise in related phenomena. A similar situation occurs when a new technology whose consequences cannot be foreseen is introduced. As Paul Slovic says, in some situations 'The technology is so new and the probabilities in question are so small that accurate risk estimates cannot be based on empirical observation.'[86] In his film *Containment* (2015), Peter Gallison has shown the difficulties we might encounter in trying to effectively communicate with future generations, very remote from us in time. What language should we use to warn these generations, living 200,000 years from now, of the danger of radioactive waste disposal sites? There are no experts on the future, on entirely new problems, so all we can realistically expect from science is to experimentally learn from mistakes.

These three factors – casuistry, the complexity of the real world and the trans-scientific nature of some phenomena – mean that the expectation that experts produce effective solutions is very often unfounded. But the failures and shortcomings of science are not proof of corruption, ineptitude, ill-will or excessive self-confidence. They often stem from the very nature of scientific research. Science needs time to work out effective solutions, to make and gradually eliminate mistakes. Politics usually demands immediate recommendations and information about the long-term consequences of specific actions. As epidemiologist Dylan Green stated candidly with regard to fighting the COVID-19 pandemic:

> I've been asked to generate modeling results in a matter of weeks (in a disease which I/we know very little about) which I previously would have done over the course of several months, with structured input and validation from collaborators on a disease I have studied for a decade. This ultimately leads to simpler rather than more complicated efforts, as well as difficult decisions in assumptions and parameterization. We do not have the luxury of waiting for better information or improvements in design, even if it takes a matter of days.[87]

The operational logic of science is incompatible with that of politics. Adapting the functioning of science to the needs of the moment necessitates a radical simplification of models of reality. This, in turn, of necessity leads to imprecision. In the case of COVID-19, the simplest models 'make basic assumptions, such as that everyone has the same chance of catching the virus from an infected person because the population is perfectly and evenly mixed, and that people with the disease are all equally infectious until they die or recover'.[88] Every model requires the baseline situation to be defined: how many people are sick; how is the virus transmitted and in what circumstances; and how do individuals typically behave (activities, lifestyle). But these things are never known with precision, so how we define them is largely arbitrary. Neil Ferguson, an epidemiologist at Imperial College London, summed it up thus: 'We're building simplified representations of reality. Models are not crystal balls.'

It is equally hard to be precise when making long-term predictions. American economics handbooks published between 1960 and 1980 kept repeating the view that the USSR would economically outdo the West. The planned economy based on centralised expert recommendations was for decades seen as more reasonable and effective. It was seen as inevitably leading to the economic supremacy of the Eastern Bloc.[89] Most economists forecasting the benefits that would accrue from the creation of the European Union foresaw a steep rise in the GDP of countries that joined the club.[90] These prognostics did not come true, but it is impossible today to determine whether it was because of flawed models or various events that happened in the meantime. Successive EU enlargements, economic crises, shifts in the international balance of power, ecological catastrophes and political crises – all of these factors influenced the ultimate economic impact of European integration. Politics, meanwhile, demands forecasts and recommendations that cannot be delivered.

As a result, it is also unrealistic to expect consensus among experts. In the absence of complete data and clear methodological guidelines for casuistry and comparing past events with current ones, it is hardly surprising that disputes between scientists are the norm, not a pathology of science. They concern especially the practical application of theory. Moreover, as Shanteau observes, the 'solution to a problem' that we typically expect experts to deliver is not one but three things: diagnosis, prognosis and treatment.[91] Success with regard to one of these three things does not automatically guarantee success with respect to another. Even if we understand a problem, we may not be able to foresee how it will unfold, and even if we grasp the unfolding we may not be able to prevent it. 'There are thousands of diagnoses and hundreds of prognoses, but relatively few treatments. It should not be surprising to find that experts may disagree at one level (diagnosis), but agree at another (treatment).'[92] It is simply unrealistic to expect consensus on all three levels. When studying macro-trends and predicting social phenomena we will be dealing with a whole array of different diagnoses, a small number of prognoses, and many potential remedies. Elsewhere we may encounter consensus with regard to diagnosis and treatment, but disagreement regarding prognosis (as in the case of climate change or the COVID-19 pandemic). Such disagreements, however, cannot be blamed on the shortcomings of science or the corruption or politicisation of scientists. They are not a sign that one of the parties has not lived up to the norms of doing science or is biased or involved in partisanship. As Tom Nichols rightly notes, 'Laypeople cannot expect experts never to be wrong; if they were capable of such accuracy, experts wouldn't need to do research and run experiments in the first place.'[93]

To conclude: our perception of expertise is erroneous in many ways. Our misperception is due to our misunderstanding of what distinguishes expertise and an expert, as is a failure to grasp the limits of scientific inquiry. As a result, our expectations with regard to expertise end up being too high. We are not very good at differentiating uncontroversial scientific truths and their imperfect applications from what politicians want us to believe for their political purposes.[94] Experts will always make mistakes, but it is relatively easy to identify the areas in which these errors will tend to happen more often. Moreover, repeated expert mistakes in some domains should not undermine the authority of science as a whole. We need to relinquish the 'cartoon' vision of a science that never makes mistakes – indeed, if it does, this can only advance scientific development and improve scientific cognition.

NOTES

1. See Christopher Power, *The Experts Speak: The Definitive Compendium of Authoritative Misinformation* (New York: Pantheon, 1984).
2. Brennan, *Against Democracy*, 17.
3. Brennan, *Against Democracy*, 68.
4. Brian Caplan, *The Myth of Rational Voter: Why Democracies Choose Bad Policies* (Princeton, NJ: Princeton University Press, 2007).
5. For example, Ilya Somin, *Democracy and Political Ignorance: Why Smaller Government is Smarter* (Stanford, CA: Stanford University Press, 2013); Landemore, *Democratic Reason*.
6. Turner, *Liberal Democracy 3.0*, 41.
7. Turner, *Liberal Democracy 3.0*, 35.
8. Turner, *Liberal Democracy 3.0*.
9. In the same spirit, Roger Koppl defines an expert as any person who is paid for their opinion (Koppl, *Expert Failure*, 38; cf. Eyal, *The Crisis of Expertise*, 19).
10. This is why according to Carlo Martini 'expertise is a social concept, and measuring expertise is more like measuring a country's wealth, or an individual's happiness: a measuring process that must be constantly updated and corrected' (Carlo Martini, 'The Epistemology of Expertise', in Miranda Fricker et al. (eds), *The Routledge Handbook of Social Epistemology* (New York: Routledge, 2020), 119), and according to Elizabeth Fricker, 'expertise is also a community-relative concept' (Elizabeth Fricker, 'Testimony and Epistemic Authority', in Jennifer Lackey and Ernest Sosa (eds), *The Epistemology of Testimony* (Oxford: Clarendon, 2006), 225–52.
11. Jamie Carlin Watson, 'What Experts Could Not Be', *Social Epistemology* 33(1) (2019): 74–87.
12. An extremely relational definition is proposed by Eyal in whose opinion expertise is not a 'thing' or set of skills, but a 'historically specific way of talking' (Eyal, *The Crisis of Expertise*, 19).

13. Karin Knorr-Cetina, *Epistemic Cultures: How the Sciences Make Knowledge* (Cambridge, MA: Harvard University Press, 1999).

14. Cf. Watson, *Expertise: A Philosophical Introduction*, ch. 2; Eyal, *The Crisis of Expertise*, 27–30.

15. See Christian Quast, 'Expertise: A Practical Explanation', *Topoi* 37(1) (2018): 12.

16. Alvin Goldman, 'Expertise', *Topoi*, 37(1) (2018): 3–10.

17. James Shanteau, 'Competence in Experts: The Role of Task Characteristics', *Organizational Behavior and Human Decision Processes* 53 (1992): 255.

18. Oliver Scholz claims that the category of 'expert' (as indeed most concepts) cannot be defined precisely, since these definitions will always differ depending on the purpose they serve (Oliver R. Scholz, 'Symptoms of Expertise: Knowledge, Understanding and Other Cognitive Goods', *Topoi*, 37 (2018): 31).

19. Scholz, 'Symptoms of Expertise', 32–3. Such symptoms may include, for example, long-time experience in a specific research area, a large quantity of knowledge; a broad and deep understanding of one's domain. Cf. Richard Foley, *Intellectual Trust in Oneself and Others* (Cambridge: Cambridge University Press, 2004).

20. Cf. Watson, *Expertise: A Philosophical Introduction*, 38–41.

21. In this spirit, Watson claims that 'experts understand a subject matter better than non-experts: they understand the meaning of subject-specific terms, how they are used, what they imply (at least generally, for the subject), and the processes used to derive them. Further, experts are able to apply their understanding of a domain of information in new and unique contexts; this would seem to require both a competence with the information in a subject matter and the capacity to see connections among concepts in that domain and the creativity to apply concepts in fruitful ways to the demands of a context' (Jamie Watson, 'The Shoulders of Giants: A Case for Non-veritism about Expert Authority', *Topoi* 37 (2018): 43).

22. Quast, 'Expertise', 15.

23. Collins, *Are We All Scientific Experts Now?* 57.

24. See at: https://dictionary.cambridge.org/dictionary/english/layperson. Cf. a similar definition in Merriam Webster at: https://www.merriam-webster.com/dictionary/layman.

25. See Zofia Stemplowska, 'What's Ideal about the Ideal Theory?' *Social Theory and Practice* 34(3) (2008): 319–40; Laura Valentini, 'Ideal vs. Non-Ideal Theory: A Conceptual Map', *Philosophy Compass* 7(9) (2012): 654–64.

26. See Steven Shapin and Simon Schaffer, *Leviathan and the Air-Pump: Hobbes, Boyle, and the Experimental Life* (Princeton, NJ: Princeton University Press, 2011).

27. Alvin Goldman, *Knowledge in a Social World* (Oxford: Oxford University Press, 1999), 268.

28. Cf. Landemore, *Democratic Reason*, 177; Caplan, *The Myth of the Rational Voter*.

29. According to Watson 'Expertise (cognitive systems) = df A subject S is an expert in domain D if and only if (a) S has a certain degree of competence with the skills and information in D; (b) that degree is determined by the current state of skills and information in D; and (c) (a) is acquired through rigorous training along one of two cognitive systems paths.'

30. Alvin Goldman, 'Experts: Which Ones Should We Trust?' in Alvin Goldman and Dennis Whitcomb (eds), *Social Epistemology: Essential Readings* (Oxford: Oxford University Press, 2011), 115; Goldman, 'Expertise'.

31. Goldman, 'Experts: Which Ones Should We Trust?' 92; cf. Oliver R. Scholz, 'Experts: What They Are and How We Recognize Them – A Discussion of Alvin Goldman's Views', *Grazer Philosophische Studien* 79 (2009): 191–2.

32. Goldman, 'Expertise', 8.

33. Fricker, 'Testimony and Epistemic Authority'.

34. Jimmi Alfonso Licon, 'Sceptical Thoughts on Philosophical Expertise', *Logos & Episteme* 3(3) (2012), 449–58.

35. David Coady, *What to Believe Now? An Epistemology to Contemporary Issues* (Malden, MA: Wiley-Blackwell, 2012).

36. Cf. Bruce D. Weinstein, 'What is an Expert?' *Theoretical Medicine* 14 (1993): 66–70.

37. Coady, *What to Believe Now?* 29.

38. Coady, *What to Believe Now?* 451.

39. Watson, 'What Experts Could Not Be'.

40. Scholz, 'Experts: What They Are', 193.

41. Watson, 'The Shoulders of Giants', 45.

42. Cf. Watson, *Expertise: A Philosophical Introduction*, 61–4.

43. Watson, 'The Shoulders of Giants', 46–7.

44. And what about the fact that much of research is not even geared towards establishing the truth but towards achieving experiment reproducibility (I. Hacking, N. Cartwright, S. Shapin)? This, in turn, requires that a whole array of irregularities be left unexplained, ignored as meaningless information noise (see Nancy Cartwright, *How the Laws of Physics Lie* (Oxford and New York: Clarendon and Oxford University Press, 1983)).

45. Watson, 'What Experts Could Not Be'.

46. Cf. Scholz, 'Symptoms of Expertise', 37.

47. Scholars critical of veritism do not avoid this problem either. Watson, for instance, proposes the epistemic facility account: '(EF) A subject, S, is an expert in a subject matter, M, if and only if S (a) understands a substantial proportion of the terms, propositions, and arguments in M, along with the procedures used to formulate propositions in M, and (b) S has the ability to demonstrate (a) successfully in the discharge of her epistemic activities.' The verity of beliefs is here replaced by their plausible demonstration. According to this definition, expertise does not require innovation. It is sufficient for the expert to understand his or her own domain and to be able to explain to others what it means to be its practitioner.

48. This, according to Gil Eyal, best corresponds to the etymology of 'expertise' (Lat. *expertire* – 'to try'), which refers to experience and practice (Eyal, *The Crisis of Expertise*, 21).
49. Nico Stehr and Reiner Grundmann, *Experts: The Knowledge and Power of Expertise* (London: Routledge, 2011), x.
50. Stehr and Grundmann, *Experts*, vii.
51. In the literature we often encounter a distinction between scientific knowledge and expertise, and the scientist and the expert. For example, Stehr and Grundman see the expert as an intermediary between scientists as producers of knowledge and customers looking for ways to apply the latter in practice. Scientific knowledge as such is limited in its implementation aspect. Jasanoff also claims that it is 'expertise, not science, that translates knowledge (or non-knowledge) into decisions' (Sheila Jasanoff, 'The Practices of Objectivity in Regulatory Science', in Charles Camic, Neil Gross and Michèle Lamont (eds), *Social Knowledge in the Making* (Chicago: University of Chicago Press, 2011), 307–37). Expertise is what connects the realm of science and the realm of practice (see Eva Krick, 'Creating Participatory Expert Bodies: How the Targeted Selection of Policy Advisers can Bridge the Epistemic–Democratic Divide', in Eva Krick and Cathrine Holst (eds), *Experts and Democratic Legitimacy: Tracing the Social Ties of Expert Bodies in Europe* (London: Routledge, 2020), 33–48). The uncertainty, risk, complexity and unpredictability that typify the context of scientific knowledge implementation should therefore not influence our assessment of research (see Sheila Jasanoff, *Designs on Nature: Science and Democracy in Europe and the United States* (Princeton, NJ: Princeton University Press, 2005), 211). The work of the scientist and the work of the expert therefore differ in their methodology, success criteria, the nature of peer review and checks within the research community, as well as their predictive power. The two are easy to confuse, since scientists sometimes appear in the role of experts, backing their expert recommendations with the authority of science.
52. Steven Epstein, *Impure Science: AIDS, Activism, and the Politics of Knowledge* (Berkeley: University of California Press, 1996); Steven Epstein, 'The Construction of Lay Expertise: AIDS Activism and the Forging of Credibility in the Reform of Clinical Trials', *Science, Technology, & Human Values* 20(4) (1995): 408–37; Alan Irwin, *Citizen Science: A Study of People, Expertise and Sustainable Development* (London: Routledge, 1995); Brian Wynne, 'Misunderstood Misunderstanding: Social Identities and Public Uptake of Science', in Alan Irwin and Brian Wynne (eds), *Misunderstanding Science?* (Cambridge: Cambridge University Press, 1996), 19–46; Brian Wynne, 'May the Sheep Safely Graze? A Reflexive View of the Expert–Lay Knowledge Divide', in Scott Lash, Bronislaw Szerszynski and Brian Wynne (eds), *Risk, Environment and Modernity: Towards a New Ecology* (London: Sage, 1996), 44–83; Sheila Jasanoff, 'Technologies of Humility: Citizen Participation in Governing Science', *Minerva* 41(3) (2003): 223–44.

53. Cf. Dominique Brossard and Bruce V. Lewenstein, 'A Critical Appraisal of Models of Public Understanding of Science: Using Practice to Inform Theory', in L. Kahlor and P. A. Stout (eds). *Communicating Science: New Agendas in Communication* (New York: Routledge, 2010), 11–39.

54. Wynne, 'May the Sheep Safely Graze?; Wynne, 'Misunderstanding Misunderstandings'.

55. Harry M. Collins, 'The TEA Set: Tacit Knowledge and Scientific Networks', *Science Studies* 4 (1974): 165–86; Harry M. Collins, *Changing Order: Replication and Induction in Scientific Practice* (London: Sage, 1985); Collins, *Are We All Scientific Experts Now?* 30–2.

56. Michael Polanyi, *The Tacit Dimension* (London: Routledge, 1966); Collins, Evans and Weinel, *Experts and the Will*, 65.

57. Harry Collins and Robert Evans, *Rethinking Expertise* (Chicago: University of Chicago Press, 2007), 30.

58. Collins and Evans, 'Third Wave of Science Studies', 254.

59. Harry Collins, 'Interactional Expertise as a Third Kind of Knowledge', *Phenomenology and the Cognitive Sciences* 3(2) (2004): 125.

60. Cf. Collins and Evans, *Rethinking Expertise*, ch. 4.

61. Collins and Evans, *Rethinking Expertise*, 48–54.

62. Sheila Jasanoff, 'The Political Science of Risk Perception', *Reliability Engineering & System Safety* 59(1) (1998): 95.

63. Collins, Evans and Weinel, *Experts and the Will*, 67; Collins and Evans, *Why Democracies Need Science*, ch. 2.

64. Collins, Evans and Weinel, *Experts and the Will*, 68.

65. Paul Slovic, Baruch Fischhoff and Sarah Lichtenstein, 'Facts versus Fears: Understanding Perceived Risk', in Daniel Kahneman, Paul Slovic and Amos Tversky (eds), *Judgement under Uncertainty: Heuristics and Biases* (Cambridge: Cambridge University Press, 1992), 489.

66. Amos Tversky and Daniel Kahneman, 'Judgement under Uncertainty: Heuristics and Biases', in Daniel Kahneman, Paul Slovic and Amos Tversky (eds), *Judgement under Uncertainty: Heuristics and Biases* (Cambridge: Cambridge University Press, 1992), 18.

67. Collins, Evans and Weinel, *Experts and the Will*, 50–1.

68. See Barry Barnes, *T. S. Kuhn and Social Science* (New York: Columbia University Press, 1982).

69. Shanteau, 'Why Do Experts Disagree?' in Bo Green et al. (eds), *Risk Behaviour and Risk Management in Business Life* (Dordrecht: Kluwer Academic, 2000), 192.

70. Shanteau, 'Why Do Experts Disagree?' 192.

71. Shanteau, 'Why Do Experts Disagree?' 194.

72. Shanteau, 'Why Do Experts Disagree?' 188.

73. Cf. Lavazza and Farina, 'The Role of Experts'.

74. Reiss, 'Expertise, Agreement', 9.

75. Jason Brennan, Chris Surprenant and Eric Winsberg, 'How Government Leaders Violated Their Epistemic Duties during the SARS-CoV-2 Crisis', *Kennedy Institute Journal of Ethics* (2020): 16.

76. Turner, *Liberal Democracy 3.0*, 60–1.
77. The role of context when applying social theories is highlighted by Reiss, who says that the applicability of theoretical generalisations depends on the 'time and place of application, whether the focus is on the short-run or on the long-run; the choice of contrast; the choice of measure or indicator' (Reiss, 'Expertise, Agreement', 7;. Cf. Reiss, 'Why Do Experts Disagree', 19–21).
78. Turner, *Liberal Democracy 3.0*, 59.
79. Cf. Reiss, 'Why Do Experts Disagree', 15.
80. Karl Rogers, *On the Metaphysics of Experimental Physics* (New York: Palgrave Macmillan, 2005); Karl Rogers, *Modern Science and the Capriciousness of Nature* (New York: Palgrave Macmillan, 2006).
81. David Colander and Roland Kupers, *Complexity and the Art: Of Public Policy* (Princeton, NJ: Princeton University Press, 2014), 174.
82. Alvin M. Weinberg, 'Science and Trans-Science', *Minerva* 10(2) (1972): 209–22; Alvin M. Weinberg, *Nuclear Reactions: Science and Trans-Science* (New York: American Institute of Physics, 1992).
83. Cf. Friedman, *Power Without Knowledge*; Reiss, 'Why Do Experts Disagree?'
84. Watson, 'What Experts Could Not Be', 74–87.
85. Jasanoff, '(No?) Accounting for Expertise', 159.
86. Slovic, Fischhoff and Lichtenstein, 'Facts versus Fears', 486.
87. Cited after Brennan, Surprenant and Winsberg, 'How Government Leaders Violated Their Epistemic Duties', 13. As Brennan, Surprenant and Winsberg notice, 'A single run of the ICL [Imperial College London] model requires about 20,000 processor hours. It was impossible, on short notice, to explore how varying the (largely arbitrary) parameter values would impact the model's predictions' (ibid., 16).
88. David Adam, 'Special Report: The Simulations Driving the World's Response to COVID-19. How Epidemiologists Rushed to Model the Coronavirus Pandemic', *Nature*, 2 April 2020, available at: https://www.nature.com/articles/d41586-020-01003-6.
89. David M. Levy and Sandra J. Peart, *Escape from Democracy* (Cambridge: Cambridge University Press, 2017), ch. 6.
90. See also Cecchini Report (1988). Cf. Zsolt G. Pataki, *The Cost of Non-Europe in the Single Market ('Cecchini Revisited')* (Brussels: EPRL, 2014).
91. Shanteau, 'Why Do Experts Disagree?' 190.
92. Shanteau, 'Why Do Experts Disagree?' 190.
93. Nichols, *Death of Expertise*, 176.
94. Turner, *Liberal Democracy 3.0*, 62.

Chapter 3

LAYMEN, EXPERTS AND EPISTEMIC DEPENDENCE

Every day we put blind faith in people. We trust those who manufactured and sold us our alarm clock that it will ring on time, that our smartphone will not give us a brain tumour, and that our car will not suddenly swerve out of control. We believe that our gas stove will not explode and that we are the only ones with a set of keys to our house; that the bus driver will show up to work on time and drive us to the place where the timetable says he or she is going; that the taxi driver will not cheat us; and that the people on the street will not lynch us unprovoked, or even if provoked. From the moment we feel some kind of pain all the way until we start treatment we make dozens of leaps of faith. First, we make a choice of whether to trust conventional or alternative medicine. Then, we decide if we have more trust in public or private healthcare providers. Then, which particular doctor we will go see. Finally, we decide if we will put our faith in the prescribed therapy and the efficacy of the prescribed medicines.[1] Every day we make hundreds if not thousands of leaps of faith for which we have no immediately available reasons. We trust complete strangers so often and so blindly that we do not even notice it. Trust is the foundation of society. This social role of trust has been discussed by sociologists and political scientists, including Piotr Sztompka, Russell Hardin, Francis Fukuyama and Charles Tilly.[2] They have analysed the role of rumour in social life, how we read social expectations off indirect cues and how we subtly sound the beliefs of others, including the way we come to share those beliefs. We trust (or do not trust) the way votes are counted in an election, those who adjudicate the validity of a vote, or public opinion polls. Trust or lack thereof is the reason why social and political systems endure or collapse. It is what sparks revolutions and, often, what extinguishes them. It is the reason why social, political or economic reforms fail. Trust is the basis of the legitimacy of any political system, including liberal democracy, significantly lowering its operational costs.

Less commonly recognised is the fact that trust is also the foundation of science. Although this claim raises relatively little controversy among sociologists and philosophers,[3] the traditional and still widely held view of science is somewhat different. According to this view, science – based on replicating experiments, falsification and peer review – is the very instantiation of institutionalised mistrust. It systemically forces participants to obey an ethos founded on the Mertonian norms: communalism, universalism, disinterestedness and organised scepticism. These, meanwhile, guarantee universal criticism and prevent blind faith in the validity or invalidity of findings from having a say. However, this picture is inadequate, while modern science is essentially founded on arbitrariness and trust. The point is not only that trust is placed in norms, institutions and the 'registers of science', which ultimately means the entire scientific community.[4] The main point is that 'the scholar is only a node in a network of trust. We are not able to re-run all the research done by others, we have to accept their findings "on faith". Every quotation, every reference to another's work, is based on trust.'[5] John Hardwig's notion of epistemic dependence is a radical iteration of this view. This insight will play a key role in this book, so let us take a closer look at it.

EPISTEMIC DEPENDENCE: JOHN HARDWIG'S APPROACH

According to Hardwig the essential feature of science is not rational argumentation and the verification of research hypotheses, but mutual trust within the scientific community. The reason for this is simple and converges with Sztompka's statement made a decade later: no scholar fully understands the foundations of the assertions he or she makes. Everyone starts from the findings of others without ever verifying them for him/herself. The narrow specialisation characteristic of contemporary science enforces narrow perspectives. This problem seems to be less dire in the humanities where research often pivots on working with source texts. But as soon as we wade into social science, and to an even greater extent natural science, we inevitably have to make reference to results obtained by other scholars. Trust plays no small role when several scholars are working together on one project, especially an interdisciplinary one. Every member of such a team relies on the others and therefore cannot mistrust the results they generate.

The dark side and inevitable consequence of such trust is the growing number of cases of scientific misconduct.[6] Specialisation and the need to rely on the work of others make the verification of others' research practically impossible. The editors of academic journals are unable to verify the findings presented in the papers they receive. Most of the time they do not do it at all. Abuses are most prevalent in the biomedical sciences, which has to do with the impossibility of reproducing publicised experiments, a large and growing number of predatory journals, and the problem of ghost authorship.[7] The Reproducibility Project, within whose framework attempts were made to reproduce the experimental research described in 100 psychology papers published in 2008, showed that the results matched the authors' conclusions only in 36.1 per cent of cases, and this to a different (usually smaller) degree than what was reported in the publications. Even more frightening were the results obtained with regard to confirming pre-clinical cancer research. Only 11 per cent of the studies were successfully reproduced.[8] John P. A. Ioannidis even goes as far as to make the somewhat provocative claim that most published findings are false.[9] To show the scale of the problem, MIT graduates developed the website SCIgen which generated texts that looked like scientific papers but were in fact utterly meaningless. A number of these texts were accepted and published by respected academic journals (including *Applied Mathematics and Computation*), while some fictional authors (for example, Ike Antkare) were cited many times. Cyril Labbé (the creator of the fictional Antkare) found over 120 such nonsense papers published in peer-reviewed journals in 2005–2013.

All of this is strikingly at odds with the 'cartoon' vision of science.[10] Most shocking for a layperson must be that the approval of a text for publication is rarely, if ever, based on the replication of the research results, while a key role is played by the researchers' track records, their reputation and the renown of the academic institution they represent. Hardwig states that 'the structure of modern science acts to prevent replication, not to ensure it. It is virtually impossible to obtain funding for attempts to replicate the work of others, and academic credit normally is given only for new findings. When replication is attempted, it will not always detect fraudulent papers. In fact, replication paradoxically will support rather than unmask those fraudulent papers which happen to have correct conclusions.'[11]

The scientific community is built on trust. Sometimes it is trust in a single scholar and the proclaimed validity of his or her research. As Michael Polanyi stated, 'the amount of knowledge which we can justify from evidence directly available to us can never be large. The overwhelming proportion of our factual beliefs continue therefore to be held at second hand through trusting others, and in the great majority of cases our trust is placed in the authority of comparatively few people of widely acknowledged standing.'[12] The role of trust in science can neither be eliminated nor minimised, 'for the alternative to trust is, often, ignorance. An untrusting, suspicious attitude would impede the growth of knowledge, perhaps without even substantially reducing the risk of unreliable testimony.'[13] One of the things affected by the need for trust is the nature of relations between scientists. They differ little, if at all, from relations between experts and laypeople. Just like laypeople, the experts, even if working in the same specialised field, are often unable to assess their colleagues' arguments on their merits if they have not themselves conducted the research. Faced with research findings, they can only accept or reject them. The 'expert–layman relationship is essential to the scientific and scholarly pursuit of knowledge'.[14] In a similar vein, Shapin says that 'modern scientists, no less than the laity, hold the bulk of their knowledge, even the knowledge of their own disciplines, so to speak, by courtesy'.[15] This is the unavoidable cost of scientific super-specialisation. 'In most disciplines, those who do not trust cannot know; those who do not trust cannot have the best evidence for their beliefs.'[16] An expert can only be evaluated in one special circumstance – by another expert specialising in the same narrow topic. To understand an expert you need to be an expert yourself.

This radical notion of the role of trust in science has far-reaching (and controversial) implications. First, blindly putting one's trust in others whom we have grounds for believing to be more competent than ourselves is a rational, not an irrational choice. The 'principle of testimony', according to which 'if A has good reasons to believe that B has good reasons to believe p',[17] or to simplify it, 'if A knows that B knows p, then A knows p',[18] is the only way to gain second-hand knowledge. If we have no way of forming our own opinions about an issue, we have no choice but to trust others. Rationality, knowledge and trust do not mutually exclude but undergird one another:

> In epistemology, as in theology, believing that you are self-reliant or attempting to be self-reliant is a sin: for finite beings, epistemic inter-dependence is epistemologically better than epistemic independence. Because the epistemological individualist requires each to stand on her own epistemic feet, her position would preclude anyone from standing on the shoulders of giants. And then no one could see very much, very far, or very clearly.[19]

Secondly, the view that science is based on the autonomy and personal effort of individuals who make scientific breakthroughs (typical of the 'cartoon' vision of science) is not corroborated by real life. Experts too depend on others just like laypeople. What unites them is not so much respect for one another's achievements but epistemic subordination and dependence: 'if I were to pursue epistemic autonomy across the board, I would succeed only in holding relatively uninformed, unreliable, crude, untested, and therefore irrational beliefs'.[20]

Thirdly, since trust is always blind, it involves an element of the mysterious and unpredictable. In classical depictions of the lay–expert relationship both sides were conscious of the epistemic gulf between them. According to the principle of epistemic dependence, the expert is aware of the layman's ignorance, while the layman has no basis for trusting the expert's competence. The latter never understands the reasons behind the former's assertions. He may understand the recommendations, but not the rationale. That is why the layman will never have sufficient grounds for accepting the authority of the expert, and although their relationship may be one of trust, it may also be one of mistrust.

Fourthly, knowledge resides not in individual scientists but in the scientific community as a whole.[21] Since everyone knows much less than they think (most of our beliefs are founded on trust in the assertions of others), then the subject in which knowledge is vested turns out not to be a specific individual but the whole complex system of science made up of scholars trusting one another.[22]

If Hardwig is right about epistemic dependence then, first, the social status of an expert is not simply one of a number of factors that influence the reception and appreciation of his or her views. It is the *only* factor and the very foundation of epistemic authority.[23] Secondly, there is no merit-based yardstick that laypeople can use to judge experts or – less evidently – that experts themselves can use to judge other experts. Thirdly, post-truth is not a side-effect of our pervasive social media culture, the public showcasing of spectacular expert errors, cognitive heuristics, lay ignorance or the multi-voiced opinions published by old and new media outlets alike. The very nature of scientific research is such that it entails the possibility of disinformation and fake news. All that social media have done is shed light on and amplify these phenomena, while populist leaders have learned to make cynical use of them.

Although Hardwig's approach is radical, there is no shortage of authors who sympathise with it.[24] In a similar spirit, Steve Fuller states that 'we have more beliefs than we can justify, and hence we must rely on others to justify those beliefs'.[25] We rarely enjoy first-hand knowledge acquired by way of experience. Most of the time we rely on whatever opinions happen to be most popular in our community. The more 'knowledge-intensive' a society and the greater the epistemic division of labour among scientists, the more laypeople come to depend on experts.[26] John Ziman has written that 'there is no real alternative to the academic practice of relying heavily on the findings reported by individual scientists – or small groups of scientists – working in private. The empirical "facts" of science are products of, and belong to, research communities. Nevertheless, they originate in the experience of isolated individuals – including our ancestors – on whose say-so they are mainly accepted.'[27] Steven Shapin has gone as far as to claim that the very possibility of doubting the validity of someone's research requires considerable trust in how a discipline functions. 'It needs to be understood that trust is a *condition* for having the body of knowledge currently called science.'[28] Elizabeth Fricker argues that relying on others is rational as long as we have grounds to believe them to be more competent than us.[29] This position is shared by Piotr Sztompka and Stephen Turner.[30]

Still, few of the scholars sympathising with the notion of epistemic dependence are prepared to accept it wholesale.[31] For this reason, we can find two interpretations of Hardwig's stance in the literature. To illustrate them, I will use C. Thi Nguyen's metaphor of 'cognitive islands'.[32] Cognitive islands are academic disciplines in which the achievements of scholars cannot be assessed or critiqued by people outside the relevant domain. The cognitive island has two essential features. First, there are no methods here by which a layperson could make a merit-based assessment of an expert's output. Secondly, such an island has no points of contact with other islands where such assessment might be possible. In other words, no expert from another domain can effectively assess the competence of an inhabitant of a given cognitive island. And so, for example, a philosopher can make no apt assessment of the claims put forward by a political scientist, a sociologist or anybody else other than his or her own colleagues. The layperson will have no appreciation of the significance of any of these scholars. There are no contiguities or points of contact between islands. The philosopher does not understand the natural scientist even if he or she specialised in the philosophy of science, and the sociologist cannot make full sense of the political scientist's reasoning, even if he or she is a political sociologist. There is no way to travel from one island to another or to translate the islanders' languages.

This radical interpretation of science raises a number of doubts. First, would it not be possible to inhabit a number of islands simultaneously and hence to acquire the ability to translate from one language into another (thereby overcoming epistemic dependence)? Can one be specialised in two or more research areas? Would such multilateral specialisation pre-destine a scholar to become a translator from the language of one area into that of another? Secondly, what is the size and number of existing cognitive islands? Are they as vast as individual disciplines, or perhaps even fields? Or as tiny as subdisciplines and specialities? Are literary studies an island or, for example, research on the life and writings of Gustave Flaubert before 1857? If all of philosophy is a single island, then an aesthetics scholar should be able to evaluate an ethicist, and both of them a political philosopher. In political science, an expert on electoral systems should be able to question the assertions of an expert on international relations, municipal authorities or political marketing. If, however, post-Rawlsian analytical philosophy, EU eastern policy and seventeenth-century French aesthetic theories are all islands of their own, then no such merit-based assessments can be made. Thirdly, is it at all possible to practice interdisciplinary research? If communication between islands is impossible, is there a place for interdisciplinary studies on the cognitive island map? And, finally, are cognitive islands exceptions, rare entities in the vicinity of a 'cognitive mainland', or are they the norm in science? Can one escape a cognitive island, and where to? Is insularity a feature only of areas by definition associated with normativity (morality, aesthetics), or only of those with an empirical orientation? Depending on how we answer these questions, we can come up with two interpretations: a 'hard' and a 'soft' version of the epistemic dependence paradigm.

HARD AND SOFT EPISTEMIC DEPENDENCE

The most uncompromising version of epistemic dependence is put forward by Hardwig himself. In this variant, professional relations between scientists, especially those working in the natural sciences, are based almost entirely on trust.[33] Aside from a small number of exceptions in which they are personally familiar with and able to reconstruct the course of experiments run by others as well as competently confirm the validity of the results, they are usually doomed to rely on their professional colleagues. Practical restrictions on their time and resources mean that even if they could replicate an experiment and themselves confirm the findings, they never or almost never do so. Their research tends to overwhelmingly rely on claims made by others. And so academic journals publish articles whose truth they are unable to confirm. Peer review is not concerned with the claims and arguments put forward, but mostly with the reputation of a given scholar. Academic publications, in turn, go on to become the basis for the formulation of other theories that will set the course of future scientific development. As a result, the entire scientific edifice is a system of mutual trust.

From this standpoint, cognitive islands are the norm in the world of science. They are small, sometimes very small. They do not cover entire academic disciplines but rather narrow specialities. Sometimes, though rarely, they are inhabited by lone shipwrecked sailors conducting pioneering research whose results can be confirmed by no one other than themselves (as in the case of Joseph Weber and gravitational waves). Discussion regarding their research may, of course, focus on the methodological issue of how it was set up, but not on the way the experiments were run, since a competent critique would require having the 'tacit knowledge' obtained in the course of running them.

This radical interpretation of cognitive islands is highly controversial. Not only because it flips on its head the traditional picture of science as realising the Mertonian norms, but also for political reasons. There is no room in this reading for merit-based discussion of scientific findings, nor for the epistemic defence of democracy. The link between science and democracy is severed without appeal. Laypeople – both citizens and their political representatives – have no way of questioning the suggestions of the expert community. In the event of a scientific controversy, they should in fact wholly abstain from taking the floor and patiently wait for the scholars to resolve the dispute, only to embrace whatever decision they convey to them on faith alone. From the standpoint of political decision-making this gives rise to serious problems should a controversy drag on indefinitely in the absence of a clear scientific ruling and there is a need for immediate action. There would be no epistemic reasons to leave the decision up to laypeople in such circumstances. As a matter of fact, justifying expert government does not do better on this point either. If relations between experts do not differ from lay–expert ones, then the choice of the best course of action is in no way obvious either. Supporters of epistocracy like Brennan do not consider this consequence of narrow scientific specialisation at all.

The soft version of epistemic dependence is much less controversial and hence more popular. The nature of cognitive islands does not change here and monadicity remains their principal trait. What changes, however, is their number and size. In the hard version, science was largely conceived of as an archipelago. There was no mainland of traditional science practised in a rational and individualistic way. But the soft version presents a different picture. Here the norm is an epistemic mainland containing the majority of academic disciplines. Cognitive islands are deviations from the norm, idiosyncratic aberrations. Not all sciences border each other on the cognitive continent, of course, but each one borders at least one other science, which makes it possible to cross borders, partly understand the inhabitants of other countries, and therefore also translate the theories developed there. Thanks to this, the experts can directly or indirectly assess the competence of other experts in most of the world of science. They can understand their main claims and at least the outline of their arguments, assess their weight and consistency, and, if not, then at least judge the competence of those making them.

The same thing proves to be impossible only with regard to a small number of islands which are so separated from the rest of science that their denizens remain impenetrable to others. Scholars often attribute this nomadic status to ethics, aesthetics or even to philosophy as a whole.[34]

HOW ARE WE TO KNOW WHO IS RIGHT?

The epistemic dependence paradigm, whether in its soft or hard version, has failed to convince its critics. They reject the claim that science is insular, even if this only applies to a few areas of knowledge. The thesis that laypeople and many experts have to resign themselves to blind trust instead of rational appraisal is unacceptable to them. Instead, most of them argue that although laypeople are not always capable of independently and directly verifying every expert opinion, they can still do so most of the time. If Anthony Fauci warns against ingesting cleaning agents as a cure for COVID-19 (which Trump suggested was a plausible treatment), then any reasonable person who knows how such substances work is capable of adjudicating the Fauci vs. Trump dispute. If an expert claims that the braking distance of summer tyres in winter is longer than that of winter tyres, anyone can test it themselves. Much of the knowledge we use on a daily basis belongs to what Collins and Evans dub 'ubiquitous expertise'. We are able to put it to the test ourselves. Living in community, we simply know that you should not lick metal objects in winter (although some of us have surely tried to), consume excessive amounts of sugar, we know we have to monitor our cholesterol levels, check the condition of a used car before buying it, and that it is better to leave renovations involving work on the load-bearing elements of a house to professionals rather than do them ourselves, etc.

Of course, with regard to a staggering number of issues we are not capable of doing the experts' job or even of verifying the validity of the expert suggestions. Most of us cannot repair our own car or renovate gas pipelines or electric installations, and most of us cannot even tell if the expert has done a good job, let alone handle more complicated issues in which the dependencies are infinitely complex, like international policy planning or preventing economic recessions. Not to mention understanding experimental lab research, which requires vast theoretical and practical expertise unavailable to us in everyday experience. Yet even in such seemingly hopeless situations, when all we have is fragmentary knowledge, we are not altogether helpless as laypeople. Scholars critical of Hardwig's concept see hopes of overcoming epistemic dependence thanks to 'calibration'[35] or 'indicators' of expertise that help a layperson indirectly assess the expert's authority. Some scholars have proposed extended lists of such indicators, including formal credentials (academic titles, degrees and other tokens of recognition in the scientific and expert community),[36] personal aptitudes and character traits that are indispensable to an expert.[37]

A large number of discussions have centred on the position of Alvin Goldman, who proposed five strategies to which a layperson can turn when deciding which expert to trust. Each of these strategies allow the layperson to circumvent their lack of knowledge and competence and choose the most competent adviser. First, the layperson can independently (directly or indirectly) assess the arguments of experts who disagree. He or she can directly compare how they both score on cohesion and links between premises and conclusions (it being assumed that the layperson understands the nature, weight and gravity of the premises). If this proves to be impossible – when the argumentation is esoteric (which it usually is, because of how we define a layman)[38] – the layperson may rate the rhetorical skill of the speakers and make inferences as to their knowledgeability. The more articulate and confident an expert, and the faster and more skilfully she or he refutes their opponents' arguments, the more competent she or he seems to be. When Fauci argues that consuming disinfectants is not a way to fight coronavirus, laypeople can judge his argument based on their own knowledge and on the way the conclusion follows from the premises. If, however, Fauci categorically, albeit calmly and facetiously, discredits Trump's opinions about the origins, likely development and foreseeable end of the pandemic (about which the layperson is not well-informed), he demonstrates his competence indirectly. The layperson may draw a number of conclusions from the expert's rhetorical prowess: that he or she has thought through counter-arguments in advance; that he or she has devoted sufficient thought to the issue; and that his or her arguments are stronger than the counter-arguments advanced by his or her opponents.

This strategy is glaringly controversial. There is no connection between rhetorical prowess and competence. In fact, one might compensate for epistemic shortcomings with rhetorical competence.[39] The strategy is therefore highly unreliable and it is hard to consider it an effective way of overcoming epistemic dependence.[40] Many scientific dissenters have exploited the lay tendency to judge experts by their rhetorical skill. David Kirby, the author of the in-vogue book *Evidence of Harm* and one of the spokespeople for the anti-vaccine movement, has used his uncompromising attitude and lack of attachment to empirical data to ruthlessly maul Harvey Fineberg, head of the Institute of Medicine, and others in televised debates. Assisted by the celebrity Jenny McCarthy, he shouted down the president of the American Academy of Pediatrics David Tayloe on *Larry King Live*. In both cases he achieved unquestionable rhetorical victory. The layperson making inferences as to his competence on this basis would be making a mistake.[41]

Secondly, there are two ways in which laypeople can assess an expert's track record. First, they can look at her or his earlier statements and determine whether they later proved to be true. This is a way to assess the expert's past predictive skill. They can also consider the expert's present publications. In the first case, the expert's ability to pick up on something and make accurate predictions (unlike others, who failed to see what he or she saw) as well as the accuracy of those predictions will be indicative of the expert's standing. This will be quite simple in certain situations. The example of solar eclipse predictions is often cited in the literature.[42] Any layperson with a calendar and a watch can independently determine whether the expert has correctly predicted a solar eclipse. But most things that are of any interest from the social, political or economic perspective are not quite so obviously predictable. In most of these cases we will never be dealing with a highly accurate prognosis nor know for sure if the person who made it had any grounds for doing so. The field of economics is a flagship example. With regard to the 2008 economic crisis caused by a housing bubble, at least twelve people are usually mentioned[43] as having predicted it with a high degree of accuracy (including Peter Schiff, Niall Ferguson and George Soros). But there are also other individuals with regard to whom it is hard to determine if they had any real grounds for predicting it at all.[44] Can laypeople independently settle such cases? If they cannot assess the weight of an expert's present argumentation (and therefore turn to other strategies), then why should they be able to single-handedly assess the accuracy of the expert's past predictions? In many situations, even if the predicted state of affairs actually materialised, the layperson is not able to unequivocally determine whether the predictions were in fact accurate.

If laypeople are not capable of independently assessing the accuracy of an expert's predictions, they can try to rely on the esteem the expert enjoys in the academic community. They might do so indirectly, for example, by examining how the periodicals in which the expert has published rank. But here, too, it is easy to be fooled. Laypeople may not be able to tell academic journals apart from predatory ones. One of the famous anti-vaccine texts that has frequently been cited in public debate appeared in *Medical Hypothesis*, a periodical that is not peer-reviewed.[45] Most of the time only the experts in a given field can tell academic journals apart from pseudo- or non-academic ones.

Thirdly, laypeople may consider the size of the expert groups in favour of particular solutions. By doing so, they transfer the responsibility for selecting the most competent expert to the scientific community. At first glance, this strategy seems much more reliable than the previous one, since what is adjudicated is not the merit of a contention but the number of scientists on both sides. We therefore trust whoever can rally more supporters. The difference between this strategy and the previous one (looking at the scholar's track record), is immediately apparent. In the previous case, one of the criteria for selecting an expert was whether in the past she or he had gone against the scientific mainstream and was ultimately proven right. Nothing more strikingly proves an expert's predictive skill and competence than differing with the expert community and still being correct. In the present scenario, however, the mainstream's backing is recognised as indicative of who is right. The more the expert's opinion accords with mainstream science, the greater the renown of the scholar proclaiming it.

Referring to the size of same-opinion expert groups and especially citing the alleged consensus of the scientific community is the most popular argument used both by supporters and opponents of mainstream opinion.[46] A theory that has more proponents may indicate that the scientific community is relatively unanimous on a point, and therefore that the point itself is not controversial, but it can also indicate that the scientific elites have struck a deal with the industrial or pharmaceutical complex. Consensus might be indicative of a community of interest, not a community of conviction with regard to facts. But, indeed, even if there was no such community of interest in evidence, there is another doubt that calls into question the legitimacy of a simple vote count. What matters is not the number of votes, but their origin.[47] Is it still a consensus if the scholars did not arrive at their opinions independently?[48] What if the alleged consensus is actually an aggregation of leaps of faith on the part of scientists blindly trusting a handful of their colleagues? It is for these very reasons that Goldman is sceptical about this strategy. If every successive opinion is simply an unreflective iteration of those previously enounced, then the numbers can lead us astray because they are a measure not of validity but of popularity.[49] Independence in arriving at one's opinion should be a key consideration. The view proclaimed by each successive expert should not be influenced by that of her or his predecessors. Everyone should independently make their own argument, even if it ultimately proves to be the same as everyone else's. Giving increasing credence to a given claim whose proponents depend on one another would be, to quote Wittgenstein, 'as if someone were to buy several copies of the morning paper to assure himself that what it said was true'.[50] Like all other human beings, scientists succumb to fashions. Sometimes they uncritically believe gurus.[51] They trust them not because they agree with them or understand their reasoning, but because they enjoy high status in the community and publish papers in the most prestigious journals, are often cited and mentioned in public debates or have rhetorical skill. But what if the academic community as a whole puts forward a claim that only a minority of scientists are competent enough to grasp? Take as an example the scientists' appeal concerning climate change. Should we only reckon with the statements of the specialists and ignore all others? Goldman suggests that what the voices of the other scholars make evident in this case is their trust in climate studies, certainly not their grasp of the issue under discussion.

David Coady is a proponent of the 'going by the numbers' approach. With regard to the debate on climate change he claims that the main (though not sole) piece of evidence that the layperson can rely on is precisely the number of scientists in each camp. In Coady's view, the 97 per cent to 3 per cent argument is decisive not just rhetorically but meritoriously. First, even if the majority of scholars are not experts in a given domain, scholars as such are equipped with a kind of 'ubiquitous expertise' that allows them to assess the credibility of their colleagues. Laypeople are not in the habit of checking the h-index, the impact factor of journals, they do not consider SCOPUS quartiles and academic publisher rankings, scholars' education or the institutions they represent. They care little about reviews of experts' works. But scholars do. If their group – assuming they are familiar with the realia of science and academia – recognise a scholar as credible, then in keeping with the logic of Condorcet's theorem[52] their opinion should be trusted. The probability of their judgement being correct is higher than the layperson's. According to this view, the more expert supporters there are of solution x, regardless of their speciality, the higher the likelihood that x is the best solution. If a number of scholars whose reputations are unquestioned accept a researcher's findings as highly likely to be correct, it is reasonable to rely on their opinion.[53] Cody improves the strategy by advising a look at the scholar's track record. He transfers the burden of assessing the expert's previous achievements from the layman's shoulders onto the academic community.

This argument seems convincing, but it is not bulletproof. First, on what basis is the layperson to determine whether each of the members of the alleged expert community is actually an expert? If our aim is to find the most competent expert by consulting a group of experts, then how are we to know that the latter qualify? And if a layperson is assumed to be capable of assigning expert status to members of groups, then why would assessing a single expert be a problem? Even if the laypeople could attribute competence to the members of some group, they might be at a loss when trying to ascertain the existence of a scientific consensus.

How do we know there is consensus, or at least relative consensus?[54] In most cases there is no way to actually count the members of rival camps. Those who sign open letters or appeals are usually only a fraction of the specialists in a given area. In the end, in diagnosing consensus the layperson must rely on an expert or group of experts claiming to represent such consensus. This puts us back to the initial problem: how do we do just that? The gravity of this problem does not escape the attention of Collins and Evans. Their idea for how to relieve laypeople forced to make such decisions is to transfer their burden onto the Owls – the most prominent scholars in the natural and social sciences as 'voted on' by fellow scientists. Such a group would make pronouncements as to the existence of a consensus on the part of the whole scientific community. It would speak on behalf of science. The idea, however, does not seem to solve the problem of infinite regress. Who will vouch for the Owls for the benefit of the layperson? Their nomination by the academic community would make sense only if laypeople trusted that community in the first place. Otherwise their opinion would be no more credible than an appeal signed by a dozen dissident scholars repealing mainstream views. The Owls can legitimise the decisions of the expert community if and only if such legitimation already exists, if citizens already trust science and the major academic institutions but do not know if they can trust specific expert individuals.[55] But this model fails across the board when most citizens do not trust mainstream academic institutions – the national academies and academic associations.

Secondly, the argument does not rebut the charge relating to intellectual fashions. That these exist is well documented: from treating mental health conditions with electric shocks, through eugenics, once triumphant in the United States and Scandinavia,[56] through the fashion for tonsillectomy,[57] to the fluctuating popularity of neoliberalism and social liberalism among economists. Throughout history, intellectual authorities have frequently inspired such fashions which were then blindly followed and spread by other members of the scientific community.

Finally, the 'going by the numbers' completely disqualifies contributory experts of unrecognised status, whose knowledge is so highly appreciated in STS. In the above-mentioned dispute between MAFF experts and the Cumbrian sheep farmers it would have given the ministerial experts an advantage every time.

Coady is aware of the weight of some of these charges. He realises that intellectual fashions exist and that idealised scientific models developed by theorists are ineffectual. Nonetheless, his response is that trusting the scientific consensus is warranted even if it occasionally leads to mistakes. It is perfectly acceptable if the strategy works most of the time, and relying on it to identify the right answer is the best available course. There simply is not a more reliable option. But if the majority of scientists suddenly proclaim that creationism is more convincing than evolutionary theory, would that make belief in creationism rational? No, says Goldman, since it does not matter how many people believe something, but rather how independent they are in their outlook and how credible is each of their opinions taken separately.[58] Unlike Goldman, Coady argues that such faith is warranted in special social and historical circumstances.[59] There is no doubt that it was justified before the late nineteenth century when the scientific mainstream in the Anglo-Saxon world embraced the theory of evolution. Today it is unjustified. Does that mean that creationism, once thought to be true, has ceased to be true? Of course not. The rationality of expert suggestions has nothing to do with their verity. One of the most erroneous beliefs about science (belonging to the 'cartoon' vision) is that expert pronouncements are unshakable. This comes down to the belief that if an expert opinion changes, it means that there were errors in the original research that have now been rectified. But nothing is further from the truth. Changing expert recommendations are part of the development of science and are themselves brought about by adherence to the Mertonian norms that regulate scientific practice.

The fourth strategy a layperson can adopt is to look for any evidence of an expert's bias. There are times when one does not have to assess an expert's competence to have reasonable doubts about it. Even the most competent person – should they have a personal interest in promoting a certain solution – should be considered potentially biased and therefore not credible. In Wakefield's case, one of the things that ultimately discredited the claims put forward in his famous article in *The Lancet* was the discovery of the author's financial motivations: the fact that he had patented (prior to publication) a measles vaccine, all the while recommending that measles be excluded from the MMR vaccine and the fact that his study had included many children sent to him by a law firm involved in preparing a class action against vaccine producers. On the same basis, expecting rating agencies to provide a reliable assessment of companies and banks that pay them for it is imprudent, to say the least.[60]

Collins is an avowed supporter of this strategy. He considers 'local discrimination' to be the layman's most effective tool. Information regarding the expert or institution, their personal sympathies, political involvement, problematic sources of financing, personal or business associations is very important and does not require expertise to analyse. It takes no special training to note that personal pecuniary benefit is an important incentive that people from all social and professional groups, including those with academic titles, can be swayed by. Due to its universality, the strategy in question is one of the most commonly used in disputes. There is no effective rebuttal when you demonstrate someone to be deriving financial benefit from a certain decision.[61] The strategy is often employed to expose 'merchants of doubt'.[62] Unmasking the sponsors of allegedly grass-roots civic or consumer movements or pseudo independent research institutes is the most effective way of combating them. There is no need to engage in discussions with representatives of the Tobacco Institute or think tanks that question the anthropogenic causes of climate change financed by fossil fuel lobbies. In fact, such discussions only lend credibility to these opponents.

But the bias (or potential bias) argument is a double-edged sword because it can also be employed by the 'merchants of doubt' themselves. It is aptly wielded by proponents of various types of conspiracy theories. They usually divide their opponents into 'useful idiots', blind to the existence of a conspiracy and uncritically repeating the opinions of the majority, and corrupt elites whose strings are pulled by financial lobbies. Flat earthers, anti-vaxxers and chemtrails alarmists all use the same strategy – arguing that the political elites want to preserve the status quo because it is in their financial and political interest. This is why they corrupt scientists through ostracism or the allocation of research funding. From this perspective, Big Pharma coerces researchers and doctors into recommending vaccinations or prescribing specific medications, while a mutual benefit scheme makes climatologists maintain the unfounded claim that human beings have a decisive impact on climate change. Climategate is a perfect example of using this kind of 'on-site investigation' to one's own advantage.[63]

This strategy is easily exploited by those who disagree with mainstream scientific opinion. They are provoked by the scientists themselves. In some areas, the number of articles sponsored by entities with a vested interest in publishing the findings is so large that it would be hard to find papers with no financial connections (and therefore unbiased). This is the case with studies on cancer and heart disease medications, most of which are financed by pharmaceutical companies.[64] The degree to which the authors of such studies depend on private funds has led Richard Smith, the former CEO of the British Medical Publishing Group, to make the statement that 'medical journals are an extension of the marketing arm of pharmaceutical companies'.[65]

The final strategy that Goldman describes is to find an expert who will make the selection for us. It is usually seen as similar to the 'going by the numbers' strategy, the only difference being that in the former case we are talking about the whole community rather than a single expert. For that very reason I will not examine it separately here.

EPISTEMIC DEPENDENCE AND THE NOVICE/
2-EXPERTS PROBLEM

Each of the strategies described above has its proponents. Goldman has high hopes for expert track record assessment by laypeople. Coady is a firm believer in the 'going by the numbers' and putting one's trust where most of the expert voices are.[66] Collins and Evans go with 'local discrimination' and identifying consensus among scholars representing the 'core-set' of a given field. Various modifications of these strategies have also been proposed. And so Keith Lehrer and Carl Wagner believe that 'weighted average' opinions are superior to chance.[67] Other scholars recommend the Bayesian method, for example, in the form of the Delphi method.[68] None of these strategies solve the novice/2-experts problem without a controversy however.[69] Most can and have been used by proponents as well as opponents of the scientific consensus. Goldman himself admitted as much in a pessimistic tone.[70] It would also be hard to order these strategies by how effective they are in an uncontroversial manner. It might turn out that each has its specific advantages in a different context. The number of advocates backing each option cannot always be ascertained. In some situations it might prove to be difficult to establish even a tentative scientific consensus. Nor will the layperson always have access an expert's past track record or be capable of assessing it, for that matter. In the majority of cases, the layperson will be unable to independently assess the coherence of the expert narrative or the strength of the conclusions as following from the premises. Finally, it is rare for a layperson to be in possession of information that might discredit an expert.

Despite all these doubts most scholars believe that the strategies laid out above do in fact solve the problem of epistemic dependence. For example, Oliver R. Scholz says that 'N may have access to reliable indicators *that* the candidate expert has good reasons for believing *p*; and N may have access to reliable indicators *that* one expert has *better* reasons for believing his conclusion than his rival has for his'.[71] According to Scholz, Goldman's strategies really do allow the layperson to successfully adjudicate expert disagreements. I do not agree with this diagnosis. I do not believe that any of the strategies described by Goldman (in any modified form) actually solve the problem of epistemic dependence. This does not mean that I consider all of them to be equally ineffective. In my view, the only truly bulletproof strategy does not address the problem of epistemic dependence at all. The strategy I am thinking of is 'searching for evidence of expert's bias'. Hardwig was right to note that trust involves not a single but several acts of faith:

1. A knows that B says that *p*.
2. A believes . . . that B is speaking truthfully, i.e., that B is saying what she believes.
3. A believes . . . that B (unlike A) is in a position, first, to know what would be good reasons to believe *p* and, second, to have the needed reasons.
4. A believes . . . that B actually has good reasons for believing *p* when she thinks she does.[72]

Trust involves normative and epistemic beliefs regarding, on the one hand, the motivations and character of the person issuing the opinion, and, on the other hand, their competence.[73] A crisis of trust may therefore manifest itself as doubt about the individual's competence or good intentions. It may have both epistemic and non-epistemic roots.[74] In my view, in the novice/2-experts problem the layperson can only fall back on non-epistemic arguments. The latter are the only basis on which laypeople, who do not necessarily possess expertise, can draw independent conclusions. In every other strategy, the layperson ultimately has to put their trust in the opinion of a particular expert. Epistemic dependence is therefore unavoidable. Of course, one cannot escape having to trust someone (it may be an investigative journalist or a whistle-blower) even if employing the strategy of searching for evidence of an expert's bias. Yet here the layperson has to trust these information purveyors solely on the facts of the matter. The interpretation is within his or her own reach. He or she does not have to determine whether the discredited expert actually possesses expertise or assess the weight and credibility of the experts opinions. The factors causing (or potentially causing) the expert to be biased are a sufficient reason to withhold one's credence.

Of course, 'finding evidence of expert's bias' can only solve the dilemmas that laypeople (citizens and voters) face some of the time. In the majority of contentious cases the bias of a single expert will not significantly affect the argumentation strategy employed by the side he or she represents. There will always be other experts who will confirm the same findings, themselves being above suspicion. In other cases, all sides of the dispute might have financial interests (for example, because they receive sponsorship from entities interested in a given solution), but any attempt to remedy this situation will lead to absurd outcomes. For example, in order to avoid allegations of bias, the special masters handling the Omnibus Autism Proceeding (a set of cases heard in court in order to rule once and for all whether there was sound scientific evidence linking autism to vaccines) not only had to have no experience in immunology but also no links to the public health sector.[75] Similarly, the Institute of

Medicine committee tasked with assessing immunisation safety in 2001 was supposed to include only individuals who had never taken part in a vaccine trial, had never testified before a court in a similar case, and had no links to a vaccine manufacturer. As a result, the committee did not comprise any immunologists or vaccinologists.[76] The knowledge of competent decision-makers was sacrificed to avoid any bias. A similar situation occurred in the case of the silicone breast implant litigation analysed by Sheila Jasanoff. Trying to avoid being seen as biased, the judge presiding over the case, Pointer, requested the appointment of independent experts from the National Science Panel. They were supposed to settle an issue spanning toxicology, immunology, epidemiology and rheumatology. Since these experts were not allowed to have taken part in similar proceedings before, nor to have any links to implant producers, as a result four individuals were assigned to the case who had no prior practical experience.[77]

For these reasons 'finding evidence of expert's bias' can dispel lay doubts only to a very limited degree. It does not solve the problem of epistemic dependence, while only making room for a dispute between experts, none of whom can be eliminated in view of potential bias. Even though it weeds out corrupt researchers, this strategy of negative selection will not help laypeople make a positive choice. Laypeople will still be facing experts who disagree. They will then have to fall back on other strategies. It is hard to choose the best one *a priori*.

EPISTEMIC DEPENDENCE: MEDIUM VERSION

The problem of epistemic dependence is an unyielding challenge that the philosophy of science and political theory must face. Accepting the hard version of epistemic dependence requires a complete redefinition of science, the identification of alternative explanations of its success, and the abandonment of epistemic arguments for democracy and epistocracy alike. The hard version is like the world in Peter Bruegel's painting of the blind leading the blind. Everybody is holding on tightly to a number of what they consider to be reliable epistemic authorities, lavishing boundless trust upon them. The latter, in turn, are holding on to other authorities, and so on ad infinitum. As a result, nobody knows where anyone else is headed. What is more, no one knows how to terminate this deplorable state of affairs. This is why so few scholars accept this version. On the other hand, in the soft version the concept of epistemic dependence largely loses its theoretical and pragmatic significance, and is reduced to a mere oddity. In this version the world has no mysteries. Although learning about it may be a laborious task, there is nothing that might render a person unable to do so *a priori*. And even if not everyone is willing to make the effort, one can easily find competent people whose opinions may be trusted. This view of reality is really cause for optimism. Dependence can be overcome, so if anyone succumbs to the rhetoric of the opponents of science, that person is personally responsible for his or her own ignorance. The first of these worlds is a terrifying place of chaos in which we are all stumbling and erring, doomed to put our trust in charlatans and merchants of doubt. The second world is the preserve of self-satisfied, potentially all-knowing and all-talented individuals. In the first world, trust in science always rests on shaky foundations and is achievable only through indoctrination. The social authority of science is built not via rational argument but through persuasion. In the second world, intractable citizens have to be punished for their lack of trust in science. After all, they have not taken sufficient pains to understand and to trust in the scientific enterprise. In the first world, Goldman's strategies for choosing an expert make little sense, since they do not eliminate the need to trust others blindly. In the second world, meanwhile, there is no use for them. Ordinary citizens either have enough acumen to grasp scientists' claims by themselves, or they can rely on science popularisers. It is therefore little surprise that the first world so repels scholars and the second so entices them. But as attractive as the optimistic world of citizen competence may be, it is also highly unrealistic. There is no indication that laypeople can competently assess experts on points of merit. Nor are there any non-controversial strategies of choosing experts in the novice/2-experts situation.

It therefore seems necessary to come up with a moderate version of epistemic dependence. We need a paradigm that will not plunge us into apathy and discourage cognitive effort, since we will never come into possession of specialist knowledge anyway. On the other hand, we need a view that will not stoke our self-satisfaction, fuel over-confidence in our cognitive skills, or hold inflamed sceptics with a limited capacity for reasoning responsible for the phenomenon of post-truth. The answer 'All is well, all we need is a bit more effort and rational argumentation' seems bizarre at a time of ubiquitous doubt in the authority of science, when pseudo-experts so easily gain throngs of followers. We need a theory that explains the systemic causes behind this state of affairs and shows us how to improve our circumstances. Such a theory should take into account the 'insular' nature of science and the existence of epistemic dependence without imprisoning us on the cognitive islands.

Let us then return to our archipelago. Let us try to see it in a new light. This time, the cognitive islands are much bigger than in the 'hard' version. They still represent research areas, but this time they are inhabited both by theorists and practitioners who share similar interests and experiences. They study the same or very similar issues, but for the former group these are the object of theoretical reflection, while for the latter they are the object of practice. The people on the island may be, say, the producers and users of a given product or service (for example, pesticide producers and farmers, social media creators and users, etc.). The differences between them often lead to a lack of trust. The theorists look at the practitioners with little emotion and with a large dose of scepticism. They consider abstract knowledge – the outcome of cumulative experimental research and scientific theory development – superior to practical experience. On the other hand, the practitioners are wary and sceptical of the theorists. They are unsure of their intentions and consider their theories little more than occasionally useful. Although both groups inhabit the same place, they usually keep away from each other. They rarely strike up conversations or draw on each other's experience. Meanwhile, cooperation could allow them to achieve synergistic effects. This is what a cognitive island might have looked like if we defined an expert following Collins and Evans. In the moderate version, the island population is not limited to scientists. The islanders might have diplomas and represent scientific and research institutions, or they might not. But they do have to be contributory experts in a given field, so it suffices if they are experienced practitioners. They inhabit a particular kind of island not because of the general quantity of their knowledge, but because they are capable of solving practical or theoretical problems within a given domain. The cognitive islands do not overlap precisely with academic disciplines, just as reality is not neatly divided according to the conventional framework of fields of research. They are interdisciplinary and 'subject-specific' – for example, they often pertain to a particular problem. This is why on different occasions the same person, whether as practitioner or theorist, will be a contributory expert in a number of areas, and therefore an inhabitant of many different islands. Table 3.1 presents the differences between this vision and the previous ones. In the medium version of epistemic dependence understanding is possible among a wider group than in the radical (hard) version. It turns out that cognitive islands have a wide array of inhabitants, including not only professionals whose knowledge pertains to a specific problem, but also ordinary users of commodities insofar as they have contributory expertise. This makes fact-based discussion and competent assessment of expert arguments a much more frequent occurrence than the radical version would have it

Table 3.1 Cognitive islands: hard, medium and soft version

	Hard version	Medium version	Soft version
Cognitive islands	Universal and overlap neatly with academic disciplines	Universal and overlap with research areas	Few in number and of little significance
Islanders	Academics or lab practitioners	Contributory experts, including practitioners	Academics or lab practitioners
Communication between inhabitants of the same island	Possible	Requires development of interactional expertise	Everyone understands everyone else, even a layperson understands an expert
Understanding between inhabitants of different islands	Impossible	Impossible	Possible
Strategies for solving the novice/2-experts problem	Useless, since fallible	Of key significance, since the alternative is blind trust	Superfluous, since trust can be replaced by understanding

The medium version also radically alters the picture of inter-island relations. The radical version left no room at all for such a possibility, while the soft version did not foresee any obstacles to such relations. The medium version shares the radical intuitions of the hard version, but it does not despair. It posits the possibility of inter-island relations, but denies that they can ever be based on mutual understanding. Trust will always play a key role in them. This should come as no surprise. Only contributory experts in the same area can understand one another. There is no way to impart to others what can be grasped only by way of tacit knowledge gained through experience. Even those who dwell on the same island will occasionally run into communication problems. They will understand one another only once they have gained the relevant interactional expertise. In the case of the inhabitants of different cognitive islands, such understanding is impossible.

This is why inter-island relations must be based on trust, which is not to say blind trust. In practice, when seeking to assess a specialist from another area we tend to use the strategies that Goldman (and others) developed for solving the novice/2-experts problem. Therefore, we can assess the coherence of the expert's argument, her or his past-track record, and support her or his claims received from other researchers or evidence of bias. In the end, the choice is up to us. There is no non-controversial hierarchy of strategies, ranging from the least to the most reliable. For those who subscribe to the 'cartoon' vision of science, a 'headcount' will be decisive. For those who, like Feyerabend, equate science with vying for influence and power, proof of bias may be the most important factor. In practice, giving preference to one of these strategies over others will often depend on the epistemic community to which we belong or sympathise with. Peter Haas, who coined the term 'epistemic community', used it to refer to a group of experts who share the same rules of procedure, methods of conducting research and formulating arguments, interests, ontological and epistemological assumptions, as well as criteria for distinguishing science from pseudo-science.[78] After all, experts never function in a void. They are always part of wider social systems, distinguished by:

> (1) a shared set of normative and principled beliefs, which provide a value-based rationale for the social action of community members; (2) shared causal beliefs, which are derived from their analysis of practices leading or contributing to a central set of problems in their domain and which then serve as the basis for elucidating the multiple linkages between possible policy actions and desired outcomes; (3) shared notions of validity – that is, intersubjective, internally defined criteria for weighing and validating knowledge in the domain of their expertise; and (4) a common policy enterprise – that is, a set of common practices associated with a set of problems to which their professional competence is directed, presumably out of the conviction that human welfare will be enhanced as a consequence.[79]

Such groups then dwell in their own separate epistemic worlds. They use different criteria to select and interpret facts, and identify admissible arguments. They employ different procedural schemes and definitions of expertise. They differ in their value hierarchies and prescriptions for action. Although they tend to agree as to the facts, they usually interpret them in divergent ways. The differences between them are so wide that they almost never come to any agreement. This is why politicians are so keen to enlist the opinions of epistemic communities in support their own political claims. There will always be an opinion that substantiates their proposed course of action. All the more so since such communities proliferate wherever pure science adjoins applied solutions, for example, in climate change, economics or engineering. For instance, even assuming that climate change is anthropogenic, how to counteract it still remains a point of contention, and the same holds for the issue of how much time is left to make changes, whether there are effective techniques of achieving the desired results, whether they are affordable, etc. Different epistemic communities will propose different definitions of the situation and different recommendations for tackling the same issues.

We see an excellent illustration of this in the discussion between supporters of ecomodernism (ecopragmatism) and degrowth.[80] *An Ecomodernist Manifesto*, signed by eighteen activists and scholars, was published in 2015.[81] Unlike the dominant view, which sees industrialisation as the main factor behind the destabilisation of our planet's ecosystems, the authors and signatories of the manifesto still put their trust in science and the salutary effects of modernisation. They see scientific and technological progress as the only hope of averting a climate disaster. In their view, the pre-industrial period is wrongly depicted as an idyllic time that we should aspire to bring back. Instead, it would be much better to simply correct the course of human technological and economic development. Full of hope, the ecomodernists await innovations that will put an end to climate change without forcing humans to renounce free markets and consumptionism.

The answer to *An Ecomodernist Manifesto* was immediate. A highly critical *Degrowth Response to An Ecomodernist Manifesto* appeared that same year.[82] Proponents of degrowth met the optimism of the ecomodernists with pessimism, countering the view that we would evolve towards the necessary changes with the opinion that the world economy needs to be radically decelerated.

The above two documents show how very differently experts can interpret the same facts, since neither group questions the facts as they stand. They agree on origins of climate change, but they come to completely different conclusions. They both note that 75 per cent of deforestation occurred during the pre-industrial era. For the ecomodernists, the fact that only a quarter of all deforestation has happened in the last 250 years is proof of the relative harmlessness of human activity. For the degrowth movement, the same fact is proof of a catastrophic acceleration of planetary destruction (250 years is a very short time compared with the pre-industrial period of 200,000 years). Both groups also employ a completely different interpretive framework. While the ecomodernists highlight the emancipatory nature of modernisation, the proponents of degrowth underscore growing global social inequalities. While the former celebrate industrial agriculture and aquaculture, the latter point to monopolistic practices on the seed market and rich nations' subsidisation of agriculture. While the former emphasise the rise of life expectancy thanks to modernisation, the latter underline the health hazards due to environmental degradation. Finally, as the former look to atomic energy to provide the long-term solution, the latter emphasise the dangers that it poses.

As a result, each group has its own definition of rational political action. Such discrepancies are characteristic of epistemic communities which always strive to bring about 'the introduction of policy alternatives, the selection of policies, and the building of national and international coalitions in support of the policies'.[83] They are responsible for the 'circulation of causal ideas and some associated normative beliefs',[84] define the acceptable social costs of policies and identify key stakeholders. They therefore stake out the political context of any decision, thereby trying to influence the decision itself.

What is most important for us to keep in mind is the fact that epistemic communities employ different definitions of expertise and have different ways of identifying experts. They also use different hierarchies of criteria to assess expert competence. Communities with stronger links to academia which acknowledge the primacy of the Mertonian norms tend more often to appeal to the scientific consensus and mainstream views. Groups straddling science and pseudo-science, sceptical of the scientific mainstream, especially advocacy-type groups, are more likely to be swayed by the personality of particular experts, their rhetorical skill and past success. For them the current scientific consensus holds no value in and of itself. On the contrary, it may even be evidence of systemic bias, an underlying ideology and a community of interest. Other communities still may be built around extra-scientific values. Their members assess experts based on whether their views agree with the values held by the group. Table 3.2 details a number of examples showing how strategies of solving the novice/2-experts problem may be ranked hierarchically.

Table 3.2 Epistemic communities and novice/2-experts problem

Nature of the epistemic community	Close links to academia	Anti-science, populist	Close to conspiracy theories
Hierarchy used in assessing experts	Scientific consensus and 'going by the numbers'	Rhetorical skill	Evidence of bias
	Past track record	Evidence of bias	Rhetorical skill
	Evidence of bias	Past track record	

The moderate version of epistemic dependence is a compromise between two equally extreme and hard-to-accept visions of reality. It alone provides grounds for a justified, moderate optimism when it comes to lay–expert understanding. It does not hold that anyone can debate experts in any field, competently question their claims and arguments, and point out the gaps in their argumentation. It states that understanding is possible only between those who have the same or similar experience. Shared experience is the only platform on which understanding can be built. No such community obtains when we are dealing with people whose knowledge and experience differ, that is, the inhabitants of different cognitive islands. In this situation, we are doomed to trust the authorities. Unluckily for us, this is what happens in the majority of the cases discussed within the public arena.

NOTES

1. Cf. Martini, 'The Epistemology of Expertise', 116.
2. Russell Hardin, *Trust* (Cambridge: Polity, 2006); Adam B. Selingman, *The Problem of Trust* (Princeton, NJ: Princeton University Press, 1997); Barbara Misztal, *Trust in Modern Societies* (Cambridge: Polity, 1996); cf. Vincent Buskens, Rense Corten and Chris Snijders (eds), *Advances in the Sociology of Trust and Cooperation* (Berlin: De Gruyter, 2020); Reinhart Bachmann and Akbar Zaheer (eds), *Handbook of Trust Research* (Northampton: Edward Elgar, 2008); Mark Warren, 'Democratic Theory and Trust', in Mark Warren (ed.), *Democracy and Trust* (Cambridge: Cambridge University Press, 1999), 310–45; Robert B. Putnam, *Bowling Alone: The Collapse and Revival of American Community* (New York: Simon & Schuster, 2000); Robert D. Putnam, Robert Leonardi and Raffaella Y. Nanetti, *Making Democracy Work: Civil Traditions in Modern Italy* (Princeton. NJ: Princeton University Press, 1993); Charles Tilly, *Trust and Rule* (Cambridge: Cambridge University Press, 2005); Francis Fukuyama, *Trust: The Social Virtues and the Creation of Prosperity* (New York: Free Press, 1995); Kevin Vallier, *Trust in a Polarized Age* (Oxford: Oxford University Press, 2020).
3. Ziman, *Real Science*, 29; Bernard Barber, *The Logic and Limits of Trust* (New Brunswick, NJ: Rutgers University Press, 1983); Steven Shapin, *A Social History of Truth: Civility and Science in Seventeenth-Century England* (Chicago: University of Chicago Press, 1994); Steven Shapin, 'Trust, Honesty, and the Authority of Science', in Harvey V. Fineberg et al. (eds), *Society's Choices: Social and Ethical Decision Making in Biomedicine* (Washington, DC: National Academy Press, 1995), 388–408; Heather Douglass, *Science, Policy, and the Value-Free Ideal* (Pittsburgh, PA: University of Pittsburgh Press, 2009), ch. 6; Barry Barnes, *About Science* (Oxford: Blackwell, 1985), ch. 3; Philip Kitcher, 'The Division of Cognitive Labor', *Journal of Philosophy* 87(1) (1990): 5–22; Philip Kitcher, 'Authority, Deference, and the Role of Individual Reasoning in Science', in E. Mcmullin (ed.), *The Social Dimensions of Science*

(Notre Dame, IN: University of Notre Dame Press, 1992); Philip Kitcher, *The Advancement of Science: Science without Legend, Objectivity without Illusions* (Oxford: Oxford University Press, 1993); Michael Polanyi, *Personal Knowledge: Towards a Post-Critical Philosophy* (Chicago: University of Chicago Press, 1958); Kyle Powys Whyte and Robert P. Crease, 'Trust, Expertise, and the Philosophy of Science', *Synthese* 177 (2010): 411–25.

4. Sztompka, *Zaufanie*, 363.
5. Sztompka, *Zaufanie*, 365.
6. The Retraction Watch database contains a list of almost 30,000 papers (as of June 2020) which have been retracted by their authors or publishers after confirming that their content was false (see at: http://retractiondatabase. org/RetractionSearch.aspx). Cf. Harriet Zuckerman, 'Is "the Time Ripe" for Quantitative Research on Misconduct in Science?' *Quantitative Science Studies* 1(3) (2020): 945–58.
7. See at: retractionwatch.com.
8. See David Sarewitz, 'Saving Science', available at: https://www.thenewatlantis. com/publications/saving-science; C. G. Begley and L. M. Ellis, 'Raise Standards for Preclinical Cancer Research', *Nature* 483 (2012): 531–3.
9. John P. A. Ioannidis, 'Why Most Published Research Findings are False', *PLoS Medicine* 2(8) (2005).
10. Collins, Evans and Weinel, *Experts and the Will*, ch. 5.
11. John Hardwig, 'Role of Trust in Knowledge', *Journal of Philosophy* 88(12) (1991): 703.
12. Polanyi, *Personal Knowledge*, 221.
13. Hardwig, 'Role of Trust', 707.
14. John Hardwig, 'Epistemic Dependence', *Journal of Philosophy* 82(7) (1985): 336.
15. Shapin, 'Trust, Honesty, and the Authority of Science'.
16. Hardwig, 'Role of Trust', 693–4; John Hardwig, 'Evidence, Testimony, and the Problem of Individualism – a Response to Schmitt', *Social Epistemology* 2(4) (1988): 317–18.
17. Hardwig, 'Role of Trust', 697.
18. Hardwig, 'Role of Trust', 698.
19. Hardwig, 'Evidence, Testimony', 319.
20. Hardwig, 'Epistemic Dependence', 340. Cf. Friederike Hendriks, Dorothe Kienhues and Rainer Bromme, 'Trust in Science and the Science of Trust', in Bernd Blöbaum (ed.), *Progress in IS: Trust and Communication in a Digitized World: Models and Concepts of Trust Research* (Cham: Springer, 2016), 145.
21. Cf. Martin Kusch, *Knowledge by Agreement: The Programme of Communitarian Epistemology* (Oxford: Oxford University Press, 2002), ch. 5; Michael Welbourne, *The Community of Knowledge* (Aberdeen: Aberdeen University Press, 1986); Jeroen de Ridder, 'Epistemic Dependence and Collective Scientific Knowledge', *Synthese* 191 (2014): 37–53.
22. Stella Gaon and Stephen P. Norris, 'The Undecidable Grounds of Scientific Expertise', *Journal of Philosophy of Education* 35(2) (2001): 190.

23. Cf. the opposite view, propounded by Martin Hoffman (Martin Hoffman, 'How to Identify Moral Experts? An Application of Goldman's Criteria for Expert Identification to the Domain of Morality', *Analyse & Kritik* 2 (2012): 300.

24. See Abraham Schwab, 'Epistemic Trust, Epistemic Responsibility, and Medical Practice', *Journal of Medicine and Philosophy* 33 (2008): 302–20.

25. Steve Fuller, *The Knowledge Book* (London: Acumen, 2007), 4.

26. Steve Fuller, *Social Epistemology* (Bloomington: Indiana University Press, 1991), 278–9; cf. Bernard Barber, 'Trust in Science', *Minerva* 25(1/2) (1987): 123.

27. Ziman, *Real Science*, 97.

28. Shapin, 'Trust, Honesty, and the Authority of Science'.

29. Fricker, 'Testimony and Epistemic Authority', 239–44.

30. Turner, *Liberal Democracy 3.0*, 51.

31. An example of such a researcher is Scott Brewer, who openly states that 'there is compelling reason to doubt that a nonexpert legal reasoner can acquire expert information from a scientific expert in a manner that is both epistemically and legally justified' (Scott Brewer, 'Scientific Expert Testimony and Intellectual Due Process', *Yale Law Journal* 107(6) (1998): 1541).

32. C. Thi Nguyen, 'Cognitive Islands and Runaway Echo Chambers: Problems for Epistemic Dependence on Experts', *Synthese* 197(7) (2020): 2803–21.

33. Cf. Mark Owen Webb, 'Why I Know About as Much as You: A Reply to Hardwig', *Journal of Philosophy* 90(5) (1993): 260–70.

34. See Michael Cholbi, 'Moral Expertise and the Credentials Problem', *Ethical Theory and Moral Practice* 10 (2007): 323–34; Scott LaBarge, 'Socrates and Moral Expertise', in Lisa Rasmussen (ed.), *Ethics Expertise: History, Contemporary Perspectives, and Applications* (Dordrecht: Springer, 2005), 15–38; Scott LaBarge, 'Socrates and the Recognition of Experts', *Apeiron: A Journal for Ancient Philosophy and Science* 30(4) (1997): 51–62; Nguyen, 'Cognitive Islands'.

35. Kitcher, *The Advancement of Science*, 230–2.

36. Martini, 'The Epistemology of Expertise', 118–19.

37. Cholbi, 'Moral Expertise and the Credentials', 325–7.

38. See Hoffman, 'How to Identify Moral Experts?' 302.

39. Scholz, 'Experts: What They Are', 200; cf. Hoffman, 'How to Identify Moral Experts?' 300, 302.

40. Catherine Holst and Anders Molander, 'Public Deliberation and the Fact of Expertise: Making Experts Accountable', *Social Epistemology. A Journal of Knowledge, Culture and Policy* (2017): 4.

41. Cf. Ben Almassi, 'Climate Change, Epistemic Trust, and Expert Trustworthiness', *Ethics and the Environment* 17(2) (2012): 34–6.

42. Goldman, 'Experts: Which Ones Should We Trust?'.

43. *Fortune* has identified only eight such individuals (cf. '8 Who saw the crisis coming . . . and 8 who didn't', available at: https://archive.fortune.com/galleries/2008/fortune/0808/gallery.whosawitcoming.fortune/index.html, last accessed 26 June 2021.

44. Cf. Dirk J. Bezemer, '"No One Saw This Coming" Understanding Financial Crisis Through Accounting Models', *Accounting Organizations and Society* 35(7) (2010): 676–88.

45. S. Bernard, A. Enayati, L. Redwood, H. Roger and T. Binstock, 'Autism: A Novel Form of Mercury Poisoning', *Medical Hypotheses* 56(4) (2001): 462–71.

46. This strategy is the basis of the Frye Standard, which for several decades defined how scientific evidence was weighed by American courts (from the 1970s to the 1990s). According to this standard, if a piece of evidence is to be admitted by a court it has be the outcome of applying a 'generally accepted' method deemed reliable by the relevant scientific community. Towards the end of the twentieth century the Daubert Standard, which transfers responsibility for judging the scientific facts as reliable to the judges, gradually became more dominant.

47. Adam Elga, 'How to Disagree about How to Disagree', in Richard Feldman and Ted Warfield (eds), *Disagreement* (Oxford: Oxford University Press, 2010), 177–8.

48. Cf. David Coady, 'Epistemology and Climate Change', in Miranda Fricker et al. (eds), *The Routledge Handbook of Social Epistemology* (New York: Routledge, 2019), 469–70.

49. Holst and Molander, 'Public Deliberation', 5.

50. Ludwig Wittgenstein, *Philosophical Investigations*, trans. G. E. M. Anscombe (Oxford: Blackwell, 1997), para. 265.

51. Cf. Friedman, *Power Without Knowledge*, 232, 246.

52. Franz Dietrich and Kai Spiekermann, 'Epistemic Democracy with Defensible Premises', *Economics and Philosophy* 29(1) (2013): 87–120; Bernard Grofman, Guillermo Owen and Scott Feld, 'Thirteen Theorems in Search of the Truth', *Theory and Decision* 15 (1983): 261–78.

53. David Coady, 'When Experts Disagree', *Episteme* 3(1/2) (2006): 70; Coady, 'Epistemology and Climate Change', 470.

54. See the complicated procedure for determining the degree of consensus among scientists as to the anthropogenic origins of climate change described in John Cook et al., 'Quantifying the Consensus on Anthropogenic Global Warming in the Scientific Literature', *Environmental Research Letters* 8 (2013): 1–7.

55. This is why Collins and Evans simply assume the existence of a general culture of trust in expertise. They are convinced that confidence in science is a default attitude, part of our culture, while problems in the post-truth era are due to people's inability to recognise what the scientific mainstream thinks. Culturally, we believe that scientific knowledge should remain apolitical and that politics and science should be separate (Collins, Evans and Weinel, *Experts and the Will*).

56. See Edwin Black, *War Against the Weak: Eugenics and America's Campaign to Create a Master Race* (New York: Four Walls Wight Windows, 2003).

57. Collins, *Are We All Scientific Experts Now?* 6–7.

58. Goldman, 'Experts: Which Ones Should We Trust?' 125.

59. Coady, 'When Experts Disagree', 75–6; Coady, *What to Believe Now*, 45–6.
60. Cf. Levy and Peart, *Escape from Democracy*, 157–8, 194–5.
61. Cf. David Michaels, *The Triumph of Doubt* (Oxford: Oxford University Press, 2020).
62. Cf. Naomi Oreskes and Erik M. Conway, *Merchants of Doubt: How a Handful of Scientists Obscured the Truth on Issues from Tobacco Smoke to Global Warming* (New York: Bloomsbury, 2010); Leah Ceccarelli, 'Manufactured Scientific Controversy: Science, Rhetoric, and Public Debate', *Rhetoric and Public Affairs* 14(2) (2011): 195–228.
63. Cf. Collins, *Are We All Scientific Experts Now?* 11–16.
64. See Joel Lexchin, Lisa A. Bero, Benjamin Djulbegovic and Otavio Clark, 'Pharmaceutical Industry Sponsorship and Research Outcome and Quality: Systematic Review', *British Medical Journal* 326 (2003): 1167–70; M. Friedberg, B. Saffran, T. J. Stinson, W. Nelson and C. L. Bennett, 'Evaluation of Conflict of Interest in Economic Analyses of New Drugs Used in Oncology', *Journal of the American Medical Association* 282(15) (1999): 1453–7.
65. Richard Smith, 'Medical Journals Are an Extension of Marketing Arm of Pharmaceutical Companies', *PLoS Medicine* 2(5) (2005): 364–6.
66. Coady, 'When Experts Disagree'; Almassi, 'Climate Change'.
67. Keith Lehrer and Carl Wagner, *Rational Consensus in Science and Society: A Philosophical and Mathematical Study* (Dordrecht: D. Reidel, 1981), 20.
68. This involves several steps. First, every member of an expert body provides his or her own answer to the problematic question. Then, the answers are disclosed to the whole group so that everyone can correct their initial assumptions (by taking guidance from the majority and from the most competent members of the group). At the end, everyone presents their position, which might differ from their initial one. Cf. Willy Aspinall, 'A Route to More Tractable Expert Advice', *Nature* 463 (2010): 294; Cf. Mark Steyvers and Brent Miller, 'Cognition and Collective Intelligence', in T. W. Malone and M. S. Bernstein (eds), *Handbook of Collective Intelligence* (Cambridge, MA: Harvard University Press, 2015), 128–30.
69. Cf. Reiss, 'Why Do Experts Disagree?', 13.
70. Goldman, 'Experts: Which Ones Should We Trust?' 129.
71. Scholz, 'Experts: What They Are', 202.
72. Hardwig, 'Role of Trust', 699.
73. Barber, 'Trust in Science', 123–4; Annette Baier, 'Trust and Antitrust', *Ethics* 96(2) (1986): 231–60; Shapin, 'Trust, Honesty, and the Authority of Science'.
74. Scholz, 'Experts: What They Are', 199–200.
75. Seth Mnookin, *The Panic Virus: A True Story Behind the Vaccine-Autism Controversy* (New York: Simon & Schuster, 2012), 280–1.
76. Mnookin, *The Panic Virus*, 177.
77. Sheila Jasanoff, 'Science and the Statistical Victim: Modernizing Knowledge in Breast Implant Litigation', *Social Studies of Science* 32, 1 (2002): 37–69. Cf. Eyal, *The Crisis of Expertise*, 107–8.

78. See Noel Castree, *Making Sense of Nature: Representation, Politics and Democracy* (London: Routledge, 2014), p. 42.

79. Peter Haas, 'Introduction: Epistemic Communities and International Policy Coordination', *International Organization* 46(1) (1992): 3.

80. I am grateful to Ewa Bińczyk for alerting me to this debate.

81. John Asafu-Adjaye, Linus Blomqvist, Stewart Brand, Barry Brook, Ruth DeFries, Erle Ellis, Christopher Foreman, David Keith, Martin Lewis, Mark Lynas, Ted Nordhaus, Roger Pielke, Jr., Rachel Pritzker, Joyashree Roy, Mark Sagoff, Michael Shellenberger, Robert Stone, Peter Teague, *An Ecomodernist Manifesto, Technical Report*, June 2015, available at: http://www.ecomodernism.org/manifesto-english, last accessed 8 December 2021.

82. Jeremy Caradonna, Iris Borowy, Tom Green, Peter A. Victor, Maurie Cohen, Andrew Gow, Anna Ignatyeva, Matthias Schmelzer, Philip Vergragt, Josefin Wangel, Jessica Dempsey, Robert Orzanna, Sylvia Lorek, Julian Axmann, Rob Duncan, Richard B. Norgaard, Halina S. Brown, Richard Heinberg, *A Degrowth Response to An Ecomodernist Manifesto*, available at: https://www.resilience.org/stories/2015-05-06/a-degrowth-response-to-an-ecomodernist-manifesto, last accessed 8 December 2021.

83. Haas, 'Introduction: Epistemic Communities', 16.

84. Peter Haas, 'Policy Knowledge: Epistemic Communities', in Neil J. Smelser and Paul B. Baltes (eds), *International Encyclopedia of the Social & Behavioral Sciences* (Oxford: Pergamon, 2001), 11579.

Chapter 4

EPISTEMIC DEPENDENCE AND POLITICAL THEORY: DEPENDENCE CHANGES EVERYTHING

════════

We already know that defining expertise is not a simple thing. We also know that even if we manage to define it, it is by no means easy to identify an expert and that expertise has some natural limitations. We know that all too often we expect too much from experts in situations in which they cannot live up to our hopes. We know, too, that there is an epistemic gulf – an unbridgeable one, to all appearances – between laypeople and experts. Laypeople are always practically helpless when having to choose the most competent expert and the best expertise. Through the lens of this knowledge, we will now take a look at three visions of the lay–expert relationship popular in liberal democratic thought as described in Chapter 1. They are as follows: (1) citizens may acquire sufficient knowledge to take part in decision-making, as it is possible to translate expertise into lay language; (2) under favourable circumstances, for example, within the framework of minipublics, ordinary citizens can acquire decision-making competence through deliberation with experts; and (3) due to the inevitable incompetence of citizens, it is sufficient to divide decision-making into two domains – political (civic) and expert-led (technical). In my view, the notion of epistemic dependence destroys the foundations of each of the above statements, bringing them all down.

TRANSLATE IT AGAIN, SAM

The first victim of epistemic dependence is the claim that we can all take part in decision-making to an equal degree and with equal success. The notion of epistemic dependence tears this idea to shreds. Epistemic differences between people are a fact. We have different degrees of competence in different fields, we differ in our knowledge, ability to absorb information and inclination to be critical, and we all filter knowledge through pre-existing attitudes and beliefs. This means that even if lay-people's knowledge can be of some use in decision-making, not every-one's knowledge will be relevant to a given issue. If we can speak of a kind of knowledge shared by all citizens to a more or less similar degree, it is knowledge related to participation in culture, that is, knowledge of values, social norms and dominant practices. This might be accompa-nied by simplified, popular knowledge about complex technical prob-lems. Neither, however, can be said to amount to specialist knowledge and neither makes citizens effective decision-makers on technical issues. Even if citizens' popular beliefs overlap with the opinions of experts, there is still an epistemic gulf between these two groups.

This is why diversity of viewpoints and experiences – so cherished by some theorists – has no epistemic value and does not amount to collec-tive wisdom if it is not accompanied by an understanding of the nature of the processes under discussion. The aggregation of socially dispersed knowledge does not accelerate or improve decision-making. It is true that many political problems are like mazes without a map. There are either no experts on them, or we do not know who they are, and there-fore there is no justification for leaving the relevant decisions up to a small group of supposed experts. In such situations, stakeholders, and possibly even the whole political community, should be involved in mak-ing the decision. But if a problem looks like something that has already been addressed in the past, if someone knows their way around the maze we have stumbled into, then ignoring the voice of this person or putting it on a par with others would be incredibly foolish.

The solution to the problem of epistemic dependence is not to trans-late scientific theory into the language of laypeople. First, it is not clear whether such translation is possible. In the world of 'cognitive islands', there is little hope of understanding even between experts. An expert can be understood by another expert only in the same narrow domain, one who shares the same knowledge and experience. Meanwhile, the reality of scientific research often drives scholars to pursue original avenues rather than replicate the research done by others. It is rare to find two equally competent scholars who are able to evaluate each other's work. Even within one specialisation, the relationship between scholars usually involves epistemic asymmetry.

Such asymmetry obtains to an even greater extent between scholars in different fields. Some scholars, inspired by the work of Collins, see interactional expertise (IE) as a way out of this conundrum.[1] Just as a reminder, this is the type of expertise that does not require active prac-tice.[2] All it requires is a long history of consulting experts and following the discussions in a given field: 'it is possible to learn to say everything that can be said about bicycle riding, car-driving, or the use of a stick by a blind man, without ever having ridden a bike, driven a car, or been blind and used a stick'.[3] It allows one to learn how to talk to contributory experts and to understand the meaning and significance of their statements without having participated in research over the long term. Interactional expertise is the bridge connecting all specialities – the same bridge whose existence is denied by radical epistemic dependence. It facilitates a number of kinds of interdisciplinary collaboration.[4]

While this kind of expertise does not make it possible to evaluate the research of others (otherwise there would be no need for interdisciplinary collaboration), it makes it possible to understand where the research is going, to appreciate its importance and place it within the general context of the work of the team. Interactional expertise is what allows one to step outside the bounds of one's narrow specialisation. It enables peer review in funding agencies which evaluate the rationale and viability of conducting innovative research based on the opinion of reviewers with differently profiled knowledge. Interactional expertise is also what allows Collins and other sociologists of science to successfully analyse scientific processes without themselves having to replicate them.[5]

Of course, acquiring interactional expertise even in a cognate field is relatively rare, as it requires quite a lot of time and cognitive effort. Even though programmes and institutions which are supposed to facilitate this process for scholars, such as interdisciplinary centres,[6] exist, they can never replace long-term contact with experts in a particular discipline. According to Collins, interactional expertise can be achieved, and the way to go about it is through 'linguistic socialisation'.[7] This is a controversial claim, however. Those who disagree argue that gaining interactional expertise is not as simple as Collins makes it out to be.[8] Their critique boils down to two points. First, there is no empirical evidence that expertise can be acquired through conversations with experts alone. Of course, a person engaged in long-term discussions with practitioners in a given field may have the impression that he or she understands all of the terms being used. He or she will also look like an expert to the average layperson. But someone whose knowledge of a domain is 'secondhand' always differs in their understanding of the relevant terms and theories from the practitioner. Seen from the side-lines, their conversation may resemble a dialogue, but is in fact two monologues concerning completely different things. Secondly, the notion of 'linguistic socialisation' is highly imprecise, since any kind of socialisation requires embodiment and therefore practice.[9] One cannot learn a natural or technical language without physically participating in the culture of a particular group. Practice is an integral part of understanding concepts. What is more, some aspects of research practice cannot be verbalised. Experts sometimes make distinctions and judgements that they have difficulty articulating.[10] This is why Collins' vision of interactional expertise needs to be problematised. According to Rodrigo Ribeiro and Francisco Lima, it is necessary to introduce additional distinctions. Aside from pure interactional expertise (*pure*-IE), we should distinguish *special*-IE and *typical*-IE. The first is the result of 'linguistic socialisation' as described by Collins. According to Collins' critics, there is no empirical evidence of its existence.[11] The second, *special*-IE, refers to participation in a given practice and requires both communication with experts and physical contiguity. It is only through participation in the research process that one comes to properly understand to what the terms refer, to perceive the problems proper to the field and to understand the solutions under discussion. And, finally, *typical*-IE stands for full immersion in the practice, conducting research, possessing tacit knowledge and being able to propose new solutions. Here, interactional expertise inextricably co-exists with contributory expertise.

The three categories of interactional experts can be arranged according to their degree of understanding of the research area in question. The highest level of scientific self-awareness should be ascribed to the third type: '*only* practitioners/*typical*-IEs can be fully fluent in any natural or technical language'.[12] Interactional experts without contributory expertise (*special*-IE) have at most a partial understanding. Unlike practitioners, they are first of all never fluent with regard to a given issue, nor even when it comes to using the practitioners' technical language. Secondly, they are unable to exploit the practitioners' cognitive resources.[13] They cannot rival practitioners in terms of understanding the area, assessing a situation, making decisions and searching for solutions. They are not fully capable of understanding the metaphors and mental shortcuts used by practitioners.[14] Nor can they see and understand some of the problems faced by a field, the connections to other fields, and the questions that should and can be asked.[15] Moreover, according to Ribeiro and Lima,[16] persons with *pure*-IE simply do not exist and hence no time should be wasted discussing them.

If we examine the notion of 'translating' technical concepts into lay language from this perspective, it turns out that there is no way for this venture to be successful. A layperson, by definition, has no interactional expertise. Nor are there any 'shortcuts' one can take to become an interactional expert. If Ribeiro and Lima are right, discussing things with experts is certainly no shortcut. Even many months of talking to experts will not make ordinary citizens into experts. This does not mean that such communication is impossible. One can present scientific theories to laypeople in a way they can follow. Specialist terms and categories can usually be expressed in common language. The problem is not untranslatability, but the incomprehensibility of such a translation. Understanding a theory requires more than understanding its constituent parts – it entails understanding other theories which provide the interpretive context. Similarly, understanding a practice is much more than merely being able to describe it. It requires physical participation.

In this reading, the concept of epistemic dependence is reminiscent of radical theories of interpretation, such as the neopragmatism of W. V. O. Quine, Richard Rorty, Donald Davidson, Jacques Derrida and Stanley Fish. According to Fish, there is no such thing as an objective meaning and reading of a text. Each reader interprets a text through the lens of his or her prior judgements. That person's understanding is always conditioned by her or his prior knowledge, gained in the course of socialisation in different interpretive communities. Each one of us lives in at least a couple of such communities, each of which teaches its members different strategies for reading and interpreting texts.[17] If the recipient and author of a text are to achieve understanding, they must at least in part belong to the same communities. Even if that is the case, the understanding between them will rarely be complete and the translation faithful. 'We now always God in Paraiso?', Japanese Christians ask a Jesuit in Martin Scorsese's *Silence* (2016), failing to grasp the ideas of baptism, heaven and life after death. Without taking part in a given research practice, without observing it from up close, one cannot be 'linguistically socialised' and understand the meaning of expertise. Christiano's belief that in the case of most problems the translation of expert language into lay language will be good enough to allow citizens to independently make the most important decisions seems overly optimistic, to say the least.

The situation does not really change much when professional 'translators' – people who have interactional expertise in an area and are also well-versed in the concepts used by laypeople – take it upon themselves to do the translating.[18] They include, for example, sociologists of scientific knowledge, high-level journalists, ethnographers, anthropologists and interpreters.[19] Christiano believes that their mediation generates 'overlapping understanding', which makes most of the message understandable to all sides. 'Overlapping understanding' is the scientific equivalent of 'Chinese whispers'. Every successive translator explains as best as he or she can the message received from the previous person. The shorter the chain process, the smaller the number of intermediaries, the greater the participants' chances of understanding the intention of the original emitter. The more stages and intermediaries there are, the greater the risk of losing the meaning of the original utterance. The epistemic asymmetry separating the participants wreaks havoc on this vision, however. The layperson will not understand the interactional expert. The interactional expert understands neither the contributory expert, nor other interactional experts.[20] The way each of them understands the same issues is 'both enabled by and limited to the nature of the experiences they have within a particular practice and how such experiences combine with each other'.[21] When passing on the message, the intermediary, who him-/herself may not understand the meaning of the original, will pass on a distorted version. As a matter of fact, as Collins states, a 'necessary but not sufficient condition of translation is the achievement of interactional expertise in each of the fields between which translation is to be accomplished'.[22] The concept of deliberative polling lays bare all the shortcomings of the idea of 'translating' scientific narratives into everyday language.

A LAYMAN GOES TO SEE AN EXPERT OR THE NAKED TRUTH ABOUT DELIBERATIVE POLLING

The ideal of direct democracy has been pushed by surprisingly different political forces over the last century. Today we most often associate it with the left, but a century ago the left side of the political scene was terrified by the vision of popular rule. In early twentieth-century Britain, the newly formed Labour Party criticised civic empowerment side by side with the Conservatives. Its leader and prime minister, Ramsey Macdonald, described the referendum as 'but a clumsy and ineffective weapon which the reaction can always use more effectively than the democracy, because it, being the power to say "No" is far more useful to the few than to the many, and that will be more and more the case as the many become enlightened'.[23] According to members of the left, the referendum was a tool for holding back progressive reforms and flattering conservative sentiment. In the United States, too, attitudes towards referenda over the last century have swung like a political pendulum. Until 1978, the demand for direct citizen empowerment was characteristic of the progressive movement. Later, it was the radical democrats who advocated direct democracy. But after California passed Proposition 13 by referendum in 1978 (lowering the income tax), conservatives discovered allies in the 'wisdom of the people'. Within two years, forty-three states had enacted some form of income tax limitation by referendum, and fifteen of them had cut taxes along California's lines.

All these volte-faces, however, are unimpressive, since democratic innovations fit perfectly, according to the communist authorities in the PRC, into the project of 'Chinese democracy'. In the biggest non-democratic country in the world, deliberative polls are being practised with increasing frequency – the same polls that Western liberal democratic thinkers associate with great hopes of empowering citizens.[24] Deliberative polls are one of many forms of minipublics – the most widely discussed ways of direct involvement of citizens in decision-making processes. What they all have in common is the conviction that a randomly selected, representative group of citizens can make the best decision or give a competent opinion by talking to experts. The author of the concept of deliberative polling, James S. Fishkin, summed it up perhaps most succinctly:

> The idea is simple. Take a national random sample of the electorate and transport it from all over the country to a single place. Immerse the sample in the issues, with carefully balanced materials, with intensive, face-to-face discussions in small groups, and with questions to competing experts and politicians developed in those small groups. At the end of several days working through the issues, face to face, poll the participants in detail.[25]

Minipublics have been used successfully around the world. In British Columbia and Ontario citizens' assemblies were relied upon to draft electoral reform. In Germany, planning cells were repeatedly used for town planning, building motorways, or shaping local and national energy policy. Citizens' juries were organised for health authorities and local governments. Consensus conferences in Denmark were used to assess technological and scientific innovations through the prism of their social and ethical impact. Deliberative polls were applied to hundreds of issues. One of the most spectacular examples was a survey forecasting the development and challenges facing the EU called Tomorrow's Europe.

Polls are a paradigmatic symbol of the faith that ordinary citizens' competencies can be improved. The premise is that the laypeople taking part will gain a better understanding of reality. The experts present the most credible of all the available solutions to them, highlighting the benefits and risks associated with each. If the group of participants is socially representative then 'enlightened public opinion' can manifest itself, that is, views that the society as a whole would hold on a given topic if all its members had the will, time and resources to acquire the requisite knowledge:

> An ordinary poll models what the public thinks, given how little it thinks, how little it knows, how little it pays attention. A deliberative opinion poll, by contrast, models what the public would think if it had a better chance to think about the questions at issue.[26]

It is therefore hardly a surprise that polls have garnered praise from political theorists and practitioners alike. They have successfully been used in hundreds of cities and countries all over the world – from Canada to Uganda, Korea, Hongkong, Macao, Argentina, Brazil and my home country, Poland. They have been used to settle all kinds of issues, from whether we should stop using non-renewable sources of energy and how (Texas), through to what sports stadiums could be used for (Poznań, Poland), to understand the condition of Roma people in Bulgaria (Sofia), to discuss the legalisation of same-sex marriages (Ireland), to drafting a constitution (Iceland). The practical success of polls, however, does not match the theoretical. Indeed, polls are one of the measures most frequently demanded by democrats.[27]

Fishkin had only moderate practical hopes for his invention. He repeatedly stated that the aim of polling was to supplement rather than to replace representative democracy. Polls were to serve as a way of empowering citizens without sacrificing the effectiveness of democratic government. As such, they were to serve as a combination of participatory democracy and meritocracy. This was one of the main reasons for their popularity and for the fact that some scholars, like Jane Mansbridge, call them the 'gold standard', the benchmark by which to judge any attempt to empower citizens.[28]

But the list of critics of deliberative polling is almost as long as that of its supporters. It includes not only steadfast epistocrats like Cass Sunstein or Brennan,[29] but also democrats like Claudio Lopez-Guerra,[30] Landemore or Shapiro. They see the concept as lacking transparency or even methodological consistency, and even pandering to psychological mechanisms that pervert the results of deliberation, including the Hawthorne effect.[31] Some critics generally question the purpose of mounting an epistemic defence of minipublics, including polling. They argue that public deliberation should not be about people trying to persuade one another to accept each other's reasons in order to reach a consensus, but rather about highlighting points of contention and sources of conflict in order to shine a spotlight on the predicament of some groups of citizens.[32] This, meanwhile, does not require setting up the idealised conditions described by Fishkin.[33]

Other detractors focus on the methodological flaws of polling. They often cite the research done by Kahneman and Tversky,[34] whose findings unequivocally prove that deliberation outcomes are influenced not only by the selection and quality of the information presented to participants, but also by *how* that information is presented as well as a host of other factors which cannot be controlled.[35] They also argue that the attitudes of poll participants are chiefly shaped by personal experience and cannot be changed just by talking.[36] Many prejudicial views and deep-seated beliefs simply cannot be eradicated. As a result, polls rarely lead to the emergence of 'enlightened public opinion'. Their outcomes tend to reflect existing social prejudice.

There is no doubt that some of these arguments are off the mark. The fact that polls effectively prevent group polarisation – a problem with which any form of sortition democracy has to grapple – is well documented.[37] They also rarely cause supporters of opposite solutions to 'dig in' on their side of the barricade. There is also much less social pressure on poll participants than in alternative arrangements. It has also been shown that polls raise participants' knowledge about the issues under discussion by about 10 per cent,[38] and that they do bring about genuine changes of opinion. The public nature of the discussion also tends to improve the quality of the result instead of provoking dishonesty.[39]

And yet these facts do not always convince critics,[40] who point to the epistemic shortcomings of polls. For example, according to Laurel Gleason,[41] the fact that polling participants expand their knowledge and change their initial positions does not necessarily lead to better results, as Fishkin assumes.[42] Drawing this conclusion would require coming up with a set of criteria by which to judge the quality of the result. Only what sort of criteria would those be? Should they make reference to the scientific consensus (ergo, the right opinion[43] would always be the one in agreement with the opinions of the majority of scientists)? If so, then the purpose of polling would simply be to convince citizens to embrace the expert perspective. By this token, they would merely be reiterating the overwhelmingly discredited model of 'science speaking truth to power'. This would make polls a tool of scientific indoctrination rather than a venue for the rational weighing of reasons and autonomous civic opinion-making. Trying to escape this conclusion, Fishkin sees conduciveness to coherent views among the participants and the alignment of those views with the consequences of the proposed solution as indicators of effectiveness. In other words, if as a result of the discussion the participants gain more clarity in their views and are able to draw on them to select one of the proposed solutions, then the polls have served their purpose.[44] But coherent views alone have no epistemic value. If a consistent racist or sexist becomes even more consistent in their views, it will not mean that their political choices have thereby gained moral justification.[45] One may have consistent views but still be wrong.

This epistemic critique of sortition democracy, and deliberative polling as a form thereof, constitutes the most serious challenge against it in my view. The critique may follow two lines of argument. Both emphasise the role of experts in making the opinions of poll participants 'more consistent'. More frequently encountered in the literature is the charge that the autonomy of poll participants is vastly limited, and that they are manipulated not only by the experts but also by the organisers of the polling process. After all, the latter select the experts participating in the poll and oversee the selection of the materials to be presented to the participants at the starting point of the discussion.[46] This theoretically purely organisational role is of vital importance. The very act of setting up the conditions of discussion influences the outcome. A study on social perceptions of climate change recently conducted in Poland showed that asking the participants to use hand sanitiser, put on face shields and follow social distancing guidelines affected their stated willingness to make sacrifices in order to halt climate change.[47]

The materials describing potential solutions distributed to participants have an even greater impact on their opinion. They significantly circumscribe and orient the citizens' perspective, or at least define the framework of subsequent discussions, naturally impacting their outcome.[48] Theoretically, the materials are only supposed to provide insights into the subject, but instead are a source of normative pronouncements, defining key discussion points.[49] Gleason's research demonstrates the significant role that the materials distributed to participants of deliberative polls play. She reports that of 3,500 factual statements provided to participants, only 75 were questioned by them.[50] Although Fishkin responds to this charge by stating that organisers always deliver balanced materials, while the participants play an active role during the discussion, the facts seem to tell a different story.[51] This is why Gleason speaks of the 'inability [of polling] to produce new content'.[52] For the same reason, Price and Neijens argue that the fact that participants change their opinions cannot be considered proof of the effectiveness of polling. We can never be certain whether the participants' opinions were changed by a better understanding of the subject or by a biased selection of materials.[53] Nor can we be sure of the permanence of this change.

Shapiro multiplies these methodological doubts, claiming that polling outcomes are manipulated at every stage of the process. He questions the criteria used to select background materials and to hire experts. Do the organisers have appropriate qualifications to engage independent experts representing all the major scientifically valid viewpoints? Based on what criteria are the poll participants recruited? If they are to be members of stakeholder groups, then who can say which groups have greater stakes in the result? In an age of complex economic and ecological interconnectedness, are we able to identify and recruit all the relevant stakeholders?[54]

Other authors suggest that the bias of polling has its origins not just in the asymmetrical relationship between the organisers and the participants, but also in the formula itself. Polls are tendentious in the procedural sense: they are conductive to a specific type of perspective (with a tendency to favour global thinking and the community perspective) and so skew the final decision.[55] Although Lynn Sanders' concerns that court juries always represent the position of privileged groups have not been corroborated,[56] it has been shown that polling outcomes show a non-representative, high convergence towards cosmopolitan, egalitarian and communitarian views. They favour the global perspective, sustainable development and the interests of future generations, and promote the common good rather than individual interest.[57] By this token, the very choice of polling as a method of problem-solving, independently of the unavoidable manipulation of materials, influences the decision.

The second epistemic critique is linked to the first and focuses on the unavoidable, epistemically privileged position of experts vis-à-vis the other poll participants, and so on the phenomenon of epistemic dependence. The problem here is no longer confined to the conscious or unconscious manipulation of materials by the organisers or experts. Even if the materials are well-balanced and the group of experts fully representative, there is no reason to suppose that the citizens will be able to choose the best option.[58] After all, they have no merit-based, objective criteria based on which they can assess their choice of expertise.[59] The factor that bears on the final result is always 'perceived [rather than actual] credibility, trustworthiness, or expertise'.[60] At best, laypeople can take advantage of substitute strategies for assessing the arguments and evidence presented in the materials and during the lay–expert discussions, whose unreliability I addressed in the previous chapter. Faced with the need to consult the experts, the participants have no fool-proof method of assessing the quality of the background materials they have received or the competence of their advisers. Fishkin states that:

> We have found that once participants realize that the experts disagree they feel empowered to think through the issue for themselves rather than defer to the experts. We have also found in various experimental variations that the small group discussions provide a more consequential driver of opinion change than do the expert sessions.[61]

But neither the greater motivation of poll participants to settle a given issue, nor the change of their opinions mean that they will opt for the best-justified expertise available.

Fishkin tries to respond to some of these concerns. And so he assures that it is possible to balance the materials delivered to participants in such a way as to make their content uncontroversial.[62] However, because of epistemic dependence it is impossible to uncontroversially choose a person who could uncontroversially confirm that the background materials are balanced. The choice of such a person is of key importance to the whole procedure, since the facts presented as uncontroversial in the materials are also usually deemed uncontroversial during the sessions.[63] Controversial facts, on the other hand, will be problematised and discussed. Fishkin's assurances that poll organisers are able to distinguish between controversial and uncontroversial facts are insufficient. For here we run into the same question again: how do we determine who has sufficient competence to make such a distinction without controversy?[64] We are thus faced with infinite regress.[65]

I believe that there are a number of conclusions to be drawn from the epistemic critique of deliberative polling. First, polls impact participant opinions in a non-merit-based way. This happens especially through the choice of the background materials and experts. This kind of manipulation is inevitable due to the unavoidable epistemic dependence of laypeople on experts. Once selected, the experts and the materials will rarely be questioned by the poll participants, and it is on them that the final outcome will in large part depend. Nor is there any guarantee that the organisers will choose the right materials and experts.

Secondly, the above concerns raise questions about the superiority of deliberative polling over epistocratic solutions. Since, after all, polls are founded on lay trust in experts, why should the experts themselves not prepare the opinion, by consensus or by vote? After all, if the experts agree on an issue, the sole aim of polling is at best to convince the lay participants to embrace their reasons. The authorities would be perfectly right to reject the outcome of a poll whose participants dismissed uncontroversial expert knowledge. Meanwhile, if there is no agreement among experts, why should we suppose that ordinary citizens are going to be able to settle the controversy for them? A coin flip[66] would be a much fairer solution in this case, since it is less procedurally biased and at the same time avoids the systematic errors characteristic of opinions made by ordinary citizens.[67]

Finally, the epistemic critique of polling notes that participants' original competence and knowledge and not their representativeness should be the main recruitment criterion.[68] Limiting the group to a representative batch has been criticised by López-Guerra and Landemore, who claim that it negatively impacts the quality of the final result.[69] In their opinion, it means less opportunity to take advantage of socially dispersed knowledge. In my view, it is not limiting the size of the group that is the problem, but choosing participants by lot, without taking their knowledge of the subject to be discussed into account.

DIVIDED WE STAND

Confronted with the challenge of epistemic dependence, the last approach to lay–expert cooperation described in Chapter 1 – the 'division of labour' model of the public sphere – also proves to be problematic. To reiterate, supporters of this solution believe that ordinary citizens, even the least competent, can remain 'in the driver's seat in the society' as long as they set the political agenda and assess its implementation. The experts supporting them in this task will only be a helpful tool in the hands of the citizens – a tool without political agency.

This position has been widely criticised in the literature. Some authors have pointed out that it runs counter to the ideal of deliberative democracy (to which proponents of deliberative systems declare themselves to be faithful). The 'division of labour' model is reactive and conservative. It legitimises the status quo and lets the biggest flaws of politics – political polarisation, manipulation and propaganda – take their toll.[70] By the same token, it runs counter to traditional approaches to deliberative democracy, where the public sphere was supposed to be improved by inspiring citizens to deliberate and by developing their capacity to share their views and work out joint solutions.[71] Meanwhile, the systemic approach is not just reconcilable with but in fact encourages the creation of deliberative islands in a sea of non-deliberative political participation.

This critique is doubtless sound, but I would like to focus on a different type of charge brought against the 'division of labour' model here. Some critics question the very premise underlying it, that is, that citizens actually make fully autonomous decisions. In their view, without seeking the opinion of experts, citizens are neither able to identify goals worthy of being pursued, nor determine whether they have been achieved. As Peter Haas puts it:

> experts highlight issues for the agenda, frame the meaning of those issues relative to pre-existing issues, help to illuminate state interests, privilege policies and shape the international bargaining space through their influence over actors' preferences and the attendant payoff matrices. Experts potentially shape both the consequence and appropriateness for the principals who rely on their advice. While states remain the primary decision makers, framing and advice come from experts.[72]

Without consulting experts, citizens cannot get their bearings, let alone change their circumstances. Because of this, it would be a far stretch to say that they are the actual initiators of the political process, and that the political phase overrides the technical.

This line of critique has been developed consistently within STS, especially by proponents of Wave Two in social studies of science, who question the decision-making autonomy of laypeople vis-à-vis experts. Not because laypeople cannot make political decisions, but because they put excessive trust in experts who redefine the boundaries of the political.[73] According to Jasanoff and Wynne, laypeople are capable of setting the agenda (and should do so),[74] determining the goals of the community and assessing the outcomes of the solutions proposed by the experts.[75] In practice, however, experts often abuse their authority in order to declare some issues purely technical, thus reassigning successive political issues to the technical category, where laypeople have no say.[76] By doing so, they blur the divide between the political and the technical. They self-appointedly define expertise, and then attribute it to themselves,[77] only to later redefine the agenda and sway the course of public debates.[78]

In a classic case study described by Wiebe Bijker, Roland Ball and Ruud Hendricks, the Dutch *Gezondheidsraad* was supposed to play the role of the expert body in a 'division of labour' model procedure.[79] It was supposed to develop and propose strategies for achieving goals defined by the Dutch Ministry of Health. Things turned out differently in practice, however. The two phases, separate in theory, kept bumping into each other in practice. The Ministry of Health staff kept asking the experts for help in defining goals. By the time an official request was sent to the *Gezondheidsraad*, a series of informal meetings had taken place between politicians and experts. The 'division of labour' model only worked on paper.

Another example is Poland's political transformation in the 1990s, when the Polish political and economic elite's critical stance with respect to state interventionism (associated with communism) made the public see no alternative to a radically free market-oriented shift.[80] Although Solidarity declarations from the early 1980s, the Round Table agreements, the electoral announcements and the political programme of the parties founded around Lech Wałęsa had never before admitted such a possibility and had favoured a gradual and semi-socialist transformation, it only took a few years for the Polish anti-communists to bring about a 'neoliberal turn'.[81] After a series of expert consultations, they decided that diving into radical capitalism was indispensable for the political shift to occur. As Leszek Balcerowicz said, 'Now or never – we must close our eyes and jump, without testing the water at the bottom or the height of the cliff.' The Polish labour unions trusted the politicians' assurances that unemployment would be on the rise for a temporary, six-month period. What actually happened was that unemployment grew steadily for nearly a decade.[82]

Experts dominate not only political agenda-setting but also the procedure of evaluating the impact of the implemented solutions. Citizens lack the competence to assess expert recommendations and outcomes. Would the number of cases and deaths due to COVID-19 have been higher or lower if alternative vaccination schedules had been followed? What would the quality of life in Poland be like today if a less radical road of political and economic transformation had been taken after 1989? The answers are beyond the grasp of average citizens. Being trans-scientific, they also often remain beyond the reach of experts, which does not stop the latter from speculating.

Nonetheless, epistemic dependence undermines not only the autonomy and agency of citizens but that of the entire political domain. The idea of an expert self-government also proves problematic. If, following Hardwig, we accept that relations between scientists are similar to those between laypeople and experts, then Michael Polanyi's 'republic of science' turns out to be a mirage. The world of science is not ruled by rational arguments, fair competition and peer review.[83] It is not true that:

> while scientists can admittedly exercise competent judgment only over a small part of science, they can usually judge an area adjoining their own special studies that is broad enough to include some fields on which other scientists have specialised. We thus have a considerable degree of overlapping between the areas over which a scientist can exercise a sound, critical judgment. And, of course, each-scientist who is a member of a group of overlapping competences will also be a member of other groups of the same kind, so that the whole of science will be covered by chains and networks of overlapping neighbourhoods.[84]

It does not follow from the fact that 'no single scientist has a sound understanding of more than a tiny fraction of the total domain of science'[85] that science is a perfect system of stably interconnected vessels. On the contrary, it is a collection of loosely tied elements whose mutual relationships lack transparency and whose functioning is frequently hard to track.

Delineating the expert domain is also problematic. Supporters of the 'division of labour' model accept the traditional definition of an expert, referring to external indicators of competence – social and professional status. In their view, the technical stage of the decision-making process consists of discussions among the scientific community, academics, and research and laboratory staff. This is the technical and specialist discourse phase. Meanwhile, if expertise is a broad and polysemous category, it may be that there is no strict way of drawing a line between laypeople and experts. Who can we identify as experts capable of making technical decisions? Only contributory experts, or interactional ones as well? Are we only talking about the 'core-set' of a science or also experts with other specialisations?[86] And if we decide that only contributory experts should be included in the discussion regardless of social status, how do we identify experts outside the academic community? Who is to identify them?

Contrary to the assurances given by its proponents, the deliberative systems narrative seems to be tilted towards technocracy. It is experts who play a key role here. Formally, they only support citizens in finding solutions to problems but in fact they determine the content and shape of public debate, what kind of solutions are implemented and how effective they are deemed to be. It is experts who define possibilities and delineate the technical realm; they define the limits of their power and the criteria for judging the success of their self-appointed mission. As Jasanoff states, 'To label some aspects of society's responses to uncertainty "political" and some others "scientific" makes little sense when the very contours of what is certain or uncertain in policy domains get established through intense and intimate science–society negotiations.'[87] Supporters of deliberative systems are 'seduced' by an idealised picture of science, as evidenced by their belief that the scientific community does not need democratic oversight since it can handle most of its inside pathologies and ambiguities by itself.[88]

Although many supporters of the 'division of labour' model share this faith in the non-problematic nature of expertise and science, some of them are aware of the danger inherent in epistemic asymmetry. One of the precursors here was James Bohman, who recognised the existence of epistemic inequalities between citizens as a fundamental problem in *Public Deliberation*.[89] His vision of the public sphere is a pessimistic one of an infinitely complex community in which the problem of ignorance and unequal access to information cannot be overcome.[90] This is why experts must enjoy a privileged position in the decision-making process and social authority which will unfortunately enable them to 'verbally intimidate' lay voters.[91] There is no such thing as epistemic symmetry between laypeople and experts.

Catherine Holst and Anders Molander are more optimistic about the possibility of resolving the problem of epistemic dependence. In their view:

> the problems associated with distinguishing between expert and non-expert and the possibility that there may be no such thing as moral expertise are challenges not only for the justification of expert arrangements but also for any conception of democratic rule under contemporary conditions.[92]

This is the greatest challenge faced by the theory of democracy, including deliberative systems theory.[93] There is no single, simple solution to the problem, however. The strategies proposed by Goldman certainly fall short. The layperson has no way of judging which expert is proposing the best solution. We should also abandon all hopes of attaining lay–expert understanding: 'non-experts, lacking both in contributory and interactional expertise, are not in the epistemic position to assess expert reasons'.[94]

In spite of this, Holst and Molander reject the scepticism of Hardwig's position and the stalemate to which it inevitably leads. In their opinion, since laypeople cannot adjudicate expert disputes, someone else has to do it for them. Holst and Molander propose a range of institutional solutions. They argue that the problem arising in the lay–expert relationship is a matter of 'institutional design: which mechanisms can contribute to ensuring that experts are really experts and that they use their competencies in the right way in a situation where non-experts are often unable to assess the quality and soundness of expert judgements directly?'[95] Three mechanisms can do the job. First, are scientific norms which regulate how the expert community acts. These might be Mertonian, Habermasian or Tranøy's norms – what matters is that they increase scientists' critical aptitude, make it imperative to present and defend positions and arguments, and include a deliberative element.[96] This requires a functional peer-review system. Secondly, an expert evaluation system should be in place, in which the experts would be assessed by peer forums, on the one hand, and bureaucrats and competent stakeholders, on the other:

> The most obvious forum for testing judgements and detecting fallacies and biases are the forum of peers: economic experts being questioned by other economic experts, contributions by legal experts being scrutinized by other legal experts and so on. However, in a process of democratic decision-making, the testing of judgements and arguments must also be extended for epistemic reasons to other relevant disciplines and other relevant expert fora, for example, to fora comprising bureaucrats and competent stakeholders, to the legislature and even to the public sphere at large.[97]

Especially in relations with stakeholders, experts must report not only what they know, but also what they do not know. The third type of mechanism is oriented towards experts' working conditions. It is necessary to guarantee 'cognitive diversity and an adequate intellectual division of labour'.[98] Otherwise experts will be at risk of bias. The more cooperation and deliberation, the better the outcomes of expert work. The more criticism there is within the community, the better. The more interdisciplinary collaboration, the better.

However, it is hard to resist the impression that Holst and Molander's optimism is somewhat over-inflated. In light of Hardwig's theory, none of the instruments spelled out above will fulfil the hopes attached to them. Scientific norms will remain, at best, normative ideals, rarely adhered to in practice. There will never be room for organised criticism in science, since narrow specialisation will effectively prevent the cross-verification of experiments.[99] The expectation that the peer-review system will safeguard against scientific controversies and disputes, eliminating contradictory expert opinions, is unfounded. Where there is no understanding, there is no room for deliberation and mutual criticism either. In the vision of science proposed by Hardwig there is only room for trust. Finally, the greater the cognitive diversity and intellectual division of labour, the greater the epistemic dependence. Understanding is predicated upon shared beliefs and methodological assumptions. The more diverse the scientific community, the more it has to be based on trust.

Finally, even if thanks to adherence to norms and the institution of a rigorous peer-review system a single course of action, sanctioned by the entire scientific community, is always consensually chosen, the citizens do not necessarily have to accept it. If the citizens cannot appreciate the force and cogency of individual expert recommendations, they will not be able to appreciate the voice of the entire expert community. The only hope then would be popular trust in the solid foundations of the scientific edifice. But will the arrangement of science in accordance with the Mertonian norms and a rigorous peer review system automatically inspire civic trust? It seems likely only if citizens believe in the 'cartoon' vision of science (in which some of the enthusiasts of the 'division of labour' model also seem to believe).

A much more consistent critique of the 'division of labour' model based on the notion of epistemic dependence is offered by Eva Krick.[100] Unlike the previous authors, her diagnosis of the current state of democratic theory is highly pessimistic. Epistemic asymmetry between laypeople and experts is unavoidable, she says, and precludes any chance of meaningful deliberation, even within the framework of minipublics.[101] All efforts to eliminate this asymmetry, including the recommendation that the laypeople participating in minipublics themselves select the experts they will be consulting (in order to guarantee a balance of expert opinions), must fail.[102] Limiting the group of experts to members of the academic community and independent scientific institutions will at best minimise the negative consequences of epistemic dependence, without however eliminating it.[103] The problem of epistemic dependence practically invalidates the two most frequently applied strategies of involving citizens in the work of democratic innovations: open access and random selection. The first leads to bias among participants and is conducive to group uniformity and non-representativeness. Opening up such bodies to anyone leads to an over-representation of stakeholders, activists and members of interest groups. Such people's views are usually already formed, they are not likely to change them, they are not interested in deliberation but rather in pushing a certain agenda. In the case of random selection, the problem has to do with laypeople's difficulty in absorbing specialised information within a relatively short time.

It is not surprising, then, that the conclusions of this chapter are just as pessimistic as the conclusions of the entire book. Neither awareness of lay epistemic dependence on experts, nor attempts to overcome it through democratic innovations or by 'translating' the language of science into everyday language can protect against epistemic asymmetry. Laypeople can never develop contributory expertise, or even interactional expertise. They will never therefore be sufficiently competent to make conscious political decisions. And since the possibility of an informed discussion between laypeople and experts is doubtful, we come to two possible solutions. The first is to renounce the call for the direct empowerment of citizens – or at least the epistemic justification of that kind of participation. The second is to search for a space in which recognised contributory experts will be able to deliberate arm in arm with those of unrecognised status. I will take a more detailed look at the second option in the next chapter.

NOTES

1. Kathryn S. Plaisance and Eric B. Kennedy, 'A Pluralistic Approach to Interactional Expertise', *Studies in History and Philosophy of Science Part A* 47 (2014): 60–8.
2. Collins, 'Interactional Expertise as a Third Kind of Knowledge', 125–43; Harry M. Collins, 'Four Kinds of Knowledge, Two (or Maybe Three) Kinds of Embodiment, and Question of Artificial Intelligence', in Mark Wrathall and Jeff Malpas (eds), *Heidegger, Coping, and Cognitive Science: Essays in Honor of Hubert L. Dreyfus*, vol. 2 (Cambridge, MA: MIT Press, 2000), 179–95.
3. Collins, 'Interactional Expertise as a Third Kind of Knowledge', 126.
4. Frederick A. Rossini and Alan L. Porter, 'Frameworks for Integrating Interdisciplinary Research', *Research Policy* 8(1) (1979): 70–9.
5. Collins and Evans, 'The Third Wave of Science Studies', 254; Harry Collins, 'Language and Practice', *Social Studies of Science* 41(2) (2011): 273.
6. See Jonathan M. Gilligan, 'Expertise Across Disciplines: Establishing Common Ground in Interdisciplinary Disaster Research Teams', *Risk Analysis* 2019, DOI:10.1111/risa.13407.
7. Collins, 'Interactional Expertise as a Third Kind of Knowledge', 125.

8. Rodrigo Ribeiro and Francisco P. A. Lima, 'The Value of Practice: A Critique of Interactional Expertise', *Social Studies of Science* 2015: 1–30; Hubert Dreyfus, 'Responses', in Mark Wrathall and Jeff Malpas (eds), *Heidegger, Authenticity, and Modernity: Essays in Honor of Hubert Dreyfus*, vol. 1 (Cambridge, MA: MIT Press, 2000), 305–41.

9. See Evan Selinger and John Mix, 'On Interactional Expertise: Pragmatic and Ontological Considerations', *Phenomenology and the Cognitive Sciences* 3 (2004): 145–63; Evan Selinger, Hubert Dreyfus and Harry Collins, 'Interactional Expertise and Embodiment', *Studies in the History and Philosophy of Science* 38(4) (2007): 722–40.

10. See Dreyfus, 'Responses'.

11. Ribeiro and Lima, 'The Value of Practice'; Selinger, Dreyfus and Collins, 'Interactional Expertise and Embodiment', 724–5. Critics claim that the main examples cited by Collins – that of disabled Madeleine, colour-blind people and his own success at the imitation game – do not substantiate the 'minimal embodiment thesis'. In all three examples the individuals questioned were already physically immersed in the environment before their expertise was assessed.

12. Ribeiro and Lima, 'The Value of Practice', 16.

13. Ribeiro and Lima, 'The Value of Practice', 20.

14. Gilligan, 'Expertise Across Disciplines'.

15. Ribeiro and Lima, 'The Value of Practice', 9–10.

16. Ribeiro and Lima, 'The Value of Practice', 22.

17. Fish, 'Mutual Respect as a Device of Exclusion', 88–102; Stanley Fish, *Doing What Comes Naturally: Change, Rhetoric, and the Practice of Theory in Literary and Legal Studies* (Durham, NC: Duke University Press, 1989); Stanley Fish, *Is There a Text in This Class?: The Authority of Interpretive Communities* (Cambridge, MA: Harvard University Press, 1980).

18. See Whyte and Crease, 'Trust, Expertise, and the Philosophy of Science', 418.

19. Collins and Evans, 'Third Wave of Science Studies'; Collins, 'Interactional Expertise as a Third Kind of Knowledge'.

20. Cf. Maytal Perlman, 'The Value of Interactional Expertise: Perceptions of Laypeople, Interactional Experts, and Contributory Experts', *Journal of Integrative Research and Reflection* 1 (2018): 23.

21. Ribeiro and Lima, 'The Value of Practice', 23.

22. Collins and Evans, 'The Third Wave of Science Studies', 258.

23. Ramsay MacDonald, *The Socialist Movement* (London: H. Holt, 1911), 153; cf. James Meadowcroft and M. W. Waylor, 'Liberalism and the Referendum in British Political Thought 1890–1914', *Twentieth Century British History* 1(1) (1990), 35–57.

24. See James S. Fishkin, Baogang He, Robert C. Luskin and Alice Siu, 'Deliberative Democracy in an Unlikely Place: Deliberative Polling in China', *British Journal of Political Science* 40 (2010), 435–48; Baogang He and Mark E. Warren, 'Authoritarian Deliberation in China', *Daedalus* 146(3) (2017): 155–66.

25. James S. Fishkin, 'Toward Deliberative Democracy: Experimenting with an Ideal', in Stephen L. Elkin and Karol Edward Sołtan (eds), *Citizen Competence and Democratic Institutions* (University Park: Pennsylvania State University Press, 1999), 282.

26. James S. Fishkin, 'Bringing Deliberation to Democracy', *Good Society* 5(3) (1995): 45.

27. See Levy and Peart, *Escape from Democracy*, 240–1; Cristina Lafont, 'Can Democracy be Deliberative and Participatory? The Democratic Case for Political Uses of Mini-Publics', *Daedalus* 146(3) (2017): 85–105; Cristina Lafont, 'Deliberation, Participation, and Democratic Legitimacy: Should Minipublics shape Public Policy?' *Journal of Political Philosophy* 23(1) (2015): 40–63; Jane Mansbridge, 'Deliberative Polling as the Gold Standard', *Good Society* 19(1) (2010): 55–62; Parkinson, *Deliberating in the Real World*; Walter F. Baber and Robert V. Bartlett, *Deliberative Environmental Politics: Democracy and Ecological Rationality* (Cambridge, MA: MIT Press, 2005); cf. Stephen Elstub, 'The Third Generation of Deliberative Democracy', *Political Studies Review* 8 (2010): 289–301; David Van Reybrouck, *Against Elections: The Case for Democracy*, trans. L. Walters (London: Bodley Head, 2016).

28. Mansbridge, 'Deliberative Polling as the Gold Standard', 56.

29. Brennan, *Against Democracy*, 66–7.

30. Claudio López-Guerra, *Democracy and Disenfrenchisement: The Morality of Electoral Exclusion* (Oxford: Oxford University Press, 2014).

31. Recording the poll causes the participants not to present their personal opinions, but only to play a role that they believe they are expected to play.

32. Cf. Nadia Urbinati, *Democracy Disfigured: Opinion, Truth, and the People* (Cambridge, MA: Harvard University Press, 2014).

33. Albena Azmanova, 'Deliberative Conflict and "The Better Argument" Mystique', *Good Society* 19(1) (2010): 52.

34. Tversky and Kahneman, 'Judgement under Uncertainty'.

35. Vincent Price and Peter Neijens, 'Deliberative Polls: Toward Improved Measures of "Informed" Public Opinion?' *International Journal of Public Opinion Research* 10(2) (1998): 159–60.

36. Azmanova, 'Deliberative Conflict', 49. Cf. Ian Shapiro, 'Conclusion in Restraint of Democracy: Against Political Deliberation', *Daedalus* 146(3) (2017): 77–84.

37. Cass R. Sunstein, 'The Law of Group Polarization', *Journal of Political Philosophy* 10(2) (2002): 175–95. Cf. Simone Chambers, 'Deliberative Democratic Theory', *Annual Review of Political Science* 6 (2003): 319–20; Tali Mendelberg, 'The Deliberative Citizen: Theory and Evidence', in Michael X. Delli Carpini, Leonie Huddy and Robert Y. Shapiro (eds), *Research in Micropolitics, Vol. 6: Political Decision Making, Deliberation, and Participation* (Amsterdam: JAI, 2002), 156–7.

38. James S. Fishkin and Robert C. Luskin, 'Experimenting with a Democratic Ideal: Deliberative Polling and Public Opinion', *Acta Politica* 40 (2005): 291.

39. Mendelberg, 'The Deliberative Citizen', 173–4; James S. Fishkin and Robert C. Luskin, 'Deliberation and Better Citizens', 2002, available

at: http://cdd.stanford.edu/research/papers/2002/bettercitizens.pdf; J. S. Fishkin and R. C. Luskin, 'Deliberative Polling, Public Opinion, and Democracy: The Case of the National Issues Convention, 2005, p. 5, available at: http://cdd.stanford.edu/research/papers/2005/issues-convention.pdf.

40. Some scholars claim that Fishkin's findings are unconvincing, since they are in large part based on self-reports. For example, Shapiro claims that forums are often dominated by the most active participants, to the detriment of others (Ian Shapiro, 'The State of Democratic Theory: a reply to James Fishkin'. *Critical Review of International Social and Political Philosophy* 8, 1 (2005): 82), although the other participants tend not to think so. However, this doesn't necessarily mean that such dominance translates into privileging any social group.

41. Laurel S. Gleason, 'Revisiting "The Voice of the People": An Evaluation of the Claims and Consequences of Deliberative Polling', *Critical Review: A Journal of Politics and Society* 23(3) (2012): 381–4.

42. Fishkin and Luskin, 'Experimenting with a Democratic Ideal', 291–2.

43. In contrast to some democratic innovations, such as planning cells or citizens' assemblies, deliberative polls have so far had an almost exclusively consultative and opinion-forming function. They showed decision-makers how the views of randomly selected participants on a given issue change as their knowledge on the subject increases. The results were not binding on political actors.

44. Price and Neijens, 'Deliberative Polls', 158.

45. Estlund, *Democratic Authority*, 16.

46. See David Michael Ryfe, 'The Practice of Deliberative Democracy: A Study of Sixteen Organizations', *Political Communication* 19(3) (2002): 365.

47. Zofia Bieńkowska, Piotr Drygas and Przemysław Sadura, *Nie nasza wina, nie nasz problem. Katastrofa klimatyczna w oczach Polek i Polaków podczas pandemii* (Warsaw: Heinrich Boll Stiftung, 2021), 20–5.

48. Shapiro, 'The State of Democratic Theory', 80; Azmanova, 'Deliberative Conflict', 48–50; Price and Neijens, 'Deliberative Polls', 172; Parkinson, *Deliberating in the Real World*, 55–6, 144.

49. Gleason, 'Revisiting "The Voice of the People"', 374.

50. Gleason, 'Revisiting "The Voice of the People"', 384.

51. See Mansbridge, 'Deliberative Polling as the Gold Standard', 55.

52. Gleason, 'Revisiting "The Voice of the People"', 384.

53. Price and Neijens, 'Deliberative Polls', 161–2; Azmanova, 'Deliberative Conflict', 49.

54. Shapiro, 'The State of Democratic Theory', 82.

55. John Gastil, Chiara Bacci and Michael Dollinger, 'Is Deliberation Neutral? Patterns of Attitude Change During "The Deliberative Polls™"', *Journal of Public Deliberation* 6(2) (2010).

56. Sanders, 'Against Deliberation', 347–76.

57. Gastil, Bacci and Dollinger, 'Is Deliberation Neutral?', 7–8, 20–1.

58. Levy and Peart, *Escape from Democracy*, 220.

59. See Holst and Molander, 'Epistemic Democracy and the Role of Experts'; Holst and Molander, 'Public Deliberation.

60. Price and Neijens, 'Deliberative Polls', 160–1.

61. James S. Fishkin, 'Response to Critics of When the People Speak: The Deliberative Deficit and What To Do About It', *Good Society* 19 (1) (2010): 71.

62. James S. Fishkin, Robert C. Luskin and Roger Jowell, 'Considered Opinions: Deliberative Polling in Britain', *British Journal of Political Science* 32(3) (2002): 458–9; Fishkin, 'Response to Critics', 70–3; James S. Fishkin, 'Why Deliberative Polling? Reply to Gleason', *Critical Review: A Journal of Politics and Society* 23(3) (2011): 395–6.

63. Gleason, 'Revisiting "The Voice of the People"', 384.

64. Fishkin, 'Response to Critics', 71.

65. Equally unconvincing is Fishkin's idea for the advisory committee (which prepares the materials) to include all key stakeholders, including interest and consumer groups as well as industry representatives (Fishkin, 'Why Deliberative Polling?' 396–7). If that were to happen, the problem described above would only be magnified. The choice of experts and materials would then be up to interest groups that have a vested interest in presenting as undisputed facts that benefit them. Reaching a consensus might be impossible in some cases, and even if one is reached, it does not mean that the materials will be balanced (cf. Mansbridge, 'Deliberative Polling as the Gold Standard', 61).

66. Cf. Estlund, *Democratic Authority*, 75.

67. Cf. Somin, *Democracy and Political Ignorance*; Brennan, *Against Democracy*.

68. Lafont, 'Can Democracy be Deliberative and Participatory?' 88–9.

69. Landemore, *Democratic Reason*, ch. 4; López-Guerra, *Democracy and Disenfrenchisement*, 30. Cf. Jamie Terence Kelly, 'Democracy and the Rule of Small Many', *Critical Review* 26(1/2) (2014): 80–91.

70. Owen and Smith, 'Survey Article', 7.

71. Gutmann and Thompson, *Why Deliberative Democracy?* 7.

72. Peter Haas, 'Ideas, Experts, and Governance', in Monika Ambrus et al. (eds), *The Role of 'Experts' in International and European Decision-Making Processes* (Cambridge: Cambridge University Press, 2014), 20. Cf. Langdon Winner, *Autonomous Technology: Technics-out-of-Control as a Theme in Political Thought* (Cambridge, MA: MIT Press, 1977); Langdon Winner, *The Whale and the Reactor: A Search for Limits in an Age of High Technology* (Chicago: University of Chicago Press, 1986); Rogers, *Participatory Democracy*; Kitcher, *Science in a Democratic Society*, 80.

73. See Eyal, *The Crisis of Expertise*, 110–11.

74. Brian Wynne, 'Seasick of the Third Wave? Subverting the Hegemony of Propositionalism: Response to Collins & Evans', *Social Studies of Science* 33(3) (2003): 412, 402.

75. Wynne, 'Seasick of the Third Wave?' 410; Turner, *Liberal Democracy 3.0*.

76. See Levy and Peart, *Escape from Democracy*, 9–0; cf. William Easterly, *The Tyranny of Experts* (New York: Basic Books, 2013), 6–7.

77. Jasanoff, 'Breaking the Waves', 393–4.

78. Wynne, 'Seasick of the Third Wave?', 402–3.
79. Wiebe E. Bijker, Roland Bal and Ruud Hendricks, *The Paradox of Scientific Authority: The Role of Scientific Advice in Democracies* (Cambridge, MA: MIT Press, 2009).
80. See Tadeusz Kowalik, *www.polskatransformacja.pl* (Warsaw: Muza, 2009), 72, 98–9.
81. Kowalik, *www.polskatransformacja.pl*, 25.
82. See David Ost, *The Defeat of Solidarity: Anger and Politics in Postcommunist Europe* (Ithaca, NY: Cornell University Press, 2005), 51, 73–4, ch. 5.
83. Cf. Polanyi, 'The Republic of Science', 60.
84. Polanyi, 'The Republic of Science', 59.
85. Polanyi, 'The Republic of Science', 59.
86. See Arie Rip, 'Constructing Expertise: In a Third Wave of Science Studies?' *Social Studies of Science* 33(3) (2003): 419–34.
87. Jasanoff, 'Breaking the Waves', 394.
88. Christiano, 'Rational Deliberation', 45–7.
89. Bohman, *Public Deliberation*, 13, 129–30.
90. See James Bohman, 'Deliberative Democracy and the Epistemic Benefits of Diversity', *Episteme* 3(3) (2006): 175–91.
91. Bohman, *Public Deliberation*, 115, 168.
92. Holst and Molander, 'Public Deliberation', 3.
93. Holst and Molander, 'Public Deliberation', 13; Cathrine Holst and Anders Molander, 'Asymmetry, Disagreement and Biases: Epistemic Worries about Expertise', *Social Epistemology* 32(6) (2018): 359.
94. Holst and Molander, 'Public Deliberation', 4.
95. Holst and Molander, 'Public Deliberation', 2. Cf. Holst and Molander, 'Asymmetry, Disagreement', 366–7; Holst and Molander, 'Epistemic Democracy and the Role of Experts'.
96. Holst and Molander, 'Public Deliberation', 8. Similar preventive measures are suggested by Levy and Peart, in whose view scientists' accountability could be improved by creating a system of mutual monitoring, competition and universal transparency (Levy and Peart, *Escape from Democracy*, 20–1, 40).
97. Holst and Molander, 'Public Deliberation', 8.
98. Holst and Molander, 'Public Deliberation', 9.
99. Especially in the world of post-academic science, where research increasingly moves into the sub-political arena. It is done by private labs and is sponsored by private entities, while the experts and scientists conducting it are financially dependent on their sponsors. Their activities are geared towards the practical application of knowledge, not the dissemination of findings. See Ulrich Beck, *Risk Society: Towards a New Modernity*, trans. Mark Ritter (London: Sage, 1992).
100. Krick, 'Creating Participatory Expert Bodies, 33–48.
101. Krick, 'Creating Participatory Expert Bodies', 35.
102. Cf. Christiano, 'Rational Deliberation', 41.
103. Krick, 'Creating Participatory Expert Bodies', 43.

INCLUSIVE EPISTOCRACY, COMPETENCE AND THE POPULAR RULE

It seems that the notion of epistemic dependence should keep liberal political theorists and practitioners awake at night. If such dependence is indeed inevitable then democratic politics will always be faced with the spectre of manipulation, disinformation, propaganda, fabricated scientific controversies, fake news and post-truth. There is no point in waiting for better times when people will no longer trust populists. Nor is there any hope that, through participation in democratic innovations, citizens will understand the nature of the problems facing societies and states. Citizens will need to be continually redirected to true science, as opposed to pseudoscience, and persuaded that policy should be based on the findings of the former, not of the latter. The way to keep these dangers at bay is not by eliminating trolling, various abuses on social media, microtargeting or the psychological profiling of social media users. Nor will the situation be improved by better education or by setting up new channels of public debate. If epistemic dependence is an insurmountable fact, then laypeople will always be reduced to the role of passive spectators in rhetorical competitions. The vision of a political reality in which populists grow increasingly adept at exploiting this situation is so disconcerting, so at odds with the spirit of individualism and rationalism underpinning scientific and political theory, that it is the main reason why epistemic dependence is so often denied. Recognising it, we risk having to consider democracy as the most unpredictable, politically manipulable, unstable, ineffectual and irrational system of government. In such a democracy the shots will always be called by those best able to manipulate the media. Citizens will swallow almost anything provided they hear it sufficiently often, for a sufficient length of time and in sufficiently attractive form.

If the above is true, it is equally hard to make an epistemic case for representative democracy. Political representatives are just as epistemically dependent on experts as ordinary citizens. They are often experts on the legislative process, but not on the issues under discussion. Moreover, faced with a constant barrage of arguments that they do not understand, politicians are susceptible to choosing expert recommendations that best fit their own political agenda. Sometimes, as in the case of the COVID-19 pandemic, politicians' resistance to science will quickly be 'punished' by the unfolding events. But even in such circumstances there will always be a sizeable group of citizens ready to confide in opinions not backed by scientific evidence and of politicians ready to capitalise on this.

But it is not democrats who should fear epistemic dependence most. For it puts epistocrats in an even tougher bind. Expert government loses all legitimacy if the scientific community is unable to identify its most competent members. And that is precisely what happens if the peer review system is not working[1] and expert knowledge on a whole range of political issues is lacking. Epistocracies face exactly the same dilemmas as democracies. What puts them at an even greater disadvantage is the fact that epistemic arguments are the only arguments there are for epistocracy. Meanwhile, epistemic arguments for democracy are not the only ones, or even the main ones, offered in the literature. Pluralistic, anti-totalitarian and agonistic democrats emphasise that effectiveness in technical decision-making is not the main advantage of democracy.[2] The value of democracy lies in the greater legitimacy of the democratic system. Democracy is not so much a matter of getting things done as of peaceful headcount, which helps to prevent open warfare between conflicted groups;[3] it is a method of peaceful (s)election, articulation and discussion of values,[4] or of treating citizens equally and guaranteeing their freedoms.[5]

But that is not the type of conclusion I am after. I do not wish to claim that recognising epistemic dependence as a fact unequivocally precludes epistemic arguments in favour of democratic government. In my view, it is possible to arrange democratic governance so as to combine its legitimacy with technical efficacy. The way to do this is through inclusive epistocracy.

INCLUSIVE EPISTOCRACY

The notion of inclusive epistocracy may initially strike one as an oxymoron. After all, epistocracy is both exclusive and elitist. It recommends entrusting political decisions to the most competent and gifted individuals – the experts. Jason Brennan, a supporter of epistocracy, defines it as 'the rule of the knowledgeable. More precisely, a political regime is epistocratic to the extent that political power is formally distributed according to competence, skill, and the good faith to act on that skill.'[6] According to David Estlund, every version of epistocracy is based on three assumptions. First, that there are objective indicators of right political decisions; secondly, that some groups of people can make better political decisions than others, and, finally, thirdly, that those persons, because of their competence, should rule.[7] In sum, power should be wielded by those who are best suited to wield it. This does not necessarily mean the rule of Platonic philosopher kings. Epistocracy is not a strict recipe. It has dozens of variants, ranging from Plato's republic, through scholocracy and education or literacy-sensitive electoral censuses, to the inclusion of independent expert institutions (not subjected to political oversight) in the democratic system.[8] This variety means that in practice it is sometimes impossible to tell democracy apart from epistocracy. Independent central banks, financial supervision authorities, institutions that control public expenditures, specialised international supervision bodies, a politically independent civil service – all of these are expert institutions that we consider a normal part of the democratic system. In fact, we see some of them as necessary to a properly functioning democracy.

So much for practice, since in theory the separateness of democracy and epistocracy is not just possible, but also unavoidable. Democrats question each of the principles of epistocracy laid out by Estlund. Most importantly, they are sceptical as to the existence of objective indicators of correct political decisions.[9] In their view, political decisions are always entangled in normative considerations, while politics itself is nothing other than the clash of opposing values. Reducing it to 'administration of things' (something that Saint-Simon famously hoped for[10]) is wishful thinking, lying to the citizens, actually imposing certain moral judgements on them while pretending that there is no alternative. Secondly, democrats claim that there is no such thing as expert knowledge concerning matters of morality. Since all political decisions involve a normative component and there are no morality experts, there is no justification for expert government. Political decisions always concern matters such as the future of the community and the direction in which that community is going to develop, and for that reason they should be discussed and made by the community as a whole. The most trivial inventions have in the past altered entire social structures. The pill, the washing machine and other household appliances, are examples of purely technological changes that have permanently altered the nature of social and political relations.[11] Each such innovation brought in its wake the redistribution of public goods and values. This is why some authors suggest that even introducing such innovations into market circulation should be up for public debate.[12] This applies even more to issues like retirement age, social insurance, basic income or judiciary reform, which should be discussed at large. The long-term consequences, aims and values guiding such reforms should be communicated to the public and carefully analysed.

Yet even if the first two assumptions on which epistocracy is founded were correct, there would still be the doubt that Estlund expressed in his succinct question 'You might be right, but who made you boss?'[13] The fact that someone knows what to do does not automatically mean that others should follow. Epistocratic claims to power are based on 'invidious comparisons',[14] on the refusal to recognise some people as worthy of wielding power. One can hardly expect those to whom such prerogatives are denied to simply accept the sovereignty of experts. Epistocracy will never meet the 'standard of general acceptability'.[15] One cannot expect citizens to put blind trust in people who are supposedly more knowledgeable or virtuous, while they themselves are considered to be inferior. Rationally, one can doubt the superior predispositions of the alleged experts if by definition ordinary citizens are deemed to be incapable of verifying them. Epistocrats would have citizens epistemically depend on experts. That is why epistocratic government is qualified by low social legitimacy.

The inclusive epistocracy conception is based on the conviction that things do not have to be that way. Epistocracy does not have to enjoy low social legitimacy and face the expert–boss fallacy, lack of general acceptability, invidious comparisons, epistemic dependence and many other conundrums. For all of these stem from the exclusive nature of this form of government, from the formalistic distinction between experts and laypeople. Inclusive epistocracy, meanwhile, champions a different approach. It reconciles the best of epistocracy with the foundational principles of democracy: the competence of expert government with the legitimacy proper to democratic rule. It also proposes a strategy for avoiding epistemic dependence. The only condition is that we must broaden the definition of expert to include persons possessing specialist knowledge who have traditionally been perceived as laypeople. Thanks to their unique practical experience ordinary citizens can contribute to the solving of problems where traditional experts – academics and lab practitioners – fail. IE does take note of the epistemic asymmetries between citizens and sees them as inevitable. No one is an expert on everything, and some people have no expertise at all. 'Google University' will not make anyone an expert on anything. Reading internet forums or online articles will not transform laypeople into experts (at least not contributory ones). Nevertheless, ordinary citizens frequently do acquire specialist knowledge thanks to their everyday activities. IE is all about tapping this knowledge. It is the only thing that can enrich the decision-making process in a meritorious sense and rival the expertise of theorists, scientists and lab practitioners.

By redefining expertise and calling for the inclusion of unrecognised experts in decision-making, IE reconciles the ideals of participatory and deliberative democracy with those of epistocracy. From participatory democracy it takes the call to more broadly include ordinary citizens in decision-making processes. It seeks settings in which all citizens will simultaneously be stakeholders and unrecognised experts. Community policing programmes and participatory budgets are a great example of tapping such 'insider's wisdom'.[16] With regard to local problems, people's life experience is the key to effective and ergonomic problem-solving. Residents of particular neighbourhoods or housing estates not only know 'what' needs to be done, but also 'how' it might be achieved. Not only are they able to diagnose problems, they are also capable of taking part in developing effective solutions. From deliberative democracy, IE takes the ideal of conversation as the best method for devising solutions. Effective strategies can be worked out only when the views, positions and experiences of recognised and unrecognised experts are brought together in confrontation. A simple aggregation of opinions and preferences is not enough. It is an unhandy and ineffective tool. Not referendums and polls but democratic innovations are the best means of coming up with solutions. Last but not least, IE draws its ideal of including only contributory experts in deliberations from epistocracy. The key thing to consider when deciding whether to include someone in decision-making is whether they have the potential to bring new knowledge to the table. There is no epistemic rationale for deliberating on problems that citizens have no – or only anecdotal – knowledge about.

Although derived from participatory democracy and epistocracy, IE nonetheless differs from them. It differs from participatory democracy because it uses epistemic criteria in selecting the participants of the decision-making process. It differs from epistocracy in its broad definition of expert knowledge, here extended to those usually thought of as laypeople. Die-hard epistocrats like Brennan, Stephen Breyer[17] or Sunstein[18] would like to place the most important political decisions in the hands of closed bodies isolated from the impact of public opinion. They believe that it is theoretical and abstract knowledge that sets experts apart from laypeople, making them better decision makers. IE, on the contrary, does not see experts as infallible. Nor does it believe that it is easy to identify those who possess the most vital knowledge. Who such individuals are always depends on context – not only the matter at hand but also the time and place of applying theory to practice. People with no formal education may often turn out to be experts. Epistocratic conceptions of experthood most often follow the beaten, traditional and formalist, path. They define experts as professionals. IE discards this simplistic approach.

IE therefore takes the road of criticising theory-centrism in a spirit typical of Michael Oakeshott. Theory is meaningless without the ability to apply it. Oakeshott suggested that nothing of practical utility, including politics, could be learned from books alone.[19] Proficient practice requires the selective application of theoretical knowledge. In a similar vein, IE argues that one cannot simply follow a manual when solving real-life problems. What we need is the contextualisation of theoretical knowledge. In the theory of democracy, this attitude is preached by Bohman, in whose view 'deliberative roles as well as epistemic division of labour'[20] should depend on the circumstances, the context in which the decision is being made, and not be set in advance. The knowledge of the potential deliberators should be of key significance in the choice of decision-making process.[21] Sometimes this will mean having to include ordinary people in the procedure,[22] whenever their experience[23] is key when it comes to 'applying laws and agreements to specific local situations'.[24]

THE FOUR PILLARS OF INCLUSIVE EPISTOCRACY AND THEIR IMPLICATIONS

IE is based on four fundamental premises. The first is that everyone is an expert, though not everyone is a scientific expert, and no one is an expert on everything. Throughout our lives, we all acquire experience that makes us contributory experts. Most of the time this expertise has to do with our profession and consists in typical know-how. It allows us to optimally perform our daily tasks, be they writing crime fiction, playing team sports, gardening or caring for another human being. After performing these duties for a sufficiently long period, we acquire tacit knowledge that makes us experts. However, this does not mean that we all become scientific experts on these issues. When acquiring practical know-how we do not thereby automatically gain theoretical knowledge. The practitioner may in fact sometimes find it difficult to understand the theorist without first consulting the relevant literature or at least asking a lot of additional questions. Practitioners are experts only within the narrow scope of their everyday activities. Football players playing in an attacking position are usually relatively terrible when moved to defence and vice versa. Formula 1 racing car drivers do not do very well at Rallycross or NASCAR. By the same token, the parents of autistic children are expert at taking care of their offspring. But they are not contributory experts with regard to the link between vaccination and autism. Their contributory expertise is usually confined to the disease symptoms manifested by their own child.

Secondly, the effectiveness of decision-making depends on the correct identification of contributory experts. This is as crucial as it is difficult, and indeed impossible if we go with a radical reading of Hardwig. Experts do not always sport external indicators such as lab coats, diplomas or recognition among the expert community. What sets them apart is their experience and tacit knowledge. These, meanwhile, can be appreciated only by someone with similar experiential baggage. If we fail to identify the right experts, the decision will suffer because of it.

Thirdly, the right way of tapping socially dispersed knowledge is through deliberation. It is not aggregating people's views via referenda and public opinion polls. Merit-based discussion involving recognised and unrecognised experts is both possible and absolutely necessary.[25] This is not to say it will always be easy. Its success will depend on all the parties jointly developing interactional expertise. Otherwise there will be no shared understanding.

Fourthly, decision-making needs to be decentralised. Citizens' contributory expertise is usually local in nature. It is for that reason that it should be used on precisely that level. Until now most of the arguments put forward in favour of decentralisation have been normative. Supporters of what is known as stakeholder democracy have argued that citizens have a moral right to decide on issues that concern them directly, in accordance with the principle 'nothing about us without us'. Regardless of one's competence, the possibility of making autonomous decisions about one's fate has been seen by theorists as an inalienable human right. Without questioning the value of such assertions, IE advances epistemic arguments in favour of local democracy. Local democracy is valuable not only because it makes self-determination possible, but also because it is the only way of avoiding the problem of epistemic dependence. It is only at the local level that all the stakeholders may well turn out to be contributory experts who should be included in the discussion and decision. In this way, both normative and epistemic considerations support inclusive democratic procedures at the local level. Involving all citizens is the only way to make rational, autonomous and effective decisions there.

In the past, some of the above recommendations were pushed by theorists and practitioners of democracy.[26] The writings of deliberative and epistemic democrats could fill a medium-sized library. One can therefore ask what novelty IE brings to the table. In my opinion, the game-changing element of IE has to do with the notion of contributory expertise, especially the fact that knowledge of this type characterises citizens to varying degrees. As a consequence, it may be claimed that the apt use of the knowledge held by ordinary citizens strengthens political contextualism. No universal institutional solution that does not take differences in people's competence into account can be reconciled with IE. The degree to which citizens are potentially contributory experts on an issue is a crucial variable. This degree, meanwhile, depends on many factors, but first and foremost on the level of governance we are talking about. As we move higher up, citizen competence diminishes.

In this respect IE differs markedly from the other solutions proposed in the literature. Let us compare it with the version of the 'division of labour' model proposed by Josiah Ober. Ober draws his inspiration from Aristotle and the methods of political choice employed in ancient Athens. His Relevant Expertise Aggregation (REA) model is a peculiar 'middle way' between simple aggregation of citizen preferences and deliberation. REA is also an attempt to reconcile democracy with epistocracy and lay-people with experts. It has several varieties, all of them epistocratic to a greater or lesser degree. The more epistocratic ones leave agenda-setting, problem analysis, the search for competent experts who could propose solutions, and voting on solutions outside the purview of ordinary citizens. In the more democratic versions, experts present their knowledge and opinions to laypeople, while the latter assess their reputations and arguments, and then choose one of the expert solutions put forward.[27]

According to the REA, citizens should choose only from among solutions previously approved by experts. Such political decisions would enjoy both a high level of social legitimacy and a high degree of effectiveness. The possibility of populist agenda-setting and of pushing solutions at odds with scientific knowledge would be eliminated. The citizens' choice would always be optimal or suboptimal.

REA is one of a number of proposals that have experts act as a filter in the legislative process. Brennan proposes an alternative version of this position, dubbed 'universal suffrage with epistocratic veto'. However, he reverses the above order and places the epistocratic stage of the decision-making process after the democratic one. The expert council he proposes would reserve the right to veto all decisions approved by a democratic parliament. It would make sure that none of the laws enacted were contradicted by science or were short-sighted.[28] This would allow every law to enjoy both social legitimacy and to be free of scientific errors.

IE is critical of these type of solutions. After all, each of them presupposes a fixed level of competence both among citizens and experts. Ober assumes that 'experts in a given domain (say, chess masters) are more capable than others at producing a desired outcome (winning) and the probability of achieving the outcome is increased by better choices (good moves)'.[29] Compared with experts, whatever the issue under discussion may be, citizens always lack the knowledge necessary to solve problems effectively. This is why their choice should always be narrowed down to a set of alternatives approved (previously, or at a later stage) by experts. Out of concern for the effectiveness of the political system, decision-makers should essentially be stripped of the freedom to choose whatever they want. Political decision-makers turn out to be figureheads, either merely putting their seal of approval on expert-led solutions or trying to foresee the intentions of the expert council (holding veto powers) until they get it right.

IE questions this vision. According to IE, citizens' competence decreases as we move up the governance ladder, until it fades out altogether at the supra-regional level. On the local level, citizens are often experts, thus reducing them to the role of extras who merely stamp their seal of approval on expert proposals would be an epistemic waste. Here roles may be reversed. Rank-and-file citizens can bring necessary correction to expert proposals and forecasts. On the regional level, citizen competence is limited to issues related to people's local experience. It is therefore significantly circumscribed, while recognised experts and stakeholder groups play a bigger role. On the supra-regional level, citizens can do no more than rely on expertise. Here, ordinary citizens are incapable of assessing expert arguments, let alone of contributing their own.

This is why the answer to the question as to the most effective form of government depends on the level of government we are talking about. What Alfred Moore calls alternative visions of the expert–lay relationship may turn out to be wholly complementary.[30] Moore devises models of representation, participation and association. In the first model (representation), politicians set the goals to be achieved by experts and oversee the latter's work. This largely resembles the 'division of labour' model discussed in the previous chapters. The participation model promotes expert–lay cooperation within the framework of democratic innovations. It holds that 'under the right conditions of deliberative organization and support, ordinary citizens are perfectly capable of making informed judgments of complex expert claims'.[31] And, finally, the associative expertise model recommends using third-sector organisations as a reservoir of knowledge and experience. 'Civil society groups, advocacy organizations, and social movements' often bring together experts and practitioners, and are therefore excellent platforms for exchanging information and raising decision-making competence. 'The cognitive contribution of lay citizens in this model takes the form not only of the formulation of new problems, but also the assessment, scrutiny, and critique of existing claims to expertise'.[32] When applied at the same level of governance, these three models may – as Moore rightly points out – be in conflict with one another, for instance with regard to the degree of social legitimacy or the participants' self-interest. However, if we take the differences in people's competence (as suggested by IE) into consideration, it may turn out that every level of governance has its own dedicated expert–lay cooperation formula. Democratic innovations are perfectly appropriate at the local level. The representative model presents a distinct advantage at the supra-regional level. And if an issue-specific point is being discussed (and if there are professional associations or NGOs that specialise in the issue), the associative model may prove best.[33] All three models can be implemented at the regional level.

INCLUSIVE EPISTOCRACY: WHAT IS IT REALLY?

IE does not pre-determine which political model is the most appropriate one for the supra-local level of governance. It focuses on the local level, since it is only there that citizens can be contributory experts. The academic literature mentions many ways of empowering citizens directly and IE does not add to this list. However, it approaches some of them critically, claiming that they are epistemically justified only to a very small degree. Democratic innovations are the main point of reference for IE. This is not particularly surprising, since many of these innovations create a space for lay–expert cooperation on practical problems. Examples of innovations include popular assemblies (for example, open town meetings), referenda, e-democracy, as well as various types of minipublics. The latter are an internally varied family of solutions. They are also widely discussed in the literature. Minipublics involve bringing together a randomly selected, socially representative group of citizens for a period of time (usually from two to five days) in order to introduce them to expert opinions and to work out recommendations together. They differ in a number of features: the amount of time spent deliberating (deliberative polls usually take a couple of days, while citizens' assemblies may continue to function for up to a year), the number of participants (from a handful in consensus conferences, up to 500 in deliberative opinion polls), meeting frequency (from single meetings to regular ones), types of lay–expert communication (from quasi-lectures in planning cells to experts being interrogated by citizens in citizens' juries), the initiating agent (NGOs or local authorities), the degree to which participants can influence the agenda or the procedure, the final outcome (a report compiled by the moderators or a 'before' and 'after' survey in deliberative polls), the degree to which the procedure is made public, and the political consequences (a non-binding consultation or a binding obligation to take the results into account when planning future policies).

Each innovation has its advantages and weaknesses, supporters and opponents. Graham Smith analyses them all in terms of how well they bring about certain goods: inclusiveness, popular control, considered judgement and transparency.[34] This multi-aspect assessment is perfectly justified, since the innovations have been used to settle all kinds of issues, many of them involving a significant normative component. As already mentioned, in Iceland they were used to draft a constitution, in Canada and the Netherlands to develop proposals for electoral reform, while in Texas they were convened to decide whether to abandon fossil fuels. In such cases, the thing deliberated on is actually the type of community that the citizens want to bequeath to future generations. The role of experts boils down to showing the likely consequences of various choices. The principal task – that of identifying the trade-offs between values and of making a hierarchy of alternative visions of the future – must belong to the citizens. This is well illustrated by the example of Ireland, where, in 2013, a Convention on the Constitution consisting of sixty-six randomly selected, representative citizens discussed proposed amendments to the Irish constitution, including the legalisation of same-sex marriages, expanding women's rights and the removal of the offence of blasphemy from the constitution. The amendments proposed by the Convention were subsequently approved in a referendum by an overwhelming majority (79 per cent) of voters. In this case, the democratic innovation was a tool for implementing a worldview-cum-legal revolution. Such far-reaching changes would have been difficult to achieve via the standard legislative procedure.

Since IE is epistemic in nature, I shall refrain from a multi-aspectual analysis of innovations. I shall focus solely on considered judgement. From this perspective, not every innovation meets the IE criteria. Those that make better use of citizens' knowledge generally do better. Chicago Community Policing is a great example. Since 1995, the Chicago police have been organising monthly meetings with the residents of different neighbourhoods. Together, they define the safety policy targets and reflect on how to achieve them. The justification for these meetings is epistemic – it is the residents who know best which spots are dangerous, the nature of the dangers and how effective the available solutions are.[35] This enables them to have meaningful discussions with the police officers and security experts. They can correct expert assumptions and enrich expert knowledge with their own, unique experiences. Open town meetings are based on the same idea. In a classic work devoted to them, Joseph Zimmerman states that 'The open town meeting is predicated on the theory that ordinary voters possess the native intelligence to weigh the pros and cons of an issue and the political acumen to make wise decisions.'[36]

In order to put citizens' epistemic potential to its best use, innovations must meet a number of criteria. First, they have to be deliberative. Only when citizens discuss things with one another and with recognised experts can 'insider's wisdom' emerge. The opportunity to ask and answer questions, learn about different experiences and points of view, is of fundamental importance. From the IE standpoint, non-deliberative forms of political participation have no epistemic value.[37] This is why IE critically approaches all theories referring to the 'wisdom of crowds'.

In the famous opening example of James Surowiecki's *Wisdom of Crowds*, Francis Galton was at the Plymouth fair looking for proof that the intellectual aristocracy should govern thoughtless citizens, when to his astonishment he discovered something else. It turned out that a group of average individuals could be surprisingly wise in their assessment of reality. When asked to estimate the weight of a butchered ox, random guessers who had purchased lottery tickets hoping to win a monetary prize turned out to be incredibly accurate as a group. The average of the individual guesses came one pound short of the right answer. Individually, none of the guessers had come so close to the truth. As a group they turned out to be almost exact. From the IE perspective such examples, albeit interesting, are at most curiosities without practical significance. Without exchanging information and assessing arguments, participation usually boils down to the aggregation of unreasonable opinions and partial perspectives. Rarely does it produce a consistent picture of reality or lead to deeper understanding. Heuristics and prejudice – Kahneman's System 1 rather than System 2 – play a dominant role.

The flaws of non-deliberative democratic innovations are readily visible in political practice, including in the Polish experience with participatory budgeting. In their original form developed in Porto Alegre, all willing residents took part in regional assemblies. There, they decided on investment priorities and elected representatives to regional budget forums and city committees which later oversaw the implementation of the projects. This made the Brazilian budgets deliberative and inclusive institutions. They created the optimal conditions for enriching knowledge and sharing information. But even in such benign circumstances, the residents often felt helpless when faced with the complexity of the problems to be examined. Despite the considerable cognitive effort expended, the members of the city committees often had to blindly trust expert opinion.[38]

When participatory budgeting was first introduced in Poland (in Sopot) in 2011, it was in a different, non-deliberative form, with less direct citizen involvement. Any resident could submit an idea, and the principal method of choosing projects was via online vote. Although experts recommended employing deliberation at every stage of the process, no room was made for an inclusive discussion on the hierarchy of problems faced by the local community and possible solutions. As a result, within a short time the budgets became an example of irrational management of relatively small public sums (from 0.5 per cent to 5 per cent of a city's budget). Quite soon certain types of project became more 'fashionable'. A brief spell of submissions followed, proposing outdoor fitness parks, dog runs, squares and recreational benches. The most extravagant graduation towers were erected in several Polish cities. The contribution of some of these projects to solving local problems cannot be said to have been very great. Only a handful of citizens showed initiative in Polish participatory budgeting. It was they who set the agenda, defined the problems to be solved and proposed solutions. Interest in participation rarely rose above 10 per cent, and over time began to decline.[39] This led some cities[40] to change the formula and switch to citizen assemblies instead. The evaluation of problems faced by the local community by a representative group of citizens in collaboration with experts became a new starting point. This deliberative transformation is in line with IE, although by solving one problem it creates another – that of exclusivity, and thus of limiting the number of perspectives taken into account.

Secondly, IE endorses the use of inclusive solutions. Diverse and multiple opinions translate into effective decisions. The requirement of inclusiveness poses a severe challenge to any sparse body, whether its members are determined by lottery or by voting. The small number of decision makers inevitably leads to the marginalisation of the voice of minority groups. A rather extreme example is the constitutional assembly from Iceland, where a group of twenty-five citizens appointed by the parliament (and previously nominated in elections) between 2010 and 2012 drafted constitutional amendments. David Van Reybrouck rightly asks 'how diverse is a constitutional assembly of twenty-five people if seven of them are in positions of leadership (at universities, museums or trades unions) and of the rest five are professors or lecturers, four are media figures, four artists, two lawyers and one a clergyman? Even the father of singer Björk, a prominent trade unionist, managed to get a place on it. There was just one farmer.'[41] From the standpoint of effectiveness, it is crucial that all interested persons be allowed to take part in deliberation.

Thirdly, deliberation needs to be a long-term process. The quality of the outcome depends directly on the amount of time spent getting over reticence or mistrust among participants as they learn to navigate a new situation.[42] It is necessary to come to agreement as to how to define the situation, to develop a glossary of terms and, if necessary, to enlist the help of an interactional expert in order to help participants understand one another. The quantity of material and information participants need to take in also frequently demands intense cognitive engagement. Taking more time also increases the creativity of the group and therefore impacts the quality of the outcome. From this standpoint, citizens' assemblies, citizens' juries, consensus conferences and planning cells have a distinct advantage over deliberative polls.[43]

Fourthly, the more free rein participants are given to shape the agenda, the better. If, rather than only tackling problems defined top-down by the organisers of the procedure, they can also independently define the original situation, the effectiveness of the procedure as a whole increases. An ill-defined problem may be impossible to solve. In this respect, as Smith rightly observed, 'citizens' juries and consensus conferences provide an opportunity for citizens to be creative in their decision-making, working together to develop novel solutions to policy problems. They also provide an opportunity for citizens to collectively justify their reasoning in the reports that are produced. In comparison, in deliberative polling, participants have little opportunity for creativity, since they are required to give their responses to pre-prepared questions.'[44]

These four conclusions clearly suggest that popular assemblies best comply with the requirements of IE. They are at once inclusive and deliberative, tackle local issues and meet regularly. They can potentially involve all stakeholders and contributory experts. They also carry into effect non-epistemic values – by including the majority of stakeholders they comply with 'All-Affected Interests Principle'.[45] The degree of legitimacy of the recommendations developed and therefore also their translation into a final policy seems to be much higher than in the case of minipublics. The already-cited discussion between the Cumbrian sheep farmers and MAFF experts is an excellent example of the practical application of IE.

Popular assemblies can take many forms, from New England Town Meetings, through participatory budgeting (as practised in Porto Alegre), to the already-mentioned Chicago Community Policing. In each of these cases, it is the small community, which knows local conditions best, that uses its unique knowledge to make the best decision. The local character of popular assemblies has its dark side as well, of course. Their definite downside is that the local community is rarely disinterested. They are usually biased in favour of particular solutions, pursuing their personal interests. It also usually includes a group of people with special authority, who can easily influence others. In such conditions, it is difficult to speak of deliberation in the strict sense of the word. After all, one of its key requirements is that the participants are ready to change their minds.[46] Otherwise, the conversation will come down to throwing around arguments without giving them due weight. In the absence of a readiness to make concessions, arguments are of no use. In such situations, a randomly selected, possibly representative part of a community may prove a better deliberative body. The problem of bias enters the main argument put forward by the proponents of sortition-based democracy. IE cannot answer it unequivocally. It may turn out that the bias of the local community will be a feature detrimental to deliberation. There is no escaping this.

There is, however, a glimmer of hope. Epistemic issues that boil down to problem-solving, which is what IE is concerned with, may prove less susceptible to the problem of bias than normative issues. In their case, there may be a community of interest between most of the participants in the deliberation.[47] The sheep farmers and MAFF experts described by Wynne had a common goal – to determine when it would be possible to sell sheep. Similarly, Chicago's police experts and local communities had the same task – to reduce crime. There was a community of interest and a community of purpose between them. A similar situation should also occur on several other issues.

LIMITATIONS

It is hard not to agree with most critics of epistocracy. It is true that expertise is often too abstract or detailed, that experts are too self-assured, unaware of the arbitrary nature of their assumptions, and that in the guise of strictly technical pronouncements they often smuggle in normative pronouncements, which should be the object of wide-ranging social discussion. The goal of IE is to put a stop to these negative consequences of taking advantage of expertise. By widening the circle of experts, IE differentiates perspectives and heuristics, and places emphasis on taking advantage of contextual knowledge and on the deliberative clash between the opinions of people representing different fields of knowledge. IE therefore creates the ideal conditions for heightened criticism, the inclusion of multiple perspectives and the aggregation of socially dispersed knowledge. Nevertheless, it is not flawless. The four fundamental premises of IE also spell out its equally fundamental limitations. First, being an epistocratic concept, IE can be applied only where expertise exists. As a result, when it comes to long-term political or economic predictions, normative choices or problems not previously encountered, IE will not be the right method of deciding. The purpose of IE is to exploit socially dispersed expert knowledge. If such knowledge is unavailable, IE loses its *raison d'être*. In such cases other decision-making formats, such as prediction markets or groups of superforecasters described by Phillip Tetlock and Dan Gardner,[48] may prove to be more effective.

Secondly, IE is based on the idea of aggregating the knowledge of contributory experts who are practitioners. Such people often do not enjoy special social status. The only thing that sets them apart is their experience and their tacit knowledge. The challenge IE faces is therefore to develop a method for identifying such people.[49] This is of crucial importance from the standpoint of working out objective criteria for the inclusion of citizens in decision-making procedures. One cannot simply fall back on official decisions, arbitrary as they are, in this process.[50] Unfortunately, when external markers of experthood are not in evidence, finding competent practitioners is an extremely difficult task. Despite their fallibility, Goldman's strategies have given laypeople hopes of identifying indicators that characterise the most competent expert. That these indicators are often unreliable is a whole different story. Things become immeasurably complicated when we need to identify an expert among people with no publications, no academic track record and no connection to other experts who would vouch for this person's authority. IE strives to circumvent the problem of cherry-picking experts by identifying entire groups of stakeholders who are certain to have the desired knowledge on account of their experience. The inhabitants of a specific locale, sheep-grazing and grain-growing farmers, drivers, dog owners and trainers are just a handful of examples. These groups may include individuals who do not have the knowledge we are seeking, but there is a good chance that if the group is large enough it will yield at least a couple of genuine contributory experts.

Thirdly, IE almost never proves to be useful beyond the local level of government. On the supra-local level, ordinary citizens do not have the kind of personal experience that would make them contributory experts. In areas like international trade or fiscal, demographic or cultural policy it is foolish to expect that the experience, say, of a private entrepreneur or activist, would make them a capable decision-maker. Although this argument is often invoked in politics, where businesspeople and bankers present themselves as apolitical and competent technocrats who are not bound to interest groups or representing the interests of the elites, IE shows that it is baseless. Neither the single-handed rule of a practitioner, nor deliberative polling, nor other types of lay–expert collaborative forums have any epistemic justification on the national and international level. Epistemic dependence is unavoidable here, and civic incompetence inevitable.

Fourthly, and last, IE is generally most applicable in the realm of practice. Wherever familiarity with context is irrelevant, the input of ordinary citizens can hardly be said to improve decisions. IE has no use in lab research or theoretical study. Ordinary citizens cannot contribute much to these fields.

What all this means is that IE is ill-suited to solving most political, social and economic problems. Where there are no experts, there is no place for epistocracy, even of an inclusive kind. This is why IE can be, at most, an addition to traditional representative democracy. IE cannot solve the problems of epistemic dependence, post-truth and public opinion manipulation. It is therefore indispensable to add other tools, which will limit the adverse consequences of epistemic dependence, to our toolkit. Their purpose will be not so much to render citizens competent, as to make them less susceptible to disinformation and manipulation. These mechanisms include fostering a culture of whistle-blowing, teaching critical thinking skills and raising experts' rhetorical ability.

WHISTLE-BLOWING

Since laypeople lack fool-proof methods of evaluating expert competence, it is imperative that they look for signs of potential expert incompetence. The only effective and uncontroversial strategy for identifying competent experts is 'searching for evidences of experts' bias', which requires no special competence on the layperson's part. It is a truism that financial motivation to preach certain views should disqualify an expert as a professional. Since this is the only method available to a layperson, it should be employed as widely as possible. One of the ways to do this is by developing a culture of whistle-blowing.

In Poland, as in many other post-communist countries, the function of the whistle-blower is not appreciated. The legal status of those reporting irregularities is often unregulated. Thus, they are not entitled to any special protection. Poland has been delaying the implementation of the European Parliament directive on the protection of persons who report breaches of EU law.[51] In the interim, many of those bringing to light irregularities at their workplace or in their immediate environment have been stigmatised as traitors or snitches. This practice is typical of societies like Polish, with a long tradition of mistrust in public institutions. The authorities sometimes exploit this. In the Polish political reality after 2015, those who criticised the Polish government on the international arena, especially in EU forums or international courts, risked being accused of treason. Often this accusation fell on fertile soil and was taken up by radical groups.

Meanwhile, citizens have to start viewing the disclosure of irregularities not as a moral failing but as their civic duty. Only by promoting such practices can the financial and personal connections of local and national politicians, businesspeople and experts be brought to light. Whistle-blowing should not only be supported by the media, audit bodies and law enforcement, but also by public institutions, even though they are often the object of the embarrassing disclosures. Information about irregularities taken up by investigative journalists and institutions should come from citizens.

The culture of whistle-blowing is in much better shape in well-established democracies. American investigative journalism, which saw its first spectacular successes towards the end of the nineteenth century, on many occasions brought about legislative changes or the breakup of monopolies. Today, the Bellingcat group shows that in the internet age all one needs to discover the identity of spies and assassins is inquisitiveness, persistence and some free time. The amateur journalists at Bellingcat have independently identified the would-be killers of Aleksei Navalny and Sergei Skripal as well as the provenance of the missile that downed the Malaysian Airlines plane over Ukraine.[52] Money should be invested in apolitical investigative journalism and institutional arrangements should be made to facilitate it. The burden of identifying irregularities cannot rest on the shoulders of investigative journalists and citizens alone. The media – both traditional and digital, especially independent outlets – should play a key role in this process. If they are to play it well, media pluralism is fundamental. The fact that the market is dominated by public broadcasters dependent on state financing as well as private monopolies and oligopolies effectively makes the work of investigative journalists impossible. In such circumstances, instead of contestation the media promote opinions that benefit their patrons.

It is also necessary to provide financial incentives for the media to serve as watchdogs, including to report spurious experts. In practice, instead of helping to debunk examples of pseudo-science the media often amplify them, escalating pseudo-scientific controversies. They spread disinformation instead of stamping it out. Chasing viewership and seeking to boost advertising revenues, the traditional media take up subjects popular on social media. Instead of criticising social media, they become its extension. This state of affairs can be blamed on the increasing commercialisation of the media. Pressure to feature viral topics trending on social media and to meet financial targets leads to the closure of science sections or the cutting of science staff down to a single employee. This is a problem that plagues most media publishers. It is imperative to rebuild science sections. Journalists specialising in science-related matters should check experts' backgrounds, track their sources of financing, and identify any potential bias and the reasons for it. They should eliminate people with shady reputations, financially connected and representing interest lobbies from media debates. They should also prevent situations in which experts speak out on topics that are not their speciality. They should eradicate the practice of juxtaposing or equating the voice of experts with the voice of dilettantes. Naturally, not being experts themselves, journalists cannot directly assess the competence of the people they interview. However, lack of academic qualifications, academic affiliation, experience, the existence of financial dependence or other evidence of bias are all enough to discredit an apparent expert. In debates concerning technical issues, the media should only transmit the opinions of specialists in a given field representing reputable academic institutions. Traditional media should also be an alternative to social media rather than its replica.

Of course, promoting a culture of whistle-blowing and disclosing the financial connections of experts will not solve the problem of epistemic dependence. Citizens will continue to face problems and choices they are not capable of making. Whistle-blowing and a responsible media will only guarantee that each of the alternatives presented to citizens is based on solid merit. Marginal views will remain marginal, and views shared by the majority of scientists will take centre stage.

TEACHING CRITICAL THINKING SKILLS

In his article 'Education as Socialization and as Individualization' (1989), Richard Rorty described developing students' contestatory potential as the aim of secondary and upper education.[53] He claimed that until the 1980s the American education system had been based on an all-round satisfactory assignment of roles. Elementary and secondary education inculcated students with basic facts and taught them to respect traditional political and social institutions and values. Higher education, meanwhile, taught constructive criticism of those truths. It was a training ground for contesting ideas, ideals and values, and resisting black-and-white visions of reality. This arrangement – which satisfied both liberals and conservatives – broke down when high school graduates began to leave school with too little knowledge to have something to question at university. Thus, universities had to take on the double role of educators and teachers of doubt. This had deplorable consequences for graduates' knowledge and their ability to think independently.

Today, the ability to critically analyse information is more needed than ever before.[54] The problem in our culture today is not a lack of scepticism. There is quite a lot of it in fact, with illiberal democrats making political capital out of it. The problem lies in 'half-hearted scepticism'. We live in a time of demi-scepticism. High school and university graduates today acquire enough criticism to doubt the messages of mainstream science, but not enough to apply the same critical acumen to merchants of doubt and dubious information stumbled upon online.[55] The ability to critically analyse a text and gauge the credibility of sources should be a basic skill taught much earlier than at university. Building a culture of criticism must be part of the elementary school curriculum, the moment students encounter disinformation online for the first time.

Establishing a universal culture of scepticism and ingraining the habit of checking the sources of online information will not remove laypeople's susceptibility to manipulation and the inability to resolve expert disputes. Laypeople are and will remain helpless in these situations. They will not be able to point to the most credible expert, but they will be able to identify those who are no experts. Still, education must develop people's ability to recognise the most egregious examples of manipulation and propaganda. It must teach them how to make a preliminary selection of materials, discarding those that are least credible, for example, by identifying sponsored posts and persons without qualifications. When a supposed authority is not a scientist or is a specialist in an entirely different field, that the fact should immediately grab the reader's attention. Students and citizens have to develop the habit of checking the source of any controversial information that they encounter. This will not eliminate all the controversies, but we will be doing something that Collins, Evans and Weinel consider a vital part of our culture – identifying frauds will become part of 'ubiquitous tacit knowledge'.

Learning to critically evaluate reality is an integral part of civic education and education for political participation. There is no conscious, rational citizenship and pursuit of the common good if one cannot tell manipulation from facts. Education today places too much emphasis on learning a trade, and too little on the ability to select information. We need to return to the ideal of civic education which includes teaching independent and critical thinking. As Martha Nussbaum puts it:

> Democracies have great rational and imaginative powers. But they also are prone to some serious flaws in reasoning, to parochialism, haste, sloppiness and selfishness. Education based mainly on profitability in the global market magnifies these deficiencies, producing a greedy obtuseness and a technically trained docility that threaten the very life of democracy itself.[56]

Education should also be about developing the ability to recognise the basic heuristics to which we usually fall prey: confirmation bias, anchoring, the conjunction fallacy and the framing effect. It must teach not just cooperation but also non-conformity and the ability to withstand group pressure. The proper functioning of democracy will nowadays require less and less the possession of detailed factual information, and increasingly the ability to find relevant and credible details in the flood of information.

THE RHETORICAL OFFENSIVE OF SCIENCE

In one of his analyses of Thomas Hobbes, Quentin Skinner traced the evolution of this philosopher's position on rhetoric. In his early works, Hobbes was convinced that rhetoric was quite useless. He saw flowery speech as a threat to public discourse rather than an added bonus. As an empiricist, materialist and a member of the modern scientific avant-garde, Hobbes believed that no beautiful metaphor could alter the facts. Public debate should be informed by reason and science, it should be a space for producing evidence, exchanging arguments and letting the best argument win. In *De Cive* the thinker openly states that:

> ability to render ... hearers insane (who were merely stupid before); to make men believe that a bad situation is worse than it is, and that a good situation is bad; to exaggerate hopes and to minimize risks beyond reason, is due to eloquence; not the eloquence which expounds things as they are, but the other eloquence, which by communicating the excitement of the speaker to the minds of others makes everything appear as he had seen it in his own excited mind.[57]

Dialectical skill, narrative fluency, the ability to introduce subtle tension or employ flowery metaphors are – at best – superfluous ornaments which do not enhance the style of argumentation. What counts is the logic of the argument, the link from premises to conclusions and consistency. It is these features that win disputes and should be emphasised in education. Nine years after the publication of *De Cive* Hobbes published *Leviathan* where he expounds a wholly different view, strikingly reminiscent of classical tracts on the role of rhetoric in public debate. This role is well conveyed by Cicero, according to whom although 'wisdom without eloquence is but of little advantage to states, but that eloquence without wisdom is often most mischievous, and is never advantageous to them'.[58] Wisdom without eloquence is rarely appreciated, and even more rarely heard.[59] Hobbes followed the same reasoning. He was concerned that although facts will always be appreciated by an exact mind, they will seldom speak to laypeople. Ordinary citizens are incapable of appreciating a flawless argument – worse, they are not interested in hearing it. Hence, they easily fall prey to manipulation and demagogy and are constantly misled. Even those with the best of intentions cannot recognise the stronger argument. This is why political success requires combining the power of reason and the art of eloquence. Those who would appeal only to reason, ignoring the emotions, should prepare for political calamity. In his conclusion to *Leviathan* Hobbes states: 'and yet if there be not powerful Eloquence, which procureth attention and Consent, the effect of Reason will be little'.[60]

Contemporary science has to follow in Hobbes' footsteps.[61] With his optimism and faith in reason, early Hobbes reminds us of today's academics. Their attitude is qualified by the conviction that producing facts, numbers and hard evidence will ensure victory in a word battle and win a dispute. This belief has witnessed some of the most spectacular debacles in science. For example, the cold and rational enumeration of the amounts that the British economy would lose by leaving the EU did not get through to the average Brit during the Brexit campaign. What did get through were catchy, though untrue, slogans about hordes of migrants and the £350 million that British health services would gain weekly thanks to the UK leaving. Science and scientists must learn their lesson from this and come to the same conclusions as Hobbes. The burden of combating manipulation cannot fall exclusively on the shoulders of citizens. Some of it must be borne by representatives of the scientific community. If there is no way to rationally convince laypeople of the authority of science and expertise, then one should at least minimise the impact of non-merit-based factors on societal trust in science. Citing dry data alone will fail against rhetorical devices, belligerence and exaggerated self-assurance. Laypeople cannot be blamed for rooting for the more savvy speaker, since judging rhetoric is one of the few things a layperson can do. We must stop blaming ordinary citizens, admit our own faults and change our way of communicating.[62] This is why Sarah and Jack Gorman claim that academics have to become more at ease in the public sphere, more charismatic, and adjust the tone and content of their narrative to their interlocutors' and audience's way of thinking.[63] They have to be more like Anthony Fauci – to inspire trust not only by what they say but also how they say it. They must raise their communication competence at least to match the level of their opponents. The current disproportion of rhetorical skill is much to the advantage of the latter. Scientists tend to be much worse at communicating with the public; they lack a catchy rhetoric, often have less marketing support, and they are less present on social media. This should change, and the reach and attractiveness of scientific communication should be improved. In other words, what we need is a rhetorical defensive and offensive campaign on behalf of science.

Regardless of their speciality, scientists should have at least a basic knowledge of cognitive psychology, behavioural economics and sociology of communication. These subjects should be part of their professional training. They should be able to understand laypeople, their fears and hopes, and be able to address their message to the broadest possible community. Rorty once wrote that *Uncle Tom's Cabin* did more for tolerance and improving the lot of Black Americans than any philosophical treatise.[64] Science has to be capable of telling about its successes, failures and difficulties in a compelling way, using the language of literature and popular culture. As Matthew d'Ancona rightly notes, 'more than ever, truth requires an emotional delivery system that speaks to experience, memory and hope'.[65]

Of course, this is not a task for all scientists. Not everyone can be expected to willingly and effectively take advantage of traditional and social media to popularise their findings. Of course, science popularisation could be made an evaluation criterion of science institutions and scholars. A key role in this respect should, however, be played by scientific institutions, universities and research centres. They must not only conduct research but also promote their work. Science must have capable spokespeople who defend its authority in the media. Equally as important as popularising science is providing a coordinated and rhetorically compelling response to the claims of sceptics. Signing appeals and issuing joint statements is not enough.

There is no solution to the problem of epistemic dependence that would be immune to charges. My ambition in this chapter was not to find such a formula. I considered here possible ways of avoiding confrontation with this problem. One of these is inclusive epistocracy and the suggested directions for reforming public debate. Inclusive epistocracy avoids the problem of epistemic dependence by excluding laypeople from taking part in deliberative forums. It minimises opportunities for merit-based debate between laypeople and experts. This is why it is not a hopeful candidate for solving the problems facing contemporary democracies. No form of epistocracy will ever save democracy. It is only supposed to unburden democracy when issues that the latter has trouble dealing with are involved. Also the proposed rhetorical offensive of science, training citizens in critical thinking and responsible selection of sources of information, as well as promoting a culture of whistle-blowing is more about dodging rather than confronting the problem of epistemic dependence, since these approaches exploit laypeople's only strategy of keeping unreliable experts out of public debate, that is looking for expert bias.

NOTES

1. Hardwig, 'Epistemic Dependence', 336.
2. Chantal Mouffe, 'Deliberative Democracy or Agonistic Pluralism?' *Social Research* 66(3) (1999): 745–58; Chantal Mouffe, *On the Political: Thinking in Action* (London: Routledge, 2005); Marie Paxton, *Agonistic Democracy: Rethinking Political Institutions in Pluralist Times* (London: Routledge, 2020).
3. Adam Przeworski, 'Minimalist Conception of Democracy: A Defense', in Ian Shapiro and C. Hacker-Cordón (eds), *Democracy's Value* (Cambridge: Cambridge University Press, 1999), 44–8.
4. Mouffe, *On the Political*.
5. Cf. Elisabeth Anderson, 'Democracy: Instrumental vs. Non-Instrumental Value', in Thomas Christiano and John Christman (eds), *Contemporary Debates in Political Philosophy* (Malden, MA: Wiley-Blackwell, 2009), 213–27.
6. Brennan, *Against Democracy*, 14.
7. Estlund, *Democratic Authority*, 30. Cf. David Estlund, 'Making Truth Safe for Democracy', in David Copp, Jean Hampton and John E. Roemer (eds), *The Idea of Democracy* (Cambridge: Cambridge University Press, 1993), 72.
8. Cf. Anne Jeffrey, 'Limited Epistocracy and Political Inclusion', *Episteme* 15(4) (2018), 412–32.
9. See Landemore, *Democratic Reason*, 275–7.
10. Henri Saint-Simon, 'On the Replacement of Government by Administration', in *Henri Saint-Simon (1760–1825): Selected Writings on Science, Industry and Social Organisation*, ed. Keith Taylor (London: Routledge, 2016).
11. Ha-Joon Chang, *23 Things They Don't Tell You About Capitalism* (New York: Bloomsbury, 2010).
12. Sclove, *Democracy and Technology*, 47, 56–61; Sheldon Krimsky, 'Beyond Technocracy: New Routes for Citizen Involvement in Social Risk Assessment', *Nonprofit and Voluntary Sector Quarterly* 11(1) (1982): 54–8.
13. Estlund, *Democratic Authority*, 40.
14. Estlund, *Democratic Authority*, 36–7.
15. Estlund, *Democratic Authority*, 33–6.
16. Graham Smith, *Democratic Innovations: Designing Institutions for Citizen Participation* (Cambridge: Cambridge University Press, 2009), ch. 2; Archon Fung, *Empowered Participation: Reinventing Urban Democracy* (Princeton, NJ: Princeton University Press, 2006); Fung and Wright, 'Deepening Democracy', 34; Fung, 'Putting the Public Back into Governance', 521.
17. Stephen Breyer, *Breaking the Vicious Circle: Toward Effective Risk Regulation* (Cambridge, MA: Harvard University Press, 1993).

18. Cass R. Sunstein, *Risk and Reason: Safety, Law, and the Environment* (Cambridge: Cambridge University Press, 2002). Cf. Michael Schudson, 'The Trouble with Experts – and Why Democracies Need Them', *Theory and Society* 35 (2006): 491–506.

19. Michael Oakeshott, *Rationalism in Politics: And Other Essays* (London: Meuthen, 1962).

20. Bohman, *Public Deliberation*, 163.

21. Bohman, *Public Deliberation*, 164.

22. James Bohman, 'The Coming of Age of Deliberative Democracy', *Journal of Political Philosophy* 6(6) (1998): 417–18.

23. Bohman, *Public Deliberation*, 168–9.

24. Bohman, *Public Deliberation*, 189.

25. John Dryzek, *Deliberative Democracy and Beyond: Liberals, Critics, Contestations* (Oxford: Oxford University Press, 2000), 36–8; Joshua Cohen, 'Procedure and Substance in Deliberative Democracy', in Seyla Benhabib (ed.), *Democracy and Difference: Contesting the Boundaries of the Political* (Princeton, NJ: Princeton University Press, 1996), 100; Jon Elster, 'The Market and the Forum: Three Varieties of Political Theory', in. James Bohman and William Rehg (eds), *Deliberative Democracy: Essays on Reason and Politics* (Cambridge, MA: MIT Press, 1997), 3–33.

26. See Cohen and Sabel, 'Directly-Deliberative Polyarchy', 313–42; Fung and Wright, 'Deepening Democracy', 5–41.

27. Josiah Ober, 'Democracy's Wisdom: An Aristotelian Middle Way for Collective Judgment', *American Political Science Review* 107(1) (2013): 104–22.

28. Brennan, *Against Democracy*, 215–18.

29. Josiah Ober, *Demopolis: Democracy before Liberalism in Theory and Practice* (Cambridge: Cambridge University Press, 2017), 144.

30. Alfred Moore, 'Three Models of Democratic Expertise', *Perspectives on Politics* 19(2) (2021): 553–63.

31. Moore, 'Three Models', 558.

32. Moore, 'Three Models', 559.

33. See Piotr Perczynski, 'Associo-Deliberative Democracy and Qualitative Participation', in Paul Hirst and Veit Bader (eds), *Associative Democracy: The Real Third Way* (New York: Routledge, 2005), 71–2, 82–3; P. Q. Hirst, *Associative Democracy: New Forms of Economic and Social Governance* (Amherst, MA: University of Massachusetts Press, 1994); Joshua Cohen and Joel Rogers, 'Secondary Associations and Democratic Governance', *Politics and Society* 20(4) (1992): 395; Stephen Elstub, *Towards a Deliberative and Associational Democracy* (Edinburgh: Edinburgh University Press, 2008), 113.

34. Smith, *Democratic Innovations*. Cf. Stephen Elstub, 'Mini-publics: Issues and Cases', in Stephen Elstub and Peter McLaverty (eds), *Deliberative Democracy: Issues and Cases* (Edinburgh: Edinburgh University Press, 2014), 166–88.

35. Archon Fung, 'Deliberative Democracy, Chicago Style: Grass-Roots Governance in Policing and Public Education', in Archon Fung and Erik Olin

Wright (eds), *Deepening Democracy* (London: Verso, 2003), 112. Naturally, normative judgements cannot be avoided in such situations. The choice of one of the available solutions always means greater gains or a greater burden for a particular group of citizens. Although this is inevitable, it is not a problem for IE. Of key significance is the fact that in such situations citizens have both normative competence and technical competence to make the decision.

36. Joseph F. Zimmerman, *The New England Town Meeting: Democracy in Action* (Westport, CT: Praeger, 1999), 185.

37. Van Reybrouck, *Against Elections*, 123–4. Cf. Lu Hong and Scott E. Page, 'Groups of Diverse Problem Solvers can Outperform Groups of High-ability Problem Solvers', *Proceedings of the National Academy of Sciences* 101(16) (2004): 16388.

38. Smith, *Democratic Innovations*, 53, 61.

39. In the largest cities, such as Warsaw and Kraków, it amounts to 4–5 per cent.

40. For example, Dąbrowa Górnicza, Legnica, Gorzów Wielkopolski.

41. Van Reybrouck, *Against Elections*, 128.

42. Smith, *Democratic Innovations*, 85.

43. See Clodagh Harris, 'Mini-publics: Design Choices and Legitimacy', in Stephen Elstub and Oliver Escobar (eds), *Handbook of Democratic Innovation and Governance* (Cheltenham: Edward Elgar, 2019), 46–7.

44. Smith, *Democratic Innovations*, 100.

45. See Robert E. Goodin, 'Enfranchising All Affected Interests, and Its Alternatives', *Philosophy & Public Affairs* 35 (2007): 43; Robert A. Dahl, *After the Revolution* (New Haven, CT: Yale University Press, 1970), 64.

46. Joshua Cohen, 'Reflections on Deliberative Democracy', in Thomas Christiano and John Christman (eds), *Contemporary Debates in Political Philosophy* (Malden, MA: Wiley-Blackwell, 2009), 247–63.

47. Cf. Hein Duijf, 'Should One Trust Experts? *Synthese* 199 (2021), 9290–1.

48. Philip E. Tetlock and Dan Gardner, *Superforecasting: The Art and Science of Prediction* (New York: Crown Publishers, 2015).

49. Rip, 'Constructing Expertise', 420.

50. Cf. Brennan, Surprenant and Winsberg, 'How Government Leaders Violated Their Epistemic Duties'.

51. At the time of writing (February 2022), Poland was obligated to do so until 17 December 2021.

52. See Sue Greenwood, *Future Journalism: Where We Are and Where We're Going* (New York: Routledge, 2017); Eliot Higgins, *We Are Bellingcat: Global Crime, Online Sleuths, and the Bold Future of News* (New York: Bloomsbury, 2021).

53. Richard Rorty, 'Education as Socialization and as Individualization', in Richard Rorty, *Philosophy and Social Hope* (London: Penguin, 1999), 114–26.

54. Cf. Nichols, *Death of Expertise*, 138.

55. This is why those who are sceptical about vaccine safety are for the most part university graduates. Because of this, Eyal diagnoses a kind of paradox

connected to rational faith in the authority of science. In order for the latter to be possible, citizens must be educated. But as citizens become more and more educated, the more they question the authority of science (Eyal, *The Crisis of Expertise*, 83). A similar view is held by Nichols, who believes that 'the death of expertise actually threatens to *reverse* the gains of years of knowledge among people who now assume they know more than they actually do' (Nichols, *Death of Expertise*, 20–1).

56. Martha C. Nussbaum, *Not for Profit: Why Democracy Needs the Humanities* (Princeton, NJ: Princeton University Press, 2010), 142.

57. Thomas Hobbes, *On the Citizen*, ed. Richard Tuck and Michael Silverthorne (Cambridge: Cambridge University Press, 1998), 140.

58. Cicero, 'On Rhetorical Invention', in Cicero, *The Orations*, Vol. IV, trans. Charles Duke Yonge (Loschberg: Jazzybee Verlag, printed Cratespace, Charleston, SC, 2017), I.I.1, 186.

59. Quentin Skinner, 'Hobbes's Changing Conception of Civil Science', in Quentin Skinner, *Visions of Politics, Vol. III: Hobbes and Civil Science* (Cambridge: Cambridge University Press, 2002), 67–8.

60. Thomas Hobbes, *Leviathan, or The Matter, Forme, and Power of Commonwealth Ecclesiasticall and Civill*, ed. Richard Tuck (Cambridge: Cambridge University Press, 1996), 483.

61. Cf. Lane, 'When the Experts are Uncertain', 110.

62. See d'Ancona, *Post-Truth*, ch. 5.

63. Sara E. Gorman and Jack M. Gorman, *Denying to the Grave: Why We Ignore the Science that Will Save Us* (New York: Oxford University Press, 2021), ch. 5.

64. Richard Rorty, 'Human Rights, Rationality, and Sentimentality', in Richard Rorty (ed.), *Truth and Progress: Philosophical Papers*, volume 3 (Cambridge: Cambridge University Press, 1991), 181–4.

65. d'Ancona, *Post-Truth*, 126.

EPILOGUE: LIVING IN A WORLD OF TOO HIGH EXPECTATIONS

The day of the plain man has passed. No criticism of democracy is more fashionable in our time than that which lays emphasis upon his incompetence. This is, we are told, a big and complex world, about which we have to find our way at our peril. The plain man is too ignorant and too uninterested to be able to judge the adequacy of the answers suggested to our problems . . . The plain man is simply obsolete in a world he has never been trained to understand. Either we must trust the making of fundamental decisions to experts, or there will be a breakdown in the machinery of government.[1]

Some texts are difficult to date based on their content alone. Harold Laski's essay from 1931, from which the above quote is drawn, is doubtless a striking case in point. It could easily be a voice in today's discussion on the idea and limits of democracy.

Laski claims that there is an irremovable tension between expertise and democracy. On the one hand, effective decision-making requires reliance on expertise. A policy based on intuition or ideology must be cost-effective. On the other hand, Laski warns against infinite trust in experts, and for two reasons. First, the pride of experts, who invariably think of themselves as infallible, all too often leads to bad decisions. Expertise, he states:

> breeds an inability to accept new views from the very depth of its preoccupation with its own conclusions. It too often fails to see round its subject. It sees its results out of perspective by making them the centre of relevance to which all other results must be related.[2]

'There is, in fact, no expert group which does not tend to deny that truth may possibly be found outside the boundary of its private Pyrenees.'[3] This attitude has a number of undesirable consequences. Above all,

156

experts repeatedly overestimate their ability and fail to appreciate the importance of other disciplines and experts. The expert 'unduly discounts experience which does not tally with his own',[4] 'because he practices a mystery, he tends to assume that, within his allotted field, men must accept without question the conclusions at which he has arrived'.[5] He tends not to notice that every seemingly technical decision or opinion involves choosing between values and advances some values. Moreover, the average expert is a creature of routine, unable or unwilling to adapt to new circumstances and challenges. He stubbornly interprets them through the lens of his prior knowledge, believing his prescriptions to be universal. Meanwhile, his knowledge is very rarely directly applicable to reality. He is also often driven by prejudice reflecting his social position, class or gender. All of this makes the expert in power a dangerous person, whose actions may have catastrophic consequences. This is why democratic politics must navigate between the Scylla of science and the Charybdis of common sense, between the ignorance of public opinion and the excessive self-assurance of professional experts. And there are no easy prescriptions for how to do this successfully.

Although philosophers' interest in the relationship between democracy and expertise goes back to ancient times, it is the twentieth century that has been dubbed the 'age of professional experts'.[6] The increasing professionalisation of political decision-making has sparked a growing interest in expert influence on politics. On the one hand, this discussion has been driven by the disclosure of successive empirical proofs of voter ignorance and of the ubiquitous and pervasive nature of the myths and prejudice that drive voters' political choices. From the architects of the American New Deal, through to champions of eugenics, centrally planned economies, to contemporary technocrats – epistocracy has enjoyed a considerable following throughout much of the twentieth century. It is also alive and well today as seen during the COVID-19 pandemic, when following expert recommendations was considered evidence of political reasonableness.

But the subject of expert fallibility has also returned time and again throughout the twentieth century in the literature and in public debates. Laski's pamphlet is an excellent case in point, as are the views of members of the progressive movement, the New Left, radical democrats and, finally, of today's populists. Is this discussion therefore doomed to reiterate the threadbare arguments invoked throughout the last 100 years? Not so, in my view. I believe that the last few decades have significantly advanced our understanding of social and political phenomena and of the various forms and possible modifications of the democratic system. Democratic innovations – initially posited only by radical democrats – have become an integral part of political practice in many parts of the world, from Brazil to EU member states.

Citizens' and theorists' perception of science and expertise has also changed. The former are increasingly well-educated, with plentiful access to information and opportunities to share their views. Paradoxically, Benjamin Barber's hope for the emergence of 'strong democracy' in which conscious and competent citizens would take over the helm has not been fulfilled.[7] Citizens are increasingly questioning the authority of experts – not out of ignorance or fear of the unknown, but because they believe they know better.[8] Often armed with ample evidence of expert bias and dependence on private corporations, and cognizant of past expert errors, citizens have ceased believing in the 'cartoon' vision of an infallible science.

The philosophy and sociology of scientific knowledge have also given us a whole new picture of expertise. STS and SSS scholars have problematised both the social role of experts and the idea of linear scientific progress, falsification, experiment replication, and the possibility of separating facts from values and technical problems from political ones. They have also helped us to understand the complexity of the phenomenon of expertise. Thanks to them, we know how hard it is to define expert knowledge and the expert, and to identify the limits of expert competence. Social epistemologists have shown us how problematic it is to differentiate not just between an expert and a fraud, but also between an expert and a layperson.

This knowledge should inform our understanding of political processes. Surprisingly, however, it rarely does. I think that if political theorists, especially liberal ones, looked for insight to STS more often, our current reflection on politics could shift into new gear. Meanwhile, political reflection is often based on a hurrah-optimistic and uncritical vision of science straight out of the 1950s. It stubbornly pins its hopes of solving humanity's most urgent problems on scientific progress. 'There is a connection between the rise of democracy and the growth of science . . . It cannot be a mere coincidence, however, that science actually has flourished in democratic periods'[9] – Henry Sigerist's thought from 1938 still reverberates in the mind of many a liberal today. The conviction that science and democracy are advancing along the same road, and that the advancement of one benefits the other, is a beautiful and optimistic picture which seems inadequate in an age marked by the triumph of illiberal democracy. It is therefore hardly a surprise that liberals attached to this view react with astonishment to the victories of post-truth and of illiberal democrats. It is also unsurprising that the main remedy they prescribe for post-truth is better civic education, flooding public debate with a stream of facts, and creating a space for lay–expert deliberation so that 'science can speak truth to power'. They are convinced that citizens would believe the science if they only understood it better, and that the scientific community would come to grips with the problems plaguing it if only it was granted full trust and autonomy.

In this attitude, they are reminiscent of Alfred Schütz, who in his famous essay 'The Well-informed Citizen' (1946) distinguished between three ideal types of citizen: the expert, the man on the street and the well-informed citizen. Experts possess knowledge 'restricted to a limited field, but therein . . . clear and distinct'.[10] The man in the street has only general knowledge '*sufficiently* precise for the practical purpose at hand. In all matters not connected with such practical purposes of immediate concern the man in the street accepts his sentiments and passions as guides'.[11] Finally, the well-informed citizen has neither specialist knowledge, nor follows sentiment. Instead, he seeks out information that helps him to 'arrive at *reasonably founded* opinions'.[12] The well-informed citizens is an ideal type. His or her perspective is neither too narrow like that of the expert, nor does he/she rely solely on their own intuitions like the man on the street. Only the well-informed citizen combines competence with a broad perspective. The well-informed citizen remains open to new information, not letting him-/herself fall into clichés, and he or she can weigh all the reasons. He or she is the only one suited to be a political decision-maker and his or her opinion should hold sway in a democracy. Instead of aggregating the thoughtless preferences of people on the street, politics should be responsive to the opinions of well-informed citizens.[13]

Both for Schütz and for liberal political theorists the solution to voters' irrationality is to educate them and awaken in them the desire for knowledge. The same perspective led J. S. Mill to endorse scholocracy – a form of government giving priority to the opinions of educated individuals. At the root of this view was the conviction that opposition to expertise was the result of ignorance, laziness or obscurantism.

In this book, I have argued otherwise. Education that does not teach one how to think critically and select credible information will not solve the problems of misinformation, manipulation and post-truth. Hammering in dry facts, even to the very limit of what can be absorbed, does not inoculate people against the messages spread by merchants of doubt. The age of post-truth is not only a transient phase in the development of liberal democracy. We would do better to make ourselves at home in it, rather than deny its existence or try to wait it out. Instead of shaking our fist at post-truth, we should give serious consideration to that which lies at its origin. And here, in my view, we come to the very nature of scientific research. One of the problems we encounter there is epistemic dependence – an inevitable gulf between experts and laypeople that makes it impossible for them to communicate.

In this book I have tried to show how being aware of the complex nature of the phenomenon of expertise can and should influence our vision of the role of experts in public debate. I started with the views that currently dominate liberal democratic thought. In Chapter 1, I distinguished the three most popular approaches to the problem in the said tradition. The first is based on faith in the high decision-making potential of citizens, who have very precise, albeit incomplete, knowledge about the social reality in which they live. If appropriately aggregated, this knowledge would give us the most comprehensive picture of reality and provide the best possible basis for political decisions. The second, somewhat less optimistic approach, sees citizens as capable of solving even the most difficult social problems as long as they have been subjected to the appropriate educational procedures. In other words, if citizens were only given the opportunity to familiarise themselves with the views of the scientific community and presented with the relevant facts, they would be capable of making conscious and informed decisions, including on issues requiring expertise. And, finally, the third approach is grounded in the belief that citizens do not need specialist knowledge at all in order to be in 'the driver's seat of society'. They must only be permitted to stake out goals and assess their implementation by experts. In my opinion, each of these approaches is based on a different set of epistemological premises, and by combining them in various configurations liberal political theorists run the risk of contradicting themselves.

To get a better idea of the nature of these inconsistencies, in Chapter 2, I analysed possible ways of defining expertise. I distinguished the three most popular definitions featured in the scientific literature. In the end, I chose the one highlighting the practical skills of the expert as the least controversial. According to this definition, one cannot look to formal credentials when determining if someone is an expert; instead, we should consider the person's long-term practice and ability to solve practical problems. This is why the group of experts is not limited to those working at universities and conducting lab research, but includes practitioners not associated with the world of science and unable to boast of a formal education. Anyone can be an expert as long as they have devoted an appropriate amount of time and attention to a specific issue and are hence able to solve problems occurring in a given field more effectively than others. This definition of an expert overlaps with the notion of the 'contributory expert' proposed by Harry Collins and Robert Evans.

In Chapter 3, I focused on the relationship between experts and laypeople. I made John Hardwig's conception of epistemic dependence my point of departure. I laid out two interpretations of it that are found in the literature. According to the first – radical – one, it is not only that experts and laypeople do not understand each other – experts do not even understand other experts. The increasing specialisation of science means that scholars are often unable to replicate each other's experiments and therefore to confirm their results. The functioning of science is therefore based on mutual trust between scholars. The vision of isolated 'cognitive islands' is, however, quite commonly rejected in the literature. An attenuated version is adopted much more frequently. According to this vision, epistemic dependence is a problem only in fields in which indirect criteria of expert assessment cannot be developed. It is not a norm, but a pathology of science. In fact, expert evaluation criteria that allow one to avoid epistemic dependence are usually available.

The most widely discussed set of criteria that laypeople can use when having to choose from among several mutually exclusive expert opinions is presented by Alvin Goldman. Four of these criteria are epistemic (since they ultimately boil down to assessing the competence of an expert or group of experts), and one is non-epistemic (since it does not require assessing the expert's competence). Trying to consider how one might attack these criteria, I concluded that none of the four epistemic criteria can make laypeople certain of their decision. When employing them, they will always in the end have to make their own decisions regarding the experts' credibility without any sure grounds. I decided that only the non-epistemic strategy, which tells the layperson to look for evidence of the expert's bias, allows the layperson to avoid epistemic dependence.

Taking as my point of departure the conclusions rolled out in Chapters 2 and 3, I evaluated the three approaches to the lay–expert relationship (informing contemporary liberal theory) laid out in Chapter 1. It turned out that all of them fall apart when confronted with the problem of epistemic dependence. The first, recommending universal civic empowerment, wrongly credits laypeople with the competence to decide on non-normative matters. The second, believing it is possible to educate citizens to the level of the 'well-informed citizen' – capable of debating the experts and of identifying the most trustworthy specialist – also fails. I examined its controversial nature in reference to the dispute around the notion of interactional expertise. I concluded that the claim that expert-level competence can be attained solely by conversing with experts without actually taking part in any research practices is extremely controversial. From this standpoint I examined the charges levelled at the concept of deliberative polls. Such polling is currently one of the most popular proposals for creating a platform of understanding between laypeople and experts. Deliberative polls are supposed to raise citizens' decision-making competence, combining the advantages of epistocracy and democracy. But scholars rarely focus on the disadvantages of polling, especially those stemming from the epistemic asymmetry between laypeople and experts. I concluded that randomly and representatively chosen poll participants have no way of challenging the competence and opinions of the experts consulted. I cited research showing that deliberative poll participants almost never question the information presented to them in the background materials and by the experts. And since polls do not make people question expert opinions, it is hard to see them as a solution to the problem of civic incompetence.

And, finally, as I have shown, the 'division of labour' model of the public sphere – promoted inter alia by supporters of deliberative systems – cannot realise the hopes pinned on it. The very idea of drawing a clear distinction between the political and the technical is itself already quite controversial. Doomed to epistemic dependence on experts, citizens can neither independently diagnose social problems, nor arrange them into a hierarchy, nor, finally, assess the implementation of proposals. As a result, they are far from having the independence and decisive autonomy that exponents of the 'division of labour' model readily attribute to them.

In the final chapter, I considered the implications of my prior considerations for political practice. I counselled cautious scepticism with regard to the possibility of providing epistemic justification for participatory democracy. Such justification seems viable to me only in very rare instances in which decisions are made by groups of citizens who are at once contributory experts. Since effective governance requires specialist knowledge, and laypeople are doomed to epistemic dependence on experts, only epistocracy is epistemically justified. The most effective form of epistocracy – at the same time the only one that enjoys social legitimacy – is inclusive epistocracy. This solution promotes the use of democratic innovations, although it warns against the inclusion of laypeople in them. Since only experts are capable of debating on non-normative issues, only contributory experts, including practitioners specialising in an issue, should take part in these innovations. Only they can have an equal discussion with the certified experts. Unfortunately, the applicability of this tool is very limited. The contributory expertise of such practitioners is usually restricted to local issues. Hence, the limits of employing inclusive epistocracy.

Inclusive epistocracy is the outcome of a compromise between the requirements of effectiveness, on the one hand, and political legitimacy, on the other, so between technocratic rule and populist rule. As with most compromises, it cannot fully satisfy anyone. Supporters of radical democracy see it as curtailing civic participation. From their perspective, questioning the epistemic potential of participatory democracy is an inadmissible concession to epistocracy. Nor will it satisfy proponents of epistocracy, who see it as an unfounded attempt to empower the man on the street.

For the sake of honesty, I have to make it clear that I am not the first person to propose this solution. Similar proposals have been put forward by Eva Krick and others. According to Krick, decision-making should first and foremost involve stakeholders who have the requisite knowledge. She writes: 'stakeholders often have considerable expertise in their field, which can qualify them for the double role of expert and citizen representative'.[14] Krick supports the use of democratic innovations, but remains critical of the most popular strategies of selecting their participants. She identifies three possibilities, considering two of them – open access and random selection – as misguided. The first produces biased participants and is conducive to group homogeneity and non-representativeness, since those who usually volunteer to take part in the work of such groups are people with well-established and ingrained views who are unwilling to change them. They also tend not to be socially representative and to be educated middle-class men. The random selection method, on the other hand, must contend with the problem of quickly raising participants' competence to allow them to understand the experts. Those selected are usually not interested in the subject of the discussion, which means that they cannot gain even a modicum of knowledge about the issue on the table. Under such circumstances the relationship between the democratic innovations' participants and the experts is reminiscent of that between a tutor and a student cramming for an exam. The latter has no time to thoughtfully assess the materials he or she is seeing for the first time in his or her life.

For these reasons Krick recommends what she calls targeted selection. 'Targeted selection is based on a reason-based, purposeful decision (in contrast to random selection), that is taken by an appointing authority, not the participants themselves (as under open access). Its main advantage is that rational, merit-based selection is possible.'[15] The objective is to find people who are at once experts, stakeholders and citizens representative of the broader community.[16] Krick suggests recruiting them through intermediary organisations, which themselves are also societal stakeholders: 'NGOs', 'advocacy groups', 'charities', 'civil society organisations', 'pressure groups' and 'interest associations'. I agree with Krick on the necessity of taking knowledge and the problem of epistemic asymmetry into account when recruiting the participants of democratic innovations. However, I am much more sceptical than she is when it comes to the possibility of reforming the political system through the use of such innovations. There will always be controversies regarding how their participants are selected, and their application is quite limited.

This is why the final chapter ends on a somewhat pessimistic note. In most situations, laypeople (citizens and politicians) are going to have to blindly trust the experts, their only method of challenging the specialist narrative being not to question experts' competence but their motivations. This is why it is imperative to implement mechanisms that will systemically bring expert bias to light. Only then will citizens have an effective tool of expert evaluation. I discuss three possibilities for implementing such a tool in this book: education instilling critical thinking; promoting a culture of whistle-blowing; and a rhetorical offensive on the part of science. Each of these is supposed to eliminate the problems caused by epistemic dependence in the lay–expert relationship. The rhetorical offensive of science is supposed to eliminate the disproportion that currently exists between the message of science and that of the enemies of science – the merchants of doubt. The purpose of teaching critical thinking skills is to help citizens identify the least credible sources of information. And, finally, promoting whistle-blowing is supposed to bring to light evidence of expert bias. None of these solutions can conquer post-truth or solve the problem of misinformation and manipulation. However, it is to be hoped that they will limit them to a large extent. In most cases, the burden of decision-making will fall on incompetent politicians and citizens anyway.

What is the most important message to take away from these reflections, crowned as they are with a not-so-optimistic conclusion? First, we should abandon hope of finding ideal solutions to our most burning problems and of the post-truth era coming to a swift end, or the ultimate success of liberal democracy and the education of 'well-informed citizens' who will be paragons of epistemic virtue and radically alter the shape of political debates and of politics itself. John Dewey believed that such citizens were bound to eventually emerge on the political scene in democratic countries.[17] He subscribed to an experimental vision of democracy and saw the latter as a self-perfecting mechanism. Its parts – the citizens – learn from their mistakes and ultimately develop decision-making competence. I, however, believe these hopes to be in vain. 'Well-informed citizens' will not just appear out of the blue, nor can they be educated into existence. None of the types of general education available today can make one capable of competently navigating expertise and of correctly identifying the best expert in the event of an expert dispute. Epistemic dependence is an unavoidable phenomenon. This means that the relationship between citizens and scientists will always come down to trust or lack thereof.

We are doomed to live in a world that doubts science. However, I do not think that we are doomed to live in a world of populism. This is why we have to lower our expectations. We cannot expect citizens to trust experts or to understand their recommendations. Politics must consist in managing epistemic asymmetry. It must involve navigating two extremes. The first extreme is waiting for the dawn of the enlightened citizen who will save democracy from the obtuseness of the masses, give credit to science and speak up on its behalf. Collins and Evans hope for such a world, inhabited by citizens who believe in the values of science. The other vision is that of radical scepticism with regard to science, denial of its authority and upholding the 'wisdom of the people' as the ultimate guide. This is the way of populism which subordinates everything, including science, to short-term interest. The road of liberal democracy must be the third way.

Secondly, we should curb our faith in the powers of experts, although we should not lose it altogether. On the one hand, we must remember that expertise often disappoints, and will continue to disappoint. It develops on an ad hoc basis in response to major problems that call for immediate solutions. It is often limited to showing us the reasons for our failure, rather than giving us actionable advice. This is inevitable. We expect too much of expertise – an expectation fuelled by the over-confidence of its dispatchers. Both laypeople and experts should be more aware of the limitations of science. It will spare us all disappointment and limit the supply of fuel that nourishes contemporary populism. However, we should not gravitate to the other extreme and completely doubt expertise, embracing unbridled relativism. Experts do exist, including among ordinary citizens. They stand out on account of their knowledge, skills and ability to solve specific problems. An effective democracy must learn to use them as a resource, not ignore their knowledge.

Thirdly, and finally, we should draw heavily from the science studies tradition. This will help us to look at the problem of expertise in a multi-dimensional way and break with the 'cartoon' vision of science and a monolithic view of expert knowledge. We will also start to notice experts where we previously saw just incompetent ordinary citizens. The division into experts and laypeople is not clear-cut and obvious. This lesson has been well-learned in STS, but is still not sufficiently appreciated in political theory and practice.

NOTES

1. Harold J. Laski, *The Limitations of the Expert* (London: Fabian Society, 1931), 3.
2. Laski, *The Limitations*, 4.
3. Laski, *The Limitations*, 6.
4. Laski, *The Limitations*, 6.

5. Laski, *The Limitations*, 7.
6. Steven Rayner, 'Democracy in the Age of Assessment: Reflections on the Roles of Expertise and Democracy in Public-Sector Decision Making', *Science and Public Policy* 30(3) (2003): 163.
7. Barber, *Strong Democracy*. Cf. Benjamin Barber, 'Three Scenarios for the Future of Technology and Strong Democracy', *Political Science Quarterly* 13(4) (1998/9): 585–8.
8. Daniel Innerarity, *The Democracy of Knowledge*, trans. Sandra Kinkery (New York: Bloomsbury Academic, 2013), 90–1.
9. Henry E. Sigerist, 'Science and Democracy', *Science & Society* 2(3) (1938): 291.
10. Alfred Schütz, 'The Well-Informed Citizen: An Essay on the Social Distribution of Knowledge', *Social Research* 13(4) (1946): 465.
11. Schütz, 'The Well-Informed Citizen', 465.
12. Schütz, 'The Well-Informed Citizen', 466.
13. Schütz, 'The Well-Informed Citizen', 478.
14. Krick, 'Creating Participatory Expert Bodies', 35.
15. Krick, 'Creating Participatory Expert Bodies', 40.
16. Krick, 'Creating Participatory Expert Bodies', 41.
17. Dewey, *Public and its Problems*, 208. Cf. Anderson, 'The Epistemology of Democracy', 13.

BIBLIOGRAPHY

Adam, David, 'Special Report: The Simulations Driving the World's Response to COVID-19. How Epidemiologists Rushed to Model the Coronavirus Pandemic', *Nature* 2 April 2020, available at: https://www.nature.com/articles/d41586-020-01003-6, last accessed 24 June 2021.

Adler, Jonathan, 'Testimony, Trust, Knowing', *Journal of Philosophy* 91(5) (1994): 264–75.

Almassi, Ben, 'Climate Change, Epistemic Trust, and Expert Trustworthiness', *Ethics and the Environment* 17(2) (2012): 29–49.

Andersen, Hanne and Susanne Wagenknecht, 'Epistemic Dependence in Interdisciplinary Groups', *Synthese* 190 (2013): 1881–98.

Anderson, Elisabeth, 'The Epistemology of Democracy', *Episteme: A Journal of Social Epistemology* 3(1/2) (2006): 8–22.

Anderson, Elisabeth, 'Democracy: Instrumental vs. Non-Instrumental Value', in Thomas Christiano and John Christman (eds), *Contemporary Debates in Political Philosophy*. Malden, MA: Wiley-Blackwell, 2009, 213–27.

Anderson, Elizabeth, 'Democracy, Public Policy, and Lay Assessment of Scientific Testimony', *Episteme* 8(2) (2011): 144–64.

Aspinall, Willy, 'A Route to More Tractable Expert Advice', *Nature* 463(7279) (2010): 294–5.

Azmanova, Albena, 'Deliberative Conflict and "The Better Argument" Mystique', *Good Society* 19(1) (2010): 48–54.

Baber, Walter F. and Robert V. Bartlett, *Deliberative Environmental Politics: Democracy and Ecological Rationality*. Cambridge, MA: MIT Press, 2005.

Bachmann, Reinhard and Akbar Zaheer (eds), *Handbook of Trust Research*. Northampton: Edward Elgar, 2008.

Bachrach, Peter, 'Elite Consensus and Democracy', *Journal of Politics* 24(3) (1962): 439–52.

Bachrach, Peter and Ariel Botwinick, *Power and Empowerment: A Radical Theory of Participatory Democracy*. Philadelphia, PA: Temple University Press, 1992.

Baier, Annette, 'Trust and Antitrust', *Ethics* 96(2) (1986): 231–60.

Barber, Benjamin, *Strong Democracy: Participatory Democracy for a New Age.* Berkeley: University of California Press, 1984.

Barber, Benjamin, 'Three Scenarios for the Future of Technology and Strong Democracy', *Political Science Quarterly* 13(4) (1998/9): 573–89.

Barber, Bernard, *The Logic and Limits of Trust.* New Brunswick, NJ: Rutgers University Press, 1983.

Barber, Bernard, 'Trust in Science', *Minerva* 25(1/2) (1987):

Barnes, Barry, *T. S. Kuhn and Social Science.* New York: Columbia University Press, 1982.

Barnes, Barry, *About Science.* Oxford: Blackwell, 1985.

Bättig, Michèle B. and Thomas Bernauer, 'National Institutions and Global Public Goods: Are Democracies More Cooperative in Climate Change Policy?' *International Organization* 63(2) (2009): 281–308.

Beck, Ulrich, *Risk Society: Towards a New Modernity*, trans. Mark Ritter. London: Sage, 1992.

Beck, Ulrich, 'World Risk Society as Cosmopolitan Society? Ecological Questions in a Framework of Manufactured Uncertainties', *Theory, Culture & Society* 13(4) (1996): 1–32.

Begley, C. Glenn and Lee M. Ellis, 'Raise Standards for Preclinical Cancer Research', *Nature* 483 (2012): 531–3.

Bernard, S., A. Enayati, L. Redwood, H. Roger and T. Binstock, 'Autism: A Novel Form of Mercury Poisoning', *Medical Hypotheses* 56(4) (2001): 462–71.

Bernstein, Richard J., 'Dewey's Vision of Radical Democracy', in Mooly Cochran (ed.), *The Cambridge Companion to Dewey.* Cambridge: Cambridge University Press, 2010, 188–308.

Best, Jacqueline, 'Technocratic Exceptionalism', *International Political Sociology* 12(4) (2018): 328–45.

Best, Jacqueline, 'Bring Politics Back to Monetary Policy: How Technocratic Exceptionalism Fuels Populism', *Foreign Affairs*, 6 December 2017, available at: https://www.foreignaffairs.com/articles/world/2017-12-06/bring-politicsback-monetary-policy, last accessed 30 March 2020.

Bezemer, Dirk J., '"No One Saw This Coming" Understanding Financial Crisis Through Accounting Models', *Accounting Organizations and Society* 35(7) (2010): 676–88.

Bickerton, Christopher and Carlo Invernizzi Accetti, 'Populism and Technocracy: Opposites or Complements?' *Critical Review of International Social and Political Philosophy* 20(2) (2017): 186–206.

Bieńkowska, Zofia, Piotr Drygas and Przemysław Sadura, *Nie nasza wina, nie nasz problem. Katastrofa klimatyczna w oczach Polek i Polaków podczas pandemii.* Warsaw: Heinrich Boll Stiftung, 2021.

Bijker, Wiebe, 'Why and How Technology Matters?' in Robert E. Goodin, Charles Tilly (eds), *Oxford Handbook of Contextual Analysis*. Oxford: Oxford University Press, 2006.

Bijker, Wiebe E., Roland Bal and Ruud Hendricks, *The Paradox of Scientific Authority: The Role of Scientific Advice in Democracies*. Cambridge, MA: MIT Press, 2009.

Black, Edwin, *War Against the Weak: Eugenics and America's Campaign to Create a Master Race*. New York: Four Walls Wight Windows, 2003.

Bohman, James, *Public Deliberation: Pluralism, Complexity, and Democracy*. Cambridge, MA: MIT Press, 1996.

Bohman, James, 'The Coming of Age of Deliberative Democracy', *Journal of Political Philosophy* 6(6) (1998): 400–25.

Bohman, James, 'Deliberative Democracy and the Epistemic Benefits of Diversity', *Episteme* 3(3) (2006): 175–91.

Brennan, Jason, *Against Democracy*. Princeton, NJ: Princeton University Press, 2016.

Brennan, Jason, Chris Surprenant and Eric Winsberg, 'How Government Leaders Violated Their Epistemic Duties during the SARS-CoV-2 Crisis', *Kennedy Institute Journal of Ethics* 2020: 1–38.

Brewer, Scott, 'Scientific Expert Testimony and Intellectual Due Process', *Yale Law Journal* 107(6) (1998): 1535–681.

Breyer, Stephen, *Breaking the Vicious Circle: Toward Effective Risk Regulation*. Cambridge, MA: Harvard University Press, 1993.

Brossard, Dominique and Bruce V. Lewenstein, 'A Critical Appraisal of Models of Public Understanding of Science: Using Practice to Inform Theory', in LeeAnn Kahlor and Patricia A. Stout (eds), *Communicating Science: New Agendas in Communication*. New York: Routledge, 2010, 11–39.

Brown, Mark B., *Science in Democracy: Expertise, Institutions, and Representation*. Cambridge, MA: MIT Press, 2009.

Brown, Mark B., 'Expertise and Deliberative Democracy', in Stephen Elstub and Peter McLaverty (eds), *Deliberative Democracy: Issues and Cases*. Edinburgh: Edinburgh University Press, 2014, 50–68.

Brown, Mark B., 'Politicizing Science: Conceptions of Politics in Science and Technology Studies', *Social Studies of Science* (2014): 1–28.

Bruff, Ian, 'The Rise of Authoritarian Neoliberalism', *Rethinking Marxism* 26(1) (2014): 113–29.

Buskens, Vincent, Rense Corten and Chris Snijders (eds), *Advances in the Sociology of Trust and Cooperation*. Berlin: De Gruyter, 2020.

Busuioc, Elena Madalina, *European Agencies: Law and Practices of Accountability*. Oxford: Oxford University Press, 2013.

Busuioc, Elena Madalina, 'Blurred Areas of Responsibility: European Agencies' Scientific "Opinions" Under Scrutiny', in Monika Ambrus, Karin Arts, Ellen Hey and Helena Raulus (eds), *The Role of 'Experts' in International and European Decision-Making Processes*. Cambridge: Cambridge University Press, 2014, 388–94.

Callon, Michel, 'Elements of a Sociology of Translation: Domestication of the Scallops and the Fishermen of St Brieuc Bay', in John Law (ed.), *Power, Action and Belief: A New Sociology of Knowledge?* London: Routledge, 1986, 196–233.

Caplan, Brian, *The Myth of Rational Voter: Why Democracies Choose Bad Policies*. Princeton, NJ: Princeton University Press, 2007.

Cartwright, Nancy, *How the Laws of Physics Lie*. Oxford and New York: Clarendon and Oxford University Press, 1983.

Castree, Noel, *Making Sense of Nature: Representation, Politics and Democracy*. London: Routledge, 2014.

Ceccarelli, Leah, 'Manufactured Scientific Controversy: Science, Rhetoric, and Public Debate', *Rhetoric and Public Affairs* 14(2) (2011): 195–228.

Chalmers, Adam William, 'Getting a Seat at the Table: Capital, Capture and Expert Groups in the European Union', *West European Politics* 37(5) (2014): 976–92.

Chambers, Simone, 'Deliberative Democratic Theory', *Annual Review of Political Science* 6 (2003): 307–26.

Chang, Ha-Joon, *23 Things They Don't Tell You About Capitalism*. New York: Bloomsbury, 2010.

Cholbi, Michael, 'Moral Expertise and the Credentials Problem', *Ethical Theory and Moral Practice* 10 (2007): 323–34.

Christiano, Thomas, *The Rule of the Many: Fundamental Issues in Democratic Theory*. Boulder, CO: Westview Press, 1996.

Christiano, Thomas, *The Constitution of Equality: Democratic Authority and its Limits*. Oxford: Oxford University Press, 2008.

Christiano, Thomas, *Rational Deliberation Among Experts and Citizens*, in John Parkinson and Jane Mansbridge (eds), *Deliberative Systems*. Cambridge: Cambridge University Press, 2012, 27–51.

Cicero, 'On Rhetorical Invention', in Cicero, *The Orations*, vol. IV, trans. Charles Duke Yonge. Loschberg: Jazzybee Verlag, printed Cratespace, Charleston, SC, 2017.

Coady, David, 'When Experts Disagree', *Episteme* 3(1/2) (2006): 68–79.

Coady, David, *What to Believe Now? An Epistemology to Contemporary Issues*. Malden, MA: Wiley-Blackwell, 2012.

Coady, David, 'Epistemology and Climate Change', in Miranda Fricker, Peter J. Graham, David Henderson and Nikolaj J.L.L. Pedersen (eds), *The Routledge Handbook of Social Epistemology*. New York: Routledge, 2019, 466–73.

Cohen, Joshua, 'Procedure and Substance in Deliberative Democracy', in Seyla Benhabib (ed.), *Democracy and Difference: Contesting the Boundaries of the Political*. Princeton, NJ: Princeton University Press, 1996, 95–119.

Cohen, Joshua, 'Reflections on Deliberative Democracy', in Thomas Christiano and John Christman (eds), *Contemporary Debates in Political Philosophy*. Malden, MA: Wiley-Blackwell, 2009, 247–63.

Cohen, Joshua and Archon Fung, 'Radical Democracy', *Swiss Journal of Political Science* 10(4) (2004): 23–34.

Cohen Joshua, and Joel Rogers, 'Secondary Associations and Democratic Governance', *Politics and Society* 20(4) (1992): 393–472.

Cohen Joshua and Charles Sabel, 'Directly-Deliberative Polyarchy', *European Law Journal* 3(4) (1977): 313–42.

Colander, David and Roland Kupers, *Complexity and the Art: Of Public Policy*. Princeton, NJ: Princeton University Press, 2014.

Collins, Harry M., 'The TEA Set: Tacit Knowledge and Scientific Networks', *Science Studies* 4 (1974): 165–86.

Collins, Harry M., *Changing Order: Replication and Induction in Scientific Practice*. London: Sage, 1985.

Collins, Harry M., 'Four Kinds of Knowledge, Two (or Maybe Three) Kinds of Embodiment, and Question of Artificial Intelligence', in Mark Wrathall and Jeff Malpas (eds), *Heidegger, Coping, and Cognitive Science: Essays in Honor of Hubert L. Dreyfus*, vol. 2. Cambridge, MA MIT Press, 2000, 179–95.

Collins, Harry M., 'Interactional Expertise as a Third Kind of Knowledge', *Phenomenology and the Cognitive Sciences* 3(2) (2004): 125–43.

Collins, Harry, 'Language and Practice', *Social Studies of Science* 41(2) (2011): 271–300.

Collins, Harry, *Are We All Scientific Experts Now?* Cambridge: Polity, 2014.

Collins, Harry and Robert Evans, 'Third Wave of Science Studies: Studies of Expertise and Experience', *Social Studies of Science* 32(2) (2002): 235–96.

Collins, Harry and Robert Evans, *Rethinking Expertise*. Chicago: University of Chicago Press, 2007.

Collins, Harry and Robert Evans, *Why Democracies Need Science*. Cambridge: Polity, 2017.

Collins, Harry and Gary Sanders, 'They Give You the Keys and Say "Drive It": Managers, Referred Expertise, and Other Expertises', *Studies in History and Philosophy of Science* (Special Issue: Case Studies of Expertise and Experience, ed. Harry Collins) 38(4) (2007): 621–41.

Collins, Harry M., Robert Evans and Martin Weinel, 'STS as Science or Politics?' *Social Studies of Science* 47(4) (2017): 580–6.

Collins, Harry M., Robert Evans and Martin Weinel, *Experts and the Will of the People*. London: Palgrave 2020.

Collins, Harry, Martin Weinel and Robert Evans, 'The Politics and Policy of the Third Wave: New Technologies and Society', *Critical Policy Studies* 4(2) (2010): 185–201.

Cook, John, Dana Nuccitelli, et al., 'Quantifying the Consensus on Anthropogenic Global Warming in the Scientific Literature', *Environmental Research Letters* 8 (2013): 1–7.

d'Ancona, Matthew, *Post-Truth: The New War on Truth and How to Fight Back*. London: Ebury Press, 2017.

Dahl, Robert A., *After the Revolution*. New Haven, CT: Yale University Press, 1970.

Dahl, Robert A., *Democracy and Its Critics*. New Haven, CT: Yale University Press, 1989.

de Ridder, Jeroen, 'Epistemic Dependence and Collective Scientific Knowledge', *Synthese* 191 (2014): 37–53.

Dewey, John, *The Public and Its Problems*. New York: H. Holt, 1927.

Dietrich, Franz and Kai Spiekermann, 'Epistemic Democracy with Defensible Premises', *Economics and Philosophy* 29(1) (2013): 87–120.

Douglass, Heather, *Science, Policy, and the Value-Free Ideal*. Pittsburgh, PA: University of Pittsburgh Press, 2009.

Dreyfus, Hubert, 'Responses', in Mark Wrathall and Jeff Malpas (eds), *Heidegger, Authenticity, and Modernity: Essays in Honor of Hubert Dreyfus*, vol. 1. Cambridge, MA: MIT Press, 2000, 305–41.

Dryzek, John, *Deliberative Democracy and Beyond: Liberals, Critics, Contestations*. Oxford: Oxford University Press, 2000.

Dryzek, John, 'The Forum, the System, and the Polity: Three Varieties of Democratic Theory', *Political Theory* 45 (2017): 610–36.

Duijf, Hein, 'Should One Trust Experts? *Synthese* 199 (2021): 9289–312.

Durant, Darrin, 'Models of Democracy in Social Studies of Science', *Social Studies of Science* 41 (2011): 691–714.

Easterly, William, *The Tyranny of Experts*. New York: Basic Books, 2013.

Elga, Adam, 'How to Disagree about How to Disagree', in Richard Feldman and Ted Warfield (eds), *Disagreement*. Oxford: Oxford University Press, 2010, 175–86.

Elster, Jon, 'The Market and the Forum: Three Varieties of Political Theory', in James Bohman and William Rehg (eds), *Deliberative Democracy: Essays on Reason and Politics*. Cambridge, MA: MIT Press, 1997, 3–33.

Elstub, Stephen, *Towards a Deliberative and Associational Democracy*. Edinburgh: Edinburgh University Press, 2008.

Elstub, Stephen, 'The Third Generation of Deliberative Democracy', *Political Studies Review* 8 (2010): 291–307.

Elstub, Stephen, 'Mini-publics: Issues and Cases', in Stephen Elstub and Peter McLaverty (eds), *Deliberative Democracy: Issues and Cases*. Edinburgh: Edinburgh University Press, 2014, 166–88.

Elstub, Stephen, Selen A. Ercan and Ricardo Fabrino Mendonça (eds), *Deliberative Systems in Theory and Practice*. New York: Routledge, 2021.

Epstein, Steven, 'The Construction of Lay Expertise: AIDS Activism and the Forging of Credibility in the Reform of Clinical Trials', *Science, Technology, & Human Values* 20(4) (1995): 408–37.

Epstein, Steven. *Impure Science: AIDS, Activism, and the Politics of Knowledge*. Berkeley: University of California Press, 1996.

Ercan, Selen A., Carolyn M. Hendriks and John Boswell, 'Studying Public Deliberation after the Systemic Turn: The Crucial Role for Interpretive Research', *Policy and Politics* 45 (2017): 195–212.

Esterling, Kevin M., *The Political Economy of Expertise: Information and Efficiency in American National Politics*. Ann Arbor: University of Michigan Press, 2004.

Estlund, David., 'Making Truth Safe for Democracy', in David Copp, Jean Hampton and John E. Roemer (eds), *The Idea of Democracy*. Cambridge: Cambridge University Press, 1993, 71–100.

Estlund, David M., 'Beyond Fairness and Deliberation: The Epistemic Dimension of Democratic Authority', in James Bohman and William Rehg (eds), *Deliberative Democracy: Essays on Reason and Politics* (Cambridge, MA: MIT Press, 1997), 173–204.

Estlund, David M., *Democratic Authority: A Philosophical Framework*. Princeton, NJ: Princeton University Press, 2008.

Evans, Robert, 'Science and Democracy in the Third Wave: Elective Modernism, Not Epistocracy', in Cathrine Holst (ed.), *Expertise and Democracy*. Oslo: ARENA, 2014, 85–102.

Eyal, Gil, *The Crisis of Expertise*. Cambridge: Polity, 2019.

Fischer, Frank, *Technocracy and the Politics of Expertise*. London: Sage, 1990.

Fischer, Frank, *Citizens, Experts, and the Environment*. Durham, NC: Duke University Press, 2000

Fischer, Frank, *Democracy and Expertise. Reorienting Policy Inquiry*. Oxford: Oxford University Press, 2009.

Fish, Stanley, *Is There a Text in This Class? The Authority of Interpretive Communities*. Cambridge, MA: Harvard University Press, 1980.

Fish, Stanley, *Doing What Comes Naturally: Change, Rhetoric, and the Practice of Theory in Literary and Legal Studies*. Durham, NC: Duke University Press, 1989.

Fish, Stanley, 'Mutual Respect as a Device of Exclusion', in Stephen Macedo (ed.), *Deliberative Politics: Essays on 'Democracy and Disagreement'*. New York: Oxford University Press, 1999, 88–102.

Fishkin, James S., *Democracy and Deliberation: New Directions for Democratic Control*. New Haven, CT: Yale University Press, 1991.

Fishkin, James S., 'Bringing Deliberation to Democracy', *Good Society* 5(3) (1995): 45–9.

Fishkin, James S., *The Voice of the People: Public Opinion and Democracy*. New Haven, CT: Yale University Press, 1995.

Fishkin, James S., 'Toward Deliberative Democracy: Experimenting with an Ideal', in Stephen L. Elkin and Karol Edward Sołtan (eds), *Citizen Competence and Democratic Institutions*. University Park: Pennsylvania State University Press, 1999, 279–90.

Fishkin, James S., *When the People Speak: Deliberative Democracy and Public Consultation*. Oxford: Oxford University Press, 2009.

Fishkin, James S., 'Response to Critics of When the People Speak: The Deliberative Deficit and What To Do About It', *Good Society* 19(1) (2010): 68–76.

Fishkin, James S., 'Why Deliberative Polling? Reply to Gleason', *Critical Review: A Journal of Politics and Society* 23(3) (2011): 405–12.

Fishkin, James S. and Robert C. Luskin, 'Deliberation and Better Citizens', 2002, available at: http://cdd.stanford.edu/research/papers/2002/bettercitizens.pdf.

Fishkin, James S. and Robert C. Luskin, 'Deliberative Polling, Public Opinion, and Democracy: The Case of the National Issues Convention', 2005, available at: http://cdd.stanford.edu/research/papers/2005/issues-convention.pdf.

Fishkin, James S. and Robert C. Luskin, 'Experimenting with a Democratic Ideal: Deliberative Polling and Public Opinion', *Acta Politica* 40 (2005): 284–98.

Fishkin, James S., Baogang He, Robert C. Luskin and Alice Siu, 'Deliberative Democracy in an Unlikely Place: Deliberative Polling in China', *British Journal of Political Science* 40 (2010): 435–48.

Fishkin, James S., Robert C. Luskin and Roger Jowell, 'Considered Opinions: Deliberative Polling in Britain', *British Journal of Political Science* 32(3) (2002): 458–9.

Foley, Richard, *Intellectual Trust in Oneself and Others*. Cambridge: Cambridge University Press, 2004.

Fricker, Elizabeth, 'Testimony and Epistemic Authority', in Jennifer Lackey and Ernest Sosa (eds), *The Epistemology of Testimony*. Oxford: Clarendon, 2006, 225–50.

Friedberg, M., B. Saffran, T. J. Stinson, W. Nelson and C. L. Bennett, 'Evaluation of Conflict of Interest in Economic Analyses of New Drugs Used in Oncology', *Journal of the American Medical Association* 282(15) (1999): 1453–7.

Friedman, Jeffrey, *Power Without Knowledge: A Critique of Technocracy*. Oxford: Oxford University Press, 2020.

Fuerstein, Michael, 'Epistemic Democracy and the Social Character of Knowledge', *Episteme. A Journal of Social Epistemology* 5(1) (2008): 74–93.

Fukuyama, Francis, *Trust: The Social Virtues and the Creation of Prosperity*. New York: Free Press, 1995.

Fuller, Steve, *Social Epistemology*. Bloomington: Indiana University Press, 1991.

Fuller, Steve, 'The Constitutively Social Character of Expertise', in Evan Selinger and Robert P. Crease (eds), *The Philosophy of Expertise*. New York: Columbia University Press, 2006, 342–57.

Fuller, Steve, *The Knowledge Book*. London: Acumen, 2007.

Fuller, Steve, *Post-Truth: Knowledge as a Power Game*. London: Anthem, 2018.

Fuller, Steve, *A Player's Guide to the Post-Truth Condition: The Name of the Game*. London: Anthem, 2020.

Fung, Archon, 'Deliberative Democracy, Chicago Style: Grass-Roots Governance in Policing and Public Education', in Archon Fung and Erik Olin Wright (eds), *Deepening Democracy*. London: Verso, 2003.

Fung, Archon, *Empowered Participation: Reinventing Urban Democracy*. Princeton, NJ: Princeton University Press, 2006.

Fung, Archon, 'Putting the Public Back into Governance: The Challenges of Citizen Participation and Its Future', *Public Administration Review* 75(4) (2015): 513–22.

Fung, Archon and Erik Olin Wright, 'Deepening Democracy: Innovations in Empowered Participatory Governance', *Politics and Society* 29 (2001): 5–41.

Gaon, Stella and Stephen P. Norris, 'The Undecidable Grounds of Scientific Expertise', *Journal of Philosophy of Education* 35(2) (2001): 187–201.

Gastil, John, Chiara Bacci and Michael Dollinger, 'Is Deliberation Neutral? Patterns of Attitude Change During "The Deliberative Polls™"', *Journal of Public Deliberation* 6(2) (2010): doi: https://doi.org/10.16997/jdd.107.

Gerber, Elizabeth, *The Populist Paradox: Interest Group Influence and the Promise of Direct Legislation*. Princeton, NJ: Princeton University Press, 2011.

Gieryn, Thomas F., 'Boundary-Work and the Demarcation of Science from Non-Science: Strains and Interests in Professional Ideologies of Scientists', *American Sociological Review* 48 (1983): 781–95.

Gilligan, Jonathan M., 'Expertise Across Disciplines: Establishing Common Ground in Interdisciplinary Disaster Research Teams', *Risk Analysis* 2019: DOI:10.1111/risa.13407.

Gleason, Laurel S., 'Revisiting "The Voice of the People": An Evaluation of the Claims and Consequences of Deliberative Polling', *Critical Review: A Journal of Politics and Society* 23(3) (2012): 371–92.

Goldman, Alvin, *Knowledge in a Social World*. Oxford: Oxford University Press, 1999.

Goldman, Alvin, 'Experts: Which Ones Should We Trust?' in Alvin Goldman and Dennis Whitcomb (eds.), *Social Epistemology: Essential Readings*. Oxford: Oxford University Press, 2011, 109–33.

Goldman, Alvin, 'Expertise' *Topoi* 37(1) (2018): 3–10.

Goodhart, Charles and Rosa Lastra, 'Populism and Central Bank Independence', *Open Economies Review* 29 (2018): 49–68.

Goodin, Robert E., 'Enfranchising All Affected Interests, and Its Alternatives', *Philosophy & Public Affairs* 35 (2007): 40–68.

Góra Magdalena, Cathrine Holst and Marta Warat (eds), *Expertisation and Democracy in Europe*. New York: Routledge, 2018.

Gorman, Sara E. and Jack M. Gorman, *Denying to the Grave: Why We Ignore the Science that Will Save Us*. New York: Oxford University Press, 2021.

Greenberg, Jack, *Crusaders in the Courts: Legal Battles of the Civil Rights Movement*. New York: Twelve Tables Press, 1995.

Greenwood, Sue, *Future Journalism: Where We Are and Where We're Going*. New York: Routledge, 2017.

Grofman, Bernard, Guillermo Owen and Scott Feld, 'Thirteen Theorems in Search of the Truth', *Theory and Decision* 15 (1983): 261–78.

Gutmann, Amy and Dennis Thompson, 'Moral Conflict and Political Consensus', *Ethics* 101(1) (1990): 64–88.

Gutmann, Amy and Dennis Thompson, *Democracy and Disagreement*. New York: Cambridge University Press, 1996.

Gutmann, Amy and Dennis Thompson, 'Deliberating about Bioethics', *Hastings Report* 27 (1997): 39–41.

Gutmann, Amy and Dennis Thompson, 'Deliberative Democracy Beyond Process', *Journal of Political Philosophy* 10(2) (2002): 153–74.

Gutmann, Amy and Dennis Thompson, *Why Deliberative Democracy?* Princeton, NJ: Princeton University Press, 2004.

Haas, Peter, 'Introduction: Epistemic Communities and International Policy Coordination', *International Organization* 46(1) (1992): 1–35.

Haas, Peter, 'Policy Knowledge: Epistemic Communities', in Neil J. Smelser and Paul B. Baltes (eds), *International Encyclopedia of the Social & Behavioral Sciences*. Oxford: Pergamon, 2001.

Haas, Peter, 'Ideas, Experts, and Governance' in Monika Ambrus et al. (eds), *The Role of 'Experts' in International and European Decision-Making Processes*. Cambridge: Cambridge University Press, 2014, 19–43.

Habermas, Jürgen, *Toward a Rational Society: Student Protest, Science, and Politics*, trans. Jeremy J. Shapiro. Cambridge: Polity, 1987.

Habermas, Jürgen, *Between Facts and Norms: Contributions to a Discourse Theory of Law and Democracy*, trans. William Rehg. Cambridge, MA: MIT Press, 1996.

Hardin, Russell, *Trust*. Cambridge: Polity, 2006.

Hardwig, John, 'Epistemic Dependence', *Journal of Philosophy* 82(7) (1985): 335–49.

Hardwig, John, 'Evidence, Testimony, and the Problem of Individualism: A Response to Schmitt', *Social Epistemology* 2(4) (1988): 309–21.

Hardwig, John, 'Role of Trust in Knowledge', *Journal of Philosophy* 88(12) (1991): 693–708.

Harris, Clodagh, 'Mini-publics: Design Choices and Legitimacy', in Stephen Elstub and Oliver Escobar (eds), *Handbook of Democratic Innovation and Governance*. Cheltenham: Edward Elgar, 2019, 45–59.

He, Baogang and Mark E. Warren, 'Authoritarian Deliberation in China', *Daedalus* 146(3) (2017): 155–66.

Hendriks, Friederike, Dorothe Kienhues and Rainer Bromme, 'Trust in Science and the Science of Trust', in Bernd Blöbaum (ed.), *Progress in IS: Trust and Communication in a Digitized World: Models and Concepts of Trust Research*. Cham: *Springer, 2016.*

Higgins, Eliot, *We Are Bellingcat: Global Crime, Online Sleuths, and the Bold Future of News*. New York: Bloomsbury, 2021.

Hirst, Paul Q., *Associative Democracy: New Forms of Economic and Social Governance*. Amherst, MA: University of Massachusetts Press, 1994.

Hirst, P. and Veit Bader (eds), *Associative Democracy: The Real Third Way*. New York: Frank Cass, 2005.

Hobbes, Thomas, *Leviathan, or The Matter, Forme, and Power of Commonwealth Ecclesiasticall and Civill*, ed. Richard Tuck. Cambridge: Cambridge University Press, 1996.

Hobbes, Thomas, *On the Citizen*, ed. Richard Tuck and Michael Silverthorne. Cambridge: Cambridge University Press, 1998.

Hoffman, Martin, 'How to Identify Moral Experts? An Application of Goldman's Criteria for Expert Identification to the Domain of Morality', *Analyse & Kritik* 2 (2012): 299–313.

Holst, Cathrine and Anders Molander, 'Public Deliberation and the Fact of Expertise: Making Experts Accountable, *Social Epistemology* (2017): doi. org/10.1080/02691728.2017.1317865.

Holst, Cathrine and Anders Molander, 'Asymmetry, Disagreement and Biases: Epistemic Worries about Expertise', *Social Epistemology* 32(6) (2018): 358–71.

Holst, Cathrine and Anders Molander, 'Epistemic Democracy and the Role of Experts', *Contemporary Political Theory* (2019): doi.org/10.1057/s41296-018-00299-4.

Holzer, Boris and Mads P. Sorensen, 'Rethinking Subpolitics: Beyond the "Iron Cage" of Modern Politics', *Theory, Culture & Society* 20(2) (2003): 79–102.

Hong, Lu and Scott E. Page, 'Groups of Diverse Problem Solvers can Outperform Groups of High-ability Problem Solvers', *Proceedings of the National Academy of Sciences* 101(16) (2004): 16385–9.

Innerarity, Daniel, *The Democracy of Knowledge*, trans. Sandra Kinkery. New York: Bloomsbury Academic, 2013.

Ioannidis, John P. A., 'Why Most Published Research Findings are False', *PLoS Medicine* 2(8) (2005), available at: https://doi.org/10.1371/journal.pmed.0020124.

Irwin, Alan, *Citizen Science: A Study of People, Expertise and Sustainable Development*. London: Routledge, 1995.

Jasanoff, Sheila, 'The Political Science of Risk Perception', *Reliability Engineering & System Safety* 59(1) (1998): 91–9.

Jasanoff, Sheila. 'Science and the Statistical Victim: Modernizing Knowledge in Breast Implant Litigation'. *Social Studies of Science* 32, 1 (2002): 37–69

Jasanoff, Sheila, '(No?) Accounting for Expertise', *Science and Public Policy* 30(3) (2003): 157–62.

Jasanoff, Sheila, 'Breaking the Waves in Science Studies: Comment on H.M. Collins and Robert Evans "The Third Wave of Science Studies"', *Social Studies of Science* 33(3) (2003): 389–400.

Jasanoff, Sheila, 'Technologies of Humility: Citizen Participation in Governing Science', *Minerva* 41(3) (2003): 223–44.

Jasanoff, Sheila, 'Ordering Knowledge, Ordering Society', in Sheila Jasanoff (ed.), *States of Knowledge: The Co-Production of Science and Social Order*. London: Routledge, 2004, 13–45.

Jasanoff, Sheila, *Designs on Nature: Science and Democracy in Europe and the United States*. Princeton, NJ: Princeton University Press, 2005.

Jasanoff, Sheila, 'The Practices of Objectivity in Regulatory Science', in Charles Camic, Neil Gross and Michèle Lamont (eds), *Social Knowledge in the Making*. Chicago: University of Chicago Press, 2011, 307–37.

Jeffrey, Anne, 'Limited Epistocracy and Political Inclusion', *Episteme* 15(4) (2018): 412–32.

Jones, Karen and François Schroeter, 'Moral Expertise', *Analyse & Kritik* 2 (2012): 219–23.

Kaplan, Michael, 'Prohibiting the People: Populism, Procedure and the Rhetoric of Democratic Desire', *Constellations* (2018): 1–22, DOI: 10.1111/1467-8675.12370.

Kappel, Klemens and Julie Zahle, 'The Epistemic Role of Science and Expertise in Liberal Democracy', in Miranda Fricker, Peter J. Graham, David Henderson and Nikolaj J.L.L. Pedersen (eds), *The Routledge Handbook of Social Epistemology*. New York: Routledge, 2019, 367–405.

Kaufman, Arnold, 'Human Nature and Participatory Democracy', in William E. Connolly (ed.), *The Bias of Pluralism* (New York: Atherton Press, 1969), 178–200.

Kelly, Jamie Terence, 'Democracy and the Rule of Small Many', *Critical Review* 26(1/2) (2014): 80–91.

Keyes, Ralph, *The Post-Truth Era: Dishonesty and Deception in Contemporary Life*. New York: St. Martin's Press, 2004.

Kitcher, Philip, 'The Division of Cognitive Labor', *Journal of Philosophy* 87(1) (1990): 5–22.

Kitcher, Philip, 'Authority, Deference, and the Role of Individual Reasoning in Science', in Ernan Mcmullin (ed.), *The Social Dimensions of Science*. Notre Dame, IN: University of Notre Dame Press, 1992.

Kitcher, Philip, *The Advancement of Science: Science without Legend, Objectivity without Illusions*. Oxford: Oxford University Press, 1993.

Kitcher, Philip, *Science, Truth, and Democracy*. Oxford: Oxford University Press, 2001.

Kitcher, Philip, *Science in a Democratic Society*. Amherst, NY: Prometheus, 2011.

Klarman, Michael J., *From Jim Crow to Civil Rights: The Supreme Court and the Struggle for Racial Equality*. Oxford: Oxford University Press, 2004.

Kleinman, Daniel, 'Democratizations of Science and Technology', in Daniel Kleinman (ed.), *Science, Technology and Democracy*. Albany: State University of New York Press, 2000, 139–65.

Knorr-Cetina, Karin, *Epistemic Cultures: How the Sciences Make Knowledge*. Cambridge, MA: Harvard University Press, 1999.

Koppl, Roger, *Expert Failure*. Cambridge: Cambridge University Press, 2018.

Kowalik, Tadeusz, *www.polskatransformacja.pl*. Warsaw: Muza, 2009.

Krick, Eva, 'Creating Participatory Expert Bodies: How the Targeted Selection of Policy Advisers can Bridge the Epistemic–Democratic Divide', in Eva Krick and Cathrine Holst (eds), *Experts and Democratic Legitimacy: Tracing the Social Ties of Expert Bodies in Europe*. London: Routledge, 2020, 33–48.

Krimsky, Sheldon, 'Beyond Technocracy: New Routes for Citizen Involvement in Social Risk Assessment', *Nonprofit and Voluntary Sector Quarterly* 11(1) (1982): 8–23.

Kusch, Martin, *Knowledge by Agreement: The Programme of Communitarian Epistemology*. Oxford: Oxford University Press, 2002.

Kusch, Martin, 'Towards a Political Philosophy of Risk: Experts and Publics in Deliberative Democracy', in Tim Lewens (ed.), *Risk: Philosophical Perspectives*. London: Routledge, 2007, 131–55.

LaBarge, Scott, 'Socrates and the Recognition of Experts', *Apeiron: A Journal for Ancient Philosophy and Science* 30(4) (1997): 51–62.

LaBarge, Scott, 'Socrates and Moral Expertise', in Lisa Rasmussen (ed.), *Ethics Expertise: History, Contemporary Perspectives, and Applications*. Dordrecht: Springer, 2005, 15–38.

Lafont, Cristina, 'Deliberation, Participation, and Democratic Legitimacy: Should Minipublics shape Public Policy?' *Journal of Political Philosophy* 23(1) (2015): 40–63.

Lafont, Cristina, 'Can Democracy be Deliberative and Participatory? The Democratic Case for Political Uses of Mini-Publics', *Daedalus* 146(3) (2017): 85–105.

Landemore, Hélène, 'Why the Many are Smarter than the Few and Why It Matters', *Journal of Public Deliberation* 8 (2012): 1–14.

Landemore, Hélène, *Democratic Reason: Politics, Collective Intelligence, and the Rule of the Many*. Princeton, NJ: Princeton University Press, 2013.

Landemore, Hélène, 'Yes, We Can (Make It Up on Volume): Answers to Critics', *Critical Review* 26(1/2) (2014): 184–237.

Landemore, Hélène, 'Deliberative Democracy as Open, not (just) Representative Democracy', *Daedalus* 146(3) (2017): 51–63.

Lane, Melissa, 'When the Experts are Uncertain: Scientific Knowledge and the Ethics of Democratic Judgment', *Episteme* 11(1) (2014): 97–118.

Laski, Harold J., *The Limitations of the Expert*. London: Fabian Society, 1931.

Latour, Bruno, 'Give Me a Laboratory and I Will Raise the World', in Karin Knorr-Cetina and M. Mulkay (eds), *Science Observed: Perspectives on the Social Studies of Science*. London: Sage, 1983, 142–69.

Lavazza, Andrea and Mirko Farina, 'The Role of Experts in the Covid-19 Pandemic and the Limits of Their Epistemic Authority in Democracy', *Frontiers in Public Health*, 14 July 2020, available at: https://www.frontiersin.org/articles/10.3389/fpubh.2020.00356/full, last accessed 24 June 2021.

Lehrer, Keith and Carl Wagner, *Rational Consensus in Science and Society: A Philosophical and Mathematical Study*. Dordrecht: D. Reidel, 1981.

Levy, David M. and Sandra J. Peart, *Escape from Democracy*. Cambridge: Cambridge University Press, 2017.

Lexchin, Joel, Lisa A. Bero, Benjamin Djulbegovic and Otavio Clark, 'Pharmaceutical Industry Sponsorship and Research Outcome and Quality: Systematic Review', *British Medical Journal* 326 (2003): 1167–70.

Liberatore, Angela and Silvio Funtowicz, '"Democratising" Expertise, "Expertising" Democracy: What Does It Mean, and Why Bother?' *Science and Public Policy* 30(3) (2003): 146–50.

Licon, Jimmi Alfonso, 'Sceptical Thoughts on Philosophical Expertise', *Logos & Episteme* 3(3) (2012): 449–58.

Lilla, Mark, *The Once and Future Liberal: After Identity Politics*. New York: Harper, 2017.

Long, Marilee and Jocelyn J. Steinke, 'The Thrill of Everyday Science: Images of Science and Scientists on Children's Educational Science Shows in the United States', *Public Understanding of Science* 5 (1996): 101–20.

López-Guerra, Claudio, *Democracy and Disenfrenchisement: The Morality of Electoral Exclusion*. Oxford: Oxford University Press, 2014.

MacDonald, Ramsay, *The Socialist Movement*. London: H. Holt, 1911.

Macpherson, Crawford Brough, *Life and Times of Liberal Democracy*. Oxford: Oxford University Press, 1977.

Mair, Peter, *Ruling the Void: The Hollowing out of Western Democracy*. London: Verso, 2013.

Manin, Bernard, 'On Legitimacy and Political Deliberation', *Political Theory* 15(3) (1987): 338–68.

Mansbridge, Jane, 'Everyday Talk in the Deliberative System', in Stephen Macedo (ed.), *Deliberative Politics: Essays on Democracy and Disagreement*. New York: Oxford University Press, 1999, 211–39.

Mansbridge, Jane, 'On the Idea that Participation Makes Better Citizens', in Stephen L. Elkin and Karol Edward Sołtan (eds), *Citizen Competence and Democratic Institutions*. University Park: Pennsylvania State University Press, 1999, 291–325.

Mansbridge, Jane, 'Deliberative Polling as the Gold Standard', *Good Society* 19(1) (2010): 55–62.

Mansbridge, Jane et al., 'A Systemic Approach to Deliberative Democracy', in John Parkinson and Jane Mansbridge (eds), *Deliberative Systems*. Cambridge: Cambridge University Press, 2012.

Martini, Carlo, 'The Epistemology of Expertise', in Miranda Fricker et al. (eds), *The Routledge Handbook of Social Epistemology*. New York: Routledge, 2020, 115–22.

Meadowcroft James and M. W. Waylor, 'Liberalism and the Referendum in British Political Thought 1890–1914', *Twentieth Century British History* 1(1) (1990): 35–57.

Mendelberg, Tali, 'The Deliberative Citizen: Theory and Evidence', in Michael X. Delli Carpini, Leonie Huddy and Robert Y. Shapiro (eds), *Research in Micropolitics, Vol. 6: Political Decision Making, Deliberation, and Participation*. Amsterdam: JAI, 2002, 151–93.

Mercier, Hugo, 'When Experts Argue: Explaining the Best and the Worst of Reasoning', *Argumentation* 25 (2011): 313–27.

Metz, Julia, *The European Commission, Expert Groups, and the Policy Process: Demystifying Technocratic Governance*. Basinstoke: Palgrave Macmillan, 2015.

Michael A. Neblo and Avery White, 'Politics in Translation: Communication Between Sites of the Deliberative System', in Andre Bächtiger, John S. Dryzek, Jane Mansbridge, and Mark Warren (eds), *Oxford Handbook of Deliberative Democracy*. Oxford: Oxford University Press, 2018.

Michaels, David, *The Triumph of Doubt*. Oxford: Oxford University Press, 2020.

Mintz, Alex and Nehemia Geva, 'Why Don't Democracies Fight Each Other? An Experimental Study', *Journal of Conflict Resolution* 37(3) (1993): 484–503.

Mirowski, Philip, 'Democracy, Expertise and the Post-Truth Era', 2020, draft.

Misak, Cheryl, 'A Culture of Justification: The Pragmatist's Epistemic Argument for Democracy', *Episteme* 5(1) (2008): 94–105.

Misztal, Barbara, *Trust in Modern Societies*. Cambridge: Polity, 1996.

Mnookin, Seth, *The Panic Virus: A True Story Behind the Vaccine-Autism Controversy*. New York: Simon & Schuster, 2012.

Moore, Alfred, 'Democratic Theory and Expertise: Between Competence and Consent', in Cathrine Holst (ed.), *Expertise and Democracy*. Oslo: ARENA Centre for European Studies, 2014, 49–84.

Moore, Alfred, 'Democratic Reason, Democratic Faith, and the Problem of Expertise', *Critical Review* 26(1/2) (2014): 101–14.

Moore, Alfred, *Critical Elitism: Deliberation, Democracy, and the Problem of Expertise*. New York: Cambridge University Press, 2017.

Moore, Alfred, 'Deliberative Democracy and Science', in Andre Bächtiger, John S. Dryzek, Jane Mansbridge, and Mark Warren (eds), *Oxford Handbook of Deliberative Democracy*. Oxford: Oxford University Press, 2018.

Moore, Alfred, 'Three Models of Democratic Expertise', *Perspectives on Politics* 19(2) (2021): 553–63.

Mouffe, Chantal, 'Deliberative Democracy or Agonistic Pluralism?' *Social Research* 66(3) (1999): 745–58.

Mouffe, Chantal, *On the Political: Thinking in Action*. London: Routledge, 2005.

Mounk, Yascha, *The People vs. Democracy: Why Our Freedom is in Danger and How to Save It*. Cambridge, MA: Harvard University Press, 2018.

Nguyen, C. Thi, 'Cognitive Islands and Runaway Echo Chambers: Problems for Epistemic Dependence on Experts', *Synthese* 197(7) (2020): 2803–21.

Nichols, Tom, *The Death of Expertise: The Campaign against Established Knowledge and Why it Matters*. Oxford: Oxford University Press, 2017.

Nowotny, Helga, 'Democratizing Expertise and Socially Robust Knowledge', *Science and Public Policy* 30(3) (2003): 151–6.

Nowotny, Helga, Peter Scott and Michael Gibbons, *Re-Thinking Science: Knowledge and the Public in an Age of Uncertainty*. Cambridge: Polity, 2001.

Nussbaum, Martha C., *Not for Profit: Why Democracy Needs the Humanities*. Princeton, NJ: Princeton University Press, 2010.

Oakeshott, Michael, *Rationalism in Politics: And Other Essays*. London: Meuthen, 1962.

Ober, Josiah, 'Democracy's Wisdom: An Aristotelian Middle Way for Collective Judgment', *American Political Science Review* 107(1) (2013): 104–22.

Ober, Josiah, *Demopolis: Democracy before Liberalism in Theory and Practice*. Cambridge: Cambridge University Press, 2017.

Oreskes, Naomi and Erik M. Conway, *Merchants of Doubt: How a Handful of Scientists Obscured the Truth on Issues from Tobacco Smoke to Global Warming*. New York: Bloomsbury, 2010.

Ost, David, *The Defeat of Solidarity: Anger and Politics in Postcommunist Europe*. Ithaca, NY: Cornell University Press, 2005.

Owen, David and Graham Smith, 'Survey Article: Deliberation and the Systemic Turn', *Journal of Political Philosophy* 23(2) (2015): 213–34.

Pabst, Adrian, *The Demons of Liberal Democracy*. Cambridge: Polity, 2019.

Page, Scott E., 'Making the Difference: Applying a Logic of Diversity', *Academy of Management Perspectives* 21(4) (2007): 6–20.

Page, Scott E., *The Difference: How the Power of Diversity Creates Better Groups, Firms, Schools, and Societies*. Princeton, NJ: Princeton University Press, 2007.

Parkinson, John, *Deliberating in the Real World: Problems of Legitimacy in Deliberative Democracy*. Oxford: Oxford University Press, 2006.

Parkinson, John, 'Deliberative Systems', in Andre Bächtiger, John S. Dryzek, Jane Mansbridge, and Mark Warren (eds), *Oxford Handbook of Deliberative Democracy*. Oxford: Oxford University Press, 2018.

Pataki, Zsolt G., *The Cost of Non-Europe in the Single Market ('Cecchini Revisited')*. Brussels: EPRL, 2014.

Pateman, Carole, *Participation and Democratic Theory*. Cambridge: Cambridge University Press, 1970.

Paxton, Marie, *Agonistic Democracy: Rethinking Political Institutions in Pluralist Times*. London: Routledge, 2020.

Perczynski, Piotr, 'Associo-Deliberative Democracy and Qualitative Participation', in Paul Hirst and Veit Bader (eds), *Associative Democracy: The Real Third Way*. New York: Routledge, 2005, 71–84.

Perlman, Maytal, 'The Value of Interactional Expertise: Perceptions of Laypeople, Interactional Experts, and Contributory Experts', *Journal of Integrative Research and Reflection* 1 (2018): 19–26.

Peter, Fabienne, 'Democratic Legitimacy and Proceduralist Social Epistemology', *Politics, Philosophy & Economics* 6(3) (2007): 329–53.

Peter, Fabienne, 'Pure Epistemic Proceduralism', *Episteme. A Journal of Social Epistemology* 5(1) (2008): 33–55.

Plaisance, Kathryn S. and Eric B. Kennedy, 'A Pluralistic Approach to Interactional Expertise', *Studies in History and Philosophy of Science Part A* 47 (2014): 60–8.

Polanyi, Michael, *Personal Knowledge: Towards a Post-Critical Philosophy*. Chicago: University of Chicago Press, 1958.

Polanyi, Michael, 'The Republic of Science: Its Political and Economic Theory', *Minerva* 1 (1962): 54–73.

Polanyi, Michael, *The Tacit Dimension*. London: Routledge, 1966.

Power, Christopher, *The Experts Speak: The Definitive Compendium of Authoritative Misinformation*. New York: Pantheon, 1984.

Price, Vincent and Peter Neijens, 'Deliberative Polls: Toward Improved Measures of "Informed" Public Opinion?' *International Journal of Public Opinion Research* 10(2) (1998): 147–76.

Przeworski, Adam, 'Minimalist Conception of Democracy: A Defense', in Ian Shapiro and C. Hacker-Cordón (eds), *Democracy's Value*. Cambridge: Cambridge University Press, 1999, 23–55.

Przeworski, Adam, 'Democracy and Economic Development', in Edward D. Mansfield and Richard Sisson (eds), *The Evolution of Political Knowledge*. Columbus, OH: Ohio State University Press, 2004.

Przeworski, Adam, 'Institutions Matter?' *Governemnt and Opposition* 39(2) (2004): 527–40.

Putnam, Robert D., *Bowling Alone: The Collapse and Revival of American Community*. New York: Simon & Schuster, 2000.

Putnam, Robert D., Robert Leonardi and Raffaella Y. Nanetti. *Making Democracy Work: Civil Traditions in Modern Italy*. Princeton, NJ: Princeton University Press, 1993.

Quast, Christian, 'Expertise: A Practical Explanation', *Topoi* 37(1) (2018): 11–27.

Radaelli, Claudio, 'The Public Policy of the European Union: Whither Politics of Expertise?' *Journal of European Public Policy* 6(5) (1999): 757–74.

Rawls, John, *Political Liberalism*. New York: Columbia University Press, 1996.

Rawls, John, *A Theory of Justice*, rev. edn. Oxford: Oxford University Press, 1999.

Rawls, John, *The Law of Peoples*. Cambridge, MA: Harvard University Press, 1999.

Rayner, Steven, 'Democracy in the Age of Assessment: Reflections on the Roles of Expertise and Democracy in Public-Sector Decision Making', *Science and Public Policy* 30(3) (2003): 163–70.

Reiss, Julian, 'Expertise, Agreement, and the Nature of Social Scientific Facts or: Against Epistocracy', *Social Epistemology* (2019), DOI: 10.1080/02691728.2019.1577513.

Reiss, Julian, 'Why Do Experts Disagree?' *Critical Review* (2021): 1–25, DOI: 10.1080/08913811.2020.1872948.

Ribeiro, Rodrigo and Francisco P. A. Lima, 'The Value of Practice: A Critique of Interactional Expertise', *Social Studies of Science* 2015: 1–30.

Rip, Arie, 'Constructing Expertise: In a Third Wave of Science Studies?' *Social Studies of Science* 33(3) (2003): 419–34.

Rogers, Karl, *On the Metaphysics of Experimental Physics*. New York: Palgrave Macmillan, 2005.

Rogers, Karl, *Modern Science and the Capriciousness of Nature*. New York: Palgrave Macmillan, 2006.

Rogers, Karl, *Participatory Democracy, Science and Technology: An Exploration in the Philosophy of Science*. Basingstoke: Palgrave Macmillan, 2008.

Rolin, Kristina, 'Gender and Trust in Science', *Hypatia* 17(4) (2002): 95–118.

Rorty, Richard, 'Human Rights, Rationality, and Sentimentality', in Richard Rorty (ed.), *Truth and Progress: Philosophical Papers*, vol. 3. Cambridge: Cambridge University Press, 1991, 167–85.

Rorty, Richard, 'Education as Socialization and as Individualization', in Richard Rorty, *Philosophy and Social Hope*. London: Penguin, 1999, 114–26.

Rossini, Frederick A. and Alan L. Porter, 'Frameworks for Integrating Interdisciplinary Research', *Research Policy* 8(1) (1979): 70–9.

Rostbøll, Christian F., 'The Non-instrumental Value of Democracy: The Freedom Argument', *Constellations* 22(2) (2015): 265–78.

Runciman, David, *How Democracy Ends*. London: Profile Books, 2018.

Ryfe, David Michael, 'The Practice of Deliberative Democracy: A Study of Sixteen Organizations', *Political Communication* 19(3) (2002): 359–77.

Saint-Simon, Henri, 'On the Replacement of Government by Administration', in *Henri Saint-Simon (1760–1825): Selected Writings on Science, Industry and Social Organisation*, ed. Keith Taylor. London: Routledge, 2016.

Sanders, Lynn, 'Against Deliberation', *Political Theory* 25(3) (1997): 347–76.

Sarewitz, David, 'Saving Science', available at: https://www.thenewatlantis.com/publications/saving-science, last accessed 24 June 2021.

Saward, Michael (ed.), *Democratic Innovation: Deliberation, Representation and Association*. London: Routledge, 2000.

Scholz, Oliver R., 'Experts: What They Are and How We Recognize Them – A Discussion of Alvin Goldman's Views', *Grazer Philosophische Studien* 79 (2009): 187–205.

Scholz, Oliver R., 'Symptoms of Expertise: Knowledge, Understanding and Other Cognitive Goods', *Topoi* 37 (2018): 29–37.

Schudson, Michael, 'The Trouble with Experts – and Why Democracies Need Them', *Theory and Society* 35 (2006): 491–506.

Schütz, Alfred, 'The Well-Informed Citizen: An Essay on the Social Distribution of Knowledge', *Social Research* 13(4) (1946): 463–78.

Schwab, Abraham, 'Epistemic Trust, Epistemic Responsibility, and Medical Practice', *Journal of Medicine and Philosophy* 33 (2008): 302–20.

Sclove, Richard, *Democracy and Technology*. New York: Guilford Press 1995.

Selinger, Evan and John Mix, 'On Interactional Expertise: Pragmatic and Ontological Considerations', *Phenomenology and the Cognitive Sciences* 3 (2004): 145–63.

Selinger, Evan, Hubert Dreyfus and Harry Collins, 'Interactional Expertise and Embodiment', Studies in the History and Philosophy of Science 38(4) (2007): 722–40.

Selingman, Adam B., The Problem of Trust. Princeton, NJ: Princeton University Press, 1997.

Sen, Amartya, 'Democracy as a Universal Value', Journal of Democracy 10(3) (1999): 3–17.

Shanteau, James, 'Competence in Experts: The Role of Task Characteristics', Organizational Behavior and Human Decision Processes 53 (1992): 252–66.

Shanteau, James, 'Why Do Experts Disagree?' in Bo Green, Robert Cressy, Frederic Delmar, Theodore Eisenberg, Barry Howcroft, Mervyn Lewis, Dirk Schoenmaker, James Shanteau and Robert Vivian (eds), Risk Behaviour and Risk Management in Business Life. Dordrecht: Kluwer Academic, 2000, 186–96.

Shapin, Steven, A Social History of Truth: Civility and Science in Seventeenth-Century England. Chicago: University of Chicago Press, 1994.

Shapin, Steven, 'Trust, Honesty, and the Authority of Science', in H. V. Fineberg, E.M. Bobby, R.E. Bulger (eds), Society's Choices: Social and Ethical Decision Making in Biomedicine. Washington, DC: National Academy Press, 1995, 388–408.

Shapin, Steven, 'Is There a Crisis of Truth?' 2019, available at: https://lareview-ofbooks.org/article/is-there-a-crisis-of-truth.

Shapin, Steven and Schaffer Simon, Leviathan and the Air-Pump: Hobbes, Boyle, and the Experimental Life. Princeton, NJ: Princeton University Press, 2011.

Shapio, Ian, 'The State of Democratic Theory: A Reply to James Fishkin', Critical Review of International Social and Political Philosophy 8(1) (2005): 79–83.

Shapiro, Ian, 'Conclusion in Restraint of Democracy: Against Political Deliberation', Daedalus 146(3) (2017): 77–84.

Sigerist, Henry E., 'Science and Democracy', Science and Society 2(3) (1938): 291–9.

Sismondo, Sergio, 'Post-Truth?' Social Studies of Science 47(1) (2017): 3–6.

Skinner, Quentin, 'Scientia Civilis in Classical Rhetoric and in the Early Hobbes', in Political Discourse in Early-Modern Britain, ed. Nicholas Phillipson and Quentin Skinner. Cambridge: Cambridge University Press, 1993, 67–93.

Skinner, Quentin, 'Hobbes's Changing Conception of Civil Science', in Quentin Skinner, Visions of Politics, Vol. III: Hobbes and Civil Science. Cambridge: Cambridge University Press, 2002, 66–86.

Slovic, Paul, Baruch Fischhoff and Sarah Lichtenstein, 'Facts versus Fears: Understanding Perceived Risk', in Daniel Kahneman, Paul Slovic and Amos Tversky (eds), Judgement under Uncertainty: Heuristics and Biases. Cambridge: Cambridge University Press, 1992, 463–89.

Smith, Graham, Democratic Innovations: Designing Institutions for Citizen Participation. Cambridge: Cambridge University Press, 2009.

Smith, Richard, 'Medical Journals Are an Extension of Marketing Arm of Pharmaceutical Companies', *PloS Medicine* 2(5) (2005): 364–6.

Solomon, Miriam, '"Groupthink" versus "The Wisdom of Crowds": The Social Epistemology of Deliberation and Dissent', *Southern Journal of Philosophy* XLIV (2006): 28–41.

Somin, Ilya, *Democracy and Political Ignorance: Why Smaller Government is Smarter*. Stanford, CA: Stanford University Press, 2013.

Somin, Ilya, 'Why Political Ignorance Undermines the Wisdom of the Many', *Critical Review* 26(1/2) (2014): 151–69.

Stears, Mark, *Demanding Democracy: American Radicals in Search of a New Politics*. Princeton, NJ: Princeton University Press, 2010.

Stehr, Nico and Reiner Grundmann, *Experts: The Knowledge and Power of Expertise*. London: Routledge, 2011.

Stemplowska, Zofia, 'What's Ideal about the Ideal Theory?' *Social Theory and Practice* 34(3) (2008): 319–40.

Steyvers, Mark and Miller Brent, 'Cognition and Collective Intelligence', in T. W. Malone and M. S. Bernstein (eds), *Handbook of Collective Intelligence*. Cambridge, MA: Harvard University Press, 2015, 119–37.

Stich, Stephen G. W., '"When Democracy Meets Pluralism" Landemore's Epistemic Argument for Democracy and the Problem of Value Diversity', *Critical Review* 26(1/2) (2014): 170–83.

Sunstein, Cass R., *Risk and Reason: Safety, Law, and the Environment*. Cambridge: Cambridge University Press, 2002.

Sunstein, Cass R., 'The Law of Group Polarization', *Journal of Political Philosophy* 10(2) (2002): 175–95.

Sunstein, Cass R., *Why Societies Need Dissent*. Cambridge, MA: Harvard University Press, 2003.

Sunstein, Cass R., *Infotopia: How Many Minds Produce Knowledge*. Oxford: Oxford University Press, 2006.

Sunstein, Cass R., 'Deliberating Groups versus Prediction Markets (or Hayek's Challenge to Habermas)', in Alvin Goldman and Dennis Whitcomb (eds), *Social Epistemology. Essential Readings*. Oxford: Oxford University Press, 2011, 192–213.

Surowiecki, James, *The Wisdom of Crowds*. New York: Anchor, 2005.

Sztompka, Piotr, *Zaufanie. Fundament społeczeństwa*. Kraków: Wydawnictwo Znak, 2007.

Talisse, Robert B., *Democracy after Liberalism: Pragmatism and Deliberative Politics*. New York: Routledge, 2005.

Tam, Henry, *Communitarianism: A New Agenda for Politics and Citizenship*. New York: New York University Press, 1998.

Tetlock, Philip E. and Dan Gardner, *Superforecasting: The Art and Science of Prediction*. New York: Crown Publishers, 2015.

Thompson, Dennis F., 'Deliberative Democratic Theory and Empirical Political Science', *Annual Review of Political Science* 11(1) (2008): 497–520.

Tilly, Charles, *Trust and Rule*. Cambridge: Cambridge University Press, 2005.

Turner, Stephen, *Liberal Democracy 3.0: Civil Society in an Age of Experts*. London: Palgrave, 2003.

Turner, Stephen, 'Political Epistemology, Experts, and the Aggregation of Knowledge', *Spontaneous Generations: A Journal for the History and Philosophy of Science* 1(1) (2007): 36–47.

Tversky, Amos and Daniel Kahneman, 'Judgement under Uncertainty: Heuristics and Biases', in Daniel Kahneman, Paul Slovic and Amos Tversky (eds), *Judgement under Uncertainty: Heuristics and Biases*. Cambridge: Cambridge University Press, 1992, 3–20.

Urbinati, Nadia, *Democracy Disfigured: Opinion, Truth, and the People*. Cambridge, MA: Harvard University Press, 2014.

Valentini, Laura, 'Ideal vs. Non-Ideal Theory: A Conceptual Map', *Philosophy Compass* 7(9) (2012): 654–64.

Vallier, Kevin, *Trust in a Polarized Age*. Oxford: Oxford University Press, 2020.

van, José and Donya Alinejad, 'Social Media and Trust in Scientific Expertise: Debating the Covid-19 Pandemic in The Netherlands', *Social Media and Society* 2020: 1–11, DOI: 10.1177/2056305120981057.

Van Reybrouck, David, *Against Elections: The Case for Democracy*, trans. Liz Walters. London: Bodley Head, 2016.

Vibert, Frank, *The Rise of the Unelected: Democracy and the New Separation of Powers*. Cambridge: Cambridge University Press, 2007.

Walzer, Michael, 'Deliberation, and What Else?' in Stephen Macedo (ed.), *Deliberative Politics: Essays on 'Democracy and Disagreement'*. New York: Oxford University Press, 1999.

Warren, Mark E., 'Deliberative Democracy and Authority', *American Political Science Review* 90(1) (1996): 46–60.

Warren, Mark, 'Democratic Theory and Trust', in Mark Warren (ed.), *Democracy and Trust*. Cambridge: Cambridge University Press, 1999, 310–45.

Warren, Mark, 'Deliberative Democracy', in April Carter and Geoffrey Stokes (eds), *Democratic Theory Today: Challenges for the 21st Century*. Cambridge and Malden, MA: Polity and Blackwell, 2002.

Watson, Jamie Carlin, 'The Shoulders of Giants: A Case for Non-veritism about Expert Authority', *Topoi* 37 (2018): 39–53.

Watson, Jamie Carlin, 'What Experts Could Not Be', *Social Epistemology* 33(1) (2019): 74–87.

Watson, Jamie Carlin, *Expertise: A Philosophical Introduction*. London: Bloomsbury, 2021.

Webb, Mark Owen, 'Why I Know About as Much as You: A Reply to Hardwig', *Journal of Philosophy* 90(5) (1993): 260–70.

Weinberg, Alvin M., 'Science and Trans-Science', *Minerva* 10(2) (1972): 209–22.

Weinberg, Alvin M., *Nuclear Reactions: Science and Trans-Science*. New York: American Institute of Physics, 1992.

Weinstein, Bruce D., 'What is an Expert?' *Theoretical Medicine* 14 (1993): 57–73.

Welbourne, Michael, *The Community of Knowledge*. Aberdeen: Aberdeen University Press, 1986.

Westbrook, Robert B., *John Dewey and American Democracy*. Ithaca, NY: Cornell University Press, 1991.

Whyte, Kyle Powys and Robert P. Crease, 'Trust, Expertise, and the Philosophy of Science', *Synthese* 177 (2010): 411–25.

Winner, Langdon, *Autonomous Technology: Technics-out-of-Control as a Theme in Political Thought*. Cambridge, MA: MIT Press, 1977.

Winner, Langdon, 'Do Artifacts have Politics?' *Daedalus* 109(1) (1980): 121–36.

Winner, Langdon, *The Whale and the Reactor: A Search for Limits in an Age of High Technology*. Chicago: University of Chicago Press, 1986.

Wittgenstein, Ludwig, *Philosophical Investigations*, trans. G. E. M. Anscombe. Oxford: Blackwell, 1997.

Wynne, Brian, 'May the Sheep Safely Graze? A Reflexive View of the Expert–Lay Knowledge Divide', in Scott Lash, Bronislaw Szerszynski and Brian Wynne (eds), *Risk, Environment and Modernity: Towards a New Ecology*. London: Sage, 1996, 44–83.

Wynne, Brian, 'Misunderstanding Misunderstandings: Social Identities and Public Uptake of Science', in Alan Irwin and Brian Wynne (eds), *Misunderstanding Science?* Cambridge: Cambridge University Press, 1996, 19–46.

Wynne, Brian, 'Seasick of the Third Wave? Subverting the Hegemony of Propositionalism: Response to Collins & Evans', *Social Studies of Science* 33(3) (2003): 401–17.

Young, Iris Marion, 'Justice, Inclusion, and Deliberative Democracy', in Stephen Macedo (ed.), *Deliberative Politics: Essays on 'Democracy and Disagreement'*. New York: Oxford University Press, 1999, 151–8.

Young, Iris Marion, *Inclusion and Democracy*. Oxford: Oxford University Press, 2000.

Young, Iris Marion, 'Activist Challenges to Deliberative Democracy', in James S. Fishkin and Peter Laslett (eds), *Debating Deliberative Democracy*. Oxford: Oxford University Press, 2003, 102–20.

Zakaria, Fareed, 'The Rise of Illiberal Democracy', *Foreign Affairs* 76(6) (1997): 22–43.

Zielonka, Jan, *Counter-Revolution: Liberal Europe in Retreat*. Oxford: Oxford University Press, 2018.

Ziman, John, *Real Science: What It Is, and What It Means*. Cambridge: Cambridge University Press, 2000.

Zimmerman, Joseph F., *The New England Town Meeting: Democracy in Action*. Westport, CT: Praeger, 1999.

Zuckerman, Harriet, 'Is "the Time Ripe" for Quantitative Research on Misconduct in Science?' *Quantitative Science Studies* 1(3) (2020): 945–58.

INDEX